D1568187

Fernald Library
Colby-Sawyer College
New London, New Hampshire

Presented by

MRS. FRANCES RUTTER

Gray Steel
and
Blue Water
Navy

Title Page: U.S.S. OKLAHOMA, Dreadnought-type Battleship, circa 1914.
Source: National Archives.

GRAY STEEL

AND

BLUE WATER

NAVY

The Formative Years of America's
Military-Industrial Complex
1881–1917

BENJAMIN FRANKLIN COOLING

ARCHON BOOKS

Hamden, Connecticut

1979

FERNALD LIBRARY
COLBY-SAWYER COLLEGE
NEW LONDON, N.H. 0325

VF
373
.C66
C.1

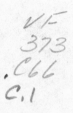

© Benjamin Franklin Cooling 1979

First published in 1979 as an Archon Book,

an imprint of THE SHOE STRING PRESS INC.

Hamden, Connecticut 06514

All rights reserved

Printed in the United States of America

5170976

6010

Library of Congress Cataloging in Publication Data

Cooling, B. Franklin.
   Gray steel and blue water Navy.

   Bibliography: p.
   Includes index.
    1. Munitions—United States—History.
  2. Ship-building—United States—History.
  3. Steel industry and trade—United States—History.
  4. Industry and state—United States—History.
  5. United States. Navy—History. I. Title.
VF373.C66   623.82′5′0973   79–17007
ISBN 0–208–01771–2

Contents

Acknowledgments

This study has been conducted primarily in official government repositories due to the paucity of steel industry records in public institutions. My gratitude for cooperation and advice must be extended to Dr. Dean Allard, Naval History Division, Department of the Navy; Dr. Samuel P. Hays, University of Pittsburgh; Dr. Meyer Fischbein, National Archives and Records Service; Dr. Kenneth P. Hagen, United States Naval Academy; Mr. Richard Glasow, Reston, Virginia; Miss Jean P. Wesner, Schwab Memorial Library, Bethlehem Steel Corporation; Mrs. Judith Weinrauch, Pennsylvania State Library; and the staffs of the Manuscript Division, Library of Congress as well as Old Army and Navy Records Branch, National Archives and Records Service, and Ms. Mary Anne Horne, U.S. Army War College Library.

I owe a particular debt of gratitude to the Center for Advanced Research of the Naval War College since this project originated as an Advanced Research Fellowship from that institution in 1973–74. Dr. James E. King and his associate at the time, Commander W.R. Pettyjohn; Commander R.M. Laske, then editor of *Naval War College Review;* and Mr. Anthony Nicolosi, Curator, Naval Historical Collection, all added greatly to the pleasure and challenges of visits and association with the U.S. Navy's senior service school at Newport, Rhode Island.

Hopefully, in the future the wealth of industrial materials will be deposited at the Eleutherian Mills Historical Library, Greenville, Wilmington, Delaware. Dr. Richmond P. Williams and his capable staff have been helpful to me in this work and the research files collected in preparation of this study will become part of that institution's collections for use by scholars and the general public.

Finally, as always, it is an honor to acknowledge the guiding hand of my graduate school mentor, Dr. Thomas C. Cochran, Benjamin Franklin Professor of History Emeritus of the University of Pennsylvania. He first started me on the quest for historical links between the business and military communities in the late nineteenth century.

Introduction

To isolate a starting point in the chain of historical causality is by definition a hopeless task. Yet there are events whose sheer magnitude gives them a claim to a certain causal autonomy. The United States Navy's search for the armor and armament of the new steel navy before World War I spawned military-industrial ties and commitments which mutually benefited industry and national defense. To view this period as the formative years of the modern military-industrial complex may seem rash. Nonetheless, linkages and a framework were created; these became more sophisticated and intricate with the passage of time and the further development of the nation as a world power.

The question of how a military establishment should secure the tools as well as the personnel of war is an enduring one. This was no less true in 1792 at the time of the French *levée en masse* than it will be when governments seek to secure laser weapons in 1992. Should a nation's military rely solely upon the private economic sector for the tools of war? Would this not incur the risk of being placed at the mercy of private monopolies with respect to design, programs, and, above all, prices? Or, should the military rely on the public sector—

arsenals, armories, government-owned plants and facilities—
which may be technologically backward in comparison with the
profit-motivated private enterprise? Should there be a third
alternative? A union of the private and public programs might
tap the best features of both sectors.

Such were the central features of the debate which ran
through the naval search for armor and ordnance before World
War I. The debate was not carried on in the United States
alone. Great Britain, France, Germany, Russia, and Japan all
groped for answers as these "super powers" of the Age of
Imperialism sought to build navies commensurate with their
quest for grandeur and global hegemony. The implications of
the debate have meaning for studies of institutions today.

We are merely on the threshold of knowledge about this
phase of naval and industrial history. Traditional and revisionist studies of the U.S. Navy, for example, all tend to focus
upon broad strategic, diplomatic, or administrative facets.[1]
Even most historians of business and technology have generally
relegated naval/military aspects of industrial product and
process development to a marginal or minor (at best) side of
their story. Merritt Roe Smith's study of Harpers Ferry and
Gaddis Smith's account of British submarine procurement
early in World War I provide notable exceptions.[2] Both naval
and business approaches omit valuable, if elusive elements in
an integrated story of how technology, business, and military
institutions became intertwined long before the current era of
the military-industrial complex.

True, some naval officials sensed the importance of this
phenomenon very early. As improbable an old salt as Admiral
of the Navy David D. Porter told Congressman Charles A.
Boutelle on 3 January 1890:

> The following exhibit of over 175 industries benefited by
> home shipbuilding has been furnished by the Harlan and
> Hollingsworth Company every item of which represents a
> *bona fide* disbursement in shipping:

Coal Miners,	Cutlers,	Oil manufacturers,
Iron Miners,	Silversmiths,	Ship chandlers,

Puddlers,
Rollsmen,
Furnacemen,
Millmen,
Riveters,
Caulkers,
Fitters-up,
Boiler-makers,
Blacksmiths,
Hammersmen,
Machinists,
Mill-wrights,
Ship-carpenters,
Joiners,
Stair-builders,
Painters,
Tinners,
Laborers,
Designers,
Draughtsmen,
Gold beaters,
Folders,
Inspectors,
Cabinet makers,
Upholsterers,
Flag makers,
Decorators,
Potters,
Glass blowers,

Loam moulders,
Cupola-tenders,
Foundrymen,
Brass finishers,
Engineers,
Stokers,
Pattern makers,
Carvers,
Brass workers,
Wire workers,
Riggers,

Compass adjusters,
Instrument makers,
Sheet brass workers,
Boiler-tube makers,
Brass-tube makers,
Tin-makers,
Plumbers,
Steam fitters,
Gas fitters,
Coppersmiths,
Lead workers,
Gum Manufacturers,
Spring makers,
Canvass makers,
Spinners,
Wire rope makers,
Stevedores,
Bell hangers,
Rope makers,
Sheet-iron makers,
Sheet-iron workers,
Bricklayers,
Boiler coverers,
Lamp makers,
Sailors,
Pilots,
Chair makers,
Anchor makers,
Steel-shape finders,

Scale makers,
Wood-working machine
  builders,
Model makers,
Sawyers,
Paper makers,
Brick makers,
Jewelers,
Hand-tool makers,
House furnishers,
Spar makers,

Ship smiths,
Mattress makers,
Mold-loft workers,
Tallow & Soap makers,
Coopers,
Block-makers,
Life-boat builders,
Stove makers,
Sail makers,
Safe makers,
Pump makers,
Nail makers,
Life preserver makers,
Blanket manufacturers,
Muslin manufacturers,
Cement makers,
Galvanizers
Hardware makers,
Oakum makers,
Pitch and Tar makers,
Electricians,
Safety valve makers
Machine-tool makers,
Saw mills,
Watchmen,
Printers,
Bookbinders,
Heaters,
Makers of electrical ap-
  paratus, annunciators, &c.,
Store keepers,
Book-keepers,
Clerks,
Insurers,
Brokers in metals,
Custom House brokers,
Paint manufacturers,
Leather belt makers,
Steel rail makers,
Type writers,
Artists,

Time keepers
Telegraphers,
Distiller makers,
Screw makers,
Grindstone makers,
Signal light makers,
Makers of marine governors,
Makers of inspirators,
Makers of ejectors,
Makers of engine indicators,

Emery wheel dealers,

Saw manufacturers,
Spar dealers,
Electric light plant furnishers,
Manufacturers of blowing
   engines
Bolt and nut works,
Engravers on metals,
Steam-steerer manufacturers,
Steam launch builders,
Brass whistle makers,
Tug boat owners,
Metallic-packing manufac-
   turers,
Sash & blind makers & turners,
Mirror makers,
Firebrick and fire-clay makers,
Bell rounders,
Marble cutters,
Makers of hoists & lifting jacks,
Tile makers,
Dealers in brushes and artists'
   supplies,

Makers of wire cloth and
   netting,
Mineral-wool manufacturers
Nickel and silver platers,
Ice machine makers
Yacht cannon makers,

White lead manufacturers,
Oil-cloth manufacturers,
Dealers in machinists'
   & iron workers' supplies,
Lumber dealers,
Cotton factors,

Jute dealers,
Rosin dealers,
Hemp growers,
Cereals,
Salt dealers,
Rubber,
Tarpaulin,
Cooks,
Waiters,
&c., &c., &c., &c., &c.,

The shipbuilder is the benefactor of every producer.[3]

This list seems naive or primitive in retrospect. Yet Porter and the managers of Harlan and Hollingsworth undoubtedly sensed important trends. The task of computing their impact is much more imposing now than it was in 1890. Still, examination of even a portion of such naval-industrial relations can uncover trends in national and regional economic and political affairs as well as foreign and domestic programs and policies. Some ingredients of the story are capitalization, profits, government standards and subsidies, manpower and technical expertise, as well as the fascination of particular business and military personalities. Focus on steelmaking, which became the glamor industry for the U.S. Navy before World War I, can clarify attitudes, philosophy, and institutional growth as well as structural unification.

For example, this era witnessed a transition from the "militia" theory of industrial preparedness practiced in the

Civil War to an integrated system which was capable of meeting the peacetime demands of an expansionist nation functioning in a hostile international climate. The needs of the U.S. Navy— like those of navies abroad—became central for stimulating industrial modernization. The U.S. Navy, rather than the army, became the first service to require industrial products more sophisticated than those normally produced by paleo-industry, i.e., rails and farm machinery. Did requirements for national defense lead domestic industry into new paths, or did the navy merely profit from developments already visible on the drawing boards of the robber barons?

Was the American steel industry in the late nineteenth century independent of large military-naval commitments? Certain firms like Bethlehem, Carnegie, and—after 1904— Midvale Steel, appeared to survive only because of military-related orders. Constantly arguing that they really did not need armor and ordnance contracts for survival, the steelmen nevertheless readily accepted each new naval contract, not only during the halcyon Big Navy years of Theodore Roosevelt, but on into the period of Wilsonian New Freedom. Concomitant with this phenomenon was the saga of "peaks and valleys" in the naval-industrial relationship, the patterns of periodic strengthening and weakening of ties between the modern steel navy and modern integrated heavy industry. Historians who rely blindly upon the printed words of the period do so at their own peril. Behind official naval reports and congressional hearings lie the personal connections and understandings forged between captains of industry, national politicians, and the admirals of American empire. Therein may be found the keys to unraveling the formative years of America's military-industrial complex.

This study merely breaks ground. It has been structured on a factual, chronological approach the details of which may seem confusing as elements of the story surface concurrently. Steel armor and ordnance remain but a portion of the military-industrial phenomena of that age. More work needs to be done to integrate procurement of small arms, provisions and clothing, noncombat equipment, and even shipbuilding itself together with what has been treated in this study. The task then remains one of revising the broader patterns of naval and business history. The subject surely merits more than the two unpublished graduate studies on the subject.[4] Eventually, these diverse—yet related—strands will be properly integrated to provide historical perspective on problems of universal interest to naval and business planners faced with evolving technology, economic and government policies, and human needs in any transitional era of national growth.

Chapter 1

Transition and Experiment

On 12 April 1884, the slate gray hull of the U.S.S. *Dolphin* slid quietly down the construction way at John Roach's shipyard in Chester, Pennsylvania. The event symbolized the launching of America's "new steel navy." Production of the little dispatch boat had consumed scarcely nine months from contract signing to launch; a mere seven months had passed since erection of the first construction frame. However, the event represented the finale to nearly twenty years of controversy about and neglect of the nation's first line of defense. Prophetically, the *Dolphin's* completion was even then shrouded in criticism, technical hassles, and verbal vituperation. But she provided a good project for introducing steel warship construction to the United States. Moreover, the vessel was the first true benchmark of the modern relationship between defense contractors and the government. This relationship has continued to the present day.

The interval between Appomattox and the launching of the *Dolphin* often has been cited as the nadir of American diplomatic and military policy. Post-Civil War America had something on its mind besides military affairs, for citizens who had just undergone a war wanted to bind up the wounds of shattered lives and homes. They wanted to exploit the burgeon-ing opportunities of industrialization, or move on to the untapped land resources of the west. The social and political implications of Reconstruction occupied the thoughts of most politicians on Capitol Hill. Economy-conscious Democrats, for example, could see little need for any expensive fleet-in-being when domestic railroad subsidies and control of a defeated, prostrate South were issues beckoning for attention.

True, intermittant diplomatic flare-ups caused concern. The French were hyperactive in Mexico; traditional enmity with Great Britain was periodically exacerbated by such events as the Fenians in Canada; and the *Virginius* affair with Spain unnerved State Department officials. But officials like Secre-tary of State William Seward were generally the only people worried about the Russian threat in Alaska, or concerned that resumption of prewar expansionist sentiment might lead to postwar international complications. After all, said Americans, that was what the State Department people were being paid to do.[1]

The traditional idea of American minutemen combined with a stockpile of veteran manpower from the victorious armies of the Union to lull the populace. Domestic needs and national introspection (if not outright isolationism) mitigated against the cries of a few anxious spokesmen of naval preparedness or a large standing army. Who really wanted to fight us anyway? asked citizens and leaders alike.

Whether styled "the Gilded Age," "the Awkward Years," the Brown Decades," or "the Search for Order," this period represented one of transition and experiment for the United States. This was true for politics, diplomacy, social develop-ment, and industrialization. Certainly the military sector was no different. Modernization in all these sectors was only at a formative stage. Perhaps "fluidity" best characterized the period. Politicians, businessmen, soldiers, and farmers all projected a bumptuous restlessness and shifting goals. Nobody seemed very clear about values or "givens." Military pro-fessionals were notably inept at enunciating and conceptualiz-ing for the general public the needs and theories of national defense. Industrial leaders, who had enjoyed windfall profits during the war, now turned their focus away from the tools of national defense. Peacetime markets, the state of technology, and reversion to traditional business pacifism all seemed more important.

The reservoir of weaponry left over from the Civil War provided both a positive good as well as a subtle evil. War reserves of cannon, ships, and other matériel always comprise part of the deterrent aspects of national defense, but they carry built-in factors of obsolescence which are but dimly perceived by the average citizen, and certainly were not by national leaders after the Civil War. To legislators of that age, a stockpile of existing battle-tried weaponry which required only the cost of storage or maintenance, seemed a far more expedient and economical mode of national defense than large appropriations for the experimentation and production of new weapons; which might not function well anyway. The American army and navy have been traditionally forced to live with the postwar problems of affluence and poverty in the guise of weapons stockpiles. The Reconstruction generation was no different.[2]

The "Reconstruction Navy" provides a particularly good case in point. The war formed a high point of American naval power. The fleet that existed in 1865 won international respect. It nearly equalled the striking power of Britain's Royal Navy— at least on paper! Over six hundred ships had been purchased, constructed, or modified as powerful steam vessels and ironclads joined a prewar squadron of sailing frigates. Here was a tribute to American naval constructors and craftsmen. The Union blockading squadrons in January 1865 boasted 471 vessels mounting 2,455 modern guns. U.S. cruisers, among the world's fastest, were thought to be capable of sweeping the seas of foreign commerce via the hoary *la guerre de course* strategy of the time. Appearance of the heavily gunned and armored monitors sent a shock wave through the international community of naval experts. But wars inevitably end, or so they did in the nineteenth century, and rapid disintegration of the army and navy has always been America's style of demobilization.[3]

The primary architects of the superb Union naval buildup in the war were also the culprits in rapid demobilization. Secretary of the Navy Gideon Welles and his capable assistant secretary, Gustavus Fox, stand out from the rather lackluster naval officials of the period between 1861 and 1884. Unfortunately, the wartime navy was dismantled largely at their instigation. Welles, while guided by his Democratic politics and New England notions of efficiency and economy, simply sensed the grass roots desires of the whole country. Long before Lee's army laid down its arms, Welles and Fox planned and executed the reduction of the navy to a level of one hundred vessels, less than one-sixth of its wartime strength. Under this stern injunction of economy, Welles should probably bear more of the onus for naval decline that has been heaped upon his successors, Adolph E. Borie, George M. Robeson, and Richard W. Thompson.

The usual picture of the latter three secretaries, battling tight budgets imposed by Congress (as reflected in their own annual reports), must be weighed against contemporary and later analysis revealing corruption and decay. By comparison with the halcyon days of the war, as well as the naval buildup of the 1890s, Borie, Robeson, and Thompson seemed to oversee a sea force filled with obsolete and rotting hulks, the padded bank accounts of friendly contractors, and rank political favoritism. Probably their actions were no worse than those of other spoilsmen of the period.

The situation seemed so bad at the time of the *Virginius* crisis that senior admiral David Porter could mutter, "Indeed, one such ship as the British iron-clad *Invincible* ought to go through a fleet like ours and put the vessels *hors de combat* in a short time, for she could either run them down, or destroy them at long range with her heavy rifled guns." Moreover, by 1878, a House committee had chopped apart the statistics of the secretary of the navy which showed a fleet of 144 vessels, including 5 first rates, 27 second rates, 30 third rates, and 24 ironclads. The members of the Naval Affairs Committee contended, however, that only 43 of these ships were fit for duty, with none of the first rates, only 9 of the second, 14 of the third, and 14 ironclads among that total. Any of these vessels would have easily succumbed to a first-class European ironclad. American warships lacked modern ordnance to penetrate the enemy's armor, armor of their own to withstand the enemy's fire, and sufficient speed to escape. Porter was quite right![4]

Still, one might ask whether or not the navy was sufficient to a normal peacetime mission of showing the flag. Most Americans felt so, as did their elected officials, and civilian administrators of the Navy Department practiced stop-gap measures in support of such a policy. The subsequent problems of the U.S. Navy can be addressed better by questioning why the caretaker, professional cadre of the service failed to keep pace with international changes in technology after Welles's departure from Washington in 1869. Surely the leaders of the navy might have known better. In retrospect, these veterans could have been expected to advocate technical modernization in order to stay abreast or preferably ahead of potential enemies.

Senior professionals like Admiral David G. Farragut, Vice Admiral David D. Porter, or Rear Admiral Louis Goldsborough may have been psychologically unprepared to cope with changes in machinery, ordnance, and ship construction in the wake of a successful war. They may have been simply captives of success. American military professionals generally prepare to fight the next war in the guise of the last. Lessons learned in combat often befuddle senior professionals as much as they challenge relatively younger, more energetic, evangelistic, or promotion-conscious junior officers.

Complacency caused by victory, the huge inventory of Civil War matériel, or vested interest in the status quo (for reasons which are both diverse and often unclear), all provide explanations for the state of the Reconstruction navy. Such complacency in any institution becomes contagious as well as stultifying. Lacking a sense of urgency, American legislators and the general public may have simply forgotten that warships, like any tools, become outdated. By the 1870s naval professionals could no longer afford the luxury of acquiescence in inertia.[5]

For one thing, foreign navies were proceeding apace with new armored steel warships, breech-loading ordnance, and sophisticated machinery. Profiting from the *Monitor-Virginia* duel, Great Britain spent £10.5 million for new ships during the eight years after the American Civil War. Heavily armored warships of the battle line, as well as lightweights like torpedo and dispatch boats, which sacrificed everything for speed, were added to the fleet. The use of iron and steel for warships became common in England during the seventies as dwindling timber supplies and the impact of steam machinery upon oak bottoms rendered a substitute for hull material highly advisable. Steel plates were used for inboard work aboard H.M.S. *Bellerophon* as early as 1868, although her traverse beams and frames remained iron. The first all-steel vessels in the Royal Navy were the *Iris* and *Mercury*, armed dispatch boats begun in 1876 and 1878 respectively, as well as six corvettes with keel, keelson, longitudinals, outside plating, and decks made from steel.

The shipbuilders of Great Britain were in the forefront of naval construction. They either built or furnished building materials for every European power of consequence except France. In 1873, a German advisory board adopted a reconstruction program for the new Imperial navy, but they continued to patronize British industry. Russia, Turkey, Spain, Holland, Italy, Denmark, Greece, Portugal, as well as non-European nations such as Japan, Chile, Peru, and Brazil, were among the purchasers of British-made armored warships. Of course, the Royal Navy remained the benchmark against which the others gauged their success.[6]

American professionals were quite aware of such developments. An occasional, but erratic spurt might be seen, as, for example, when in 1865 Admiral Porter, then superintendent of the Naval Academy, introduced a steam engine there for instructional purposes. Porter remained an enigma. He unremittingly endorsed iron monitors and gunboat-launched torpedoes for coastal defense. Yet, as senior admiral, he once ordered that all naval vessels "will be fitted out with full-sail power," and all cruising was to be done under sail with ships' captains justifying in writing any resort to auxiliary use of steam. Progressive strides always seemed to be overtaken by departmental directives retrogressive in tone.

Such ironies reflect an institution and its professional members caught in a whirlpool of uncertainty. A distraught junior officer in the late seventies gave one plausible explanation for this condition when he noted that the public always believed that the navy could improvise overnight if war threatened. "For many years," he declared, "the art of building ships was making such rapid strides that it was out of the question for us, with our small appropriations, to keep pace with European nations, and because we felt that it was just as well to save our money and remain observers, . . . so that when the time came for us to build, we might be warned by the mistakes of other nations and profit by their successes."[7]

Still, we may assume that while certain people resisted, others sponsored technological innovation and change. Functional resistance and messianism both may be viewed in sociopolitical terms since the human principals in each camp had something to lose or to gain. Victories and defeats might be calculated in terms of status, authority, or control. The watershed issue seems to have been the so-called staff-line controversy which alternately simmered and flared up between the time of the establishment of the engineer corps in 1842 and its merger with the line officers at the end of the century.

Focusing upon the propulsion plant of the steam warship, this issue may have unduly magnified a single aspect of the whole question of technological modernization and the U.S. Navy. Still, it represented the struggle between deck officers blessed with social graces, good family background, and political clout, as well as a Nelsonian approach to professional competence, and the upstart mechanics—the engineer officers—of the dirty engine room, boiler compartment, oil can, and black gang. Pushed forward and upward like many elements in American society at this time, the engineers squabbled with the deck elite over billets, peer acceptance, and career advancement.

It now appears that deck officers were fighting a rearguard action against the inevitable onslaught of modern times. But members of that group were hardly acting irrationally or irresponsibly. Their legitimate grievances ranged from rank shortchanges by Congress during wartime inflation of the officer corps to a much more rational complaint—inefficiency. Given the state of naval engineering and technology at the time, the engineer corps failed to produce the optimum in effective and efficient warships. The line officer argument seems to have had merit on this particular point.[8]

The great *cause célèbre* of the day was the U.S.S. *Wampanoag*. Supposedly "faultless in her model, and, as a steamship, the fastest in the world," the internal arrangements of munitions space, armor, living quarters, stores, as well as inefficient coal burning engines led to a Navy Department review board's declaration that she was "scarcely more than naval trash." There was much to opponents' criticism that the *Wampanoag* was really impractical given lack of overseas repair facilities and the predictable closure of neutral ports in wartime. But the controversy about machinery and propulsion simply hid other issues in the fight between traditionalists and modernists. The protagonists might also have worried about modern ordnance and protective hull material.[9]

One of the seemingly eternal verities in naval and land warfare has been the controversy of gun versus fortification (or fortified ship). Each has alternated in ascendancy since the invention of gunpowder. Whatever the experiences of heavy Civil War ordnance with land fortification, the introduction of ironclad warships necessitated development of heavier ordnance. Nearly every aspect of ordnance design, fabrication, and gunnery was ripe for overhaul by the last quarter of the nineteenth century.[10] As with machinery and propulsion, ordnance and naval architectural material were in a similar state of uncertainty. As late as 1897, one Royal Navy captain observed, "Great as have been the changes and improvements in everything connected with naval gunnery during the last thirty years, there is as yet no appearance of finality."[11]

Not that the navy and the nation lacked experimentors. Not only were there Americans like John Dahlgren, T.J. Rodman, and Robert C. Parrott, but also such foreign experts as Sir William Armstrong and Joseph Whitworth in England and Alfred Krupp in Germany. Everywhere arms makers wondered how a gun could be produced which would deliver high velocity fire without bursting. The plethora of designs, sizes, and matériel variety attested to the activity of the day.[12]

The Europeans led ordnance manufacture in this transitional era. Krupp, Armstrong, and others employed agents like Thomas Prosser and Son in New York to supply test cannon to less sophisticated customers like the United States, Italy, and Russia. Although Russia began her own heavy ordnance manufacture by the late seventies, the Americans held back. Fabrication of a series of breech-loading, forged steel tubes held together by shrinkage seemed a chancy business to private entrepreneurs when the only customers were national governments. Pervading everything was the philosophy that "rapidly changing developments in guns and armor would enable us, by waiting a few years, to take up the subject at an advanced stage and thus derive the benefit of the vast amount of experimentation continuously being carried on in other countries."

This philosophy had merit. But in the meantime both army and navy officials tested immature designs and quack inventions, while board after board was appointed with sufficient frequency to keep the matter in a constant state of agitation. Technocrats like Captain Edward M. Simpson, USN, and Army ordnance chief Brigadier General Stephen Vincent Benet fretted about steel versus solid-shot projectiles, slow or quick burning powder, cast iron, wrought iron, or all-steel cannon tubes, and conversion of old smooth-bore tubes via rifled sleeving in comparison with newer concepts of built-up steel guns. American experts were probably no more uncertain than their British, French, or German counterparts when it came to the details. But the published records of a succession of American ordnance boards confirm an impression of inertia, uncertainty, and overlap between service ordnance bureaus.[13]

The U.S. Navy actually surged slightly ahead by the end of the 1870s under the tutelage of Commodore William Jeffers as chief of ordnance. Plans were actually completed for a six-inch, built-up, steel breech-loading rifle, employing the new slow-burning brown or cocoa gunpowder from Germany. No conversions were made by naval ordnance experts after 1880, and importation of forgings and a working model led to testing at the Annapolis Proving Ground in 1882.

Ordnance was only part of the problem. Another aspect of the armament triad—that of defensive protection—posed additional difficulties for naval officials in the sixties and seventies. The *Monitor-Virginia* duel had largely resolved the wood versus metal question. But cruiser enthusiasts defied the trend, claiming wood alone provided a lightweight material necessary for *la guerre de course.* How then could one protect a ship's vulnerable innards, which housed machinery, ammunition, fire control, and crew space? Something had to thwart rifled shell penetration of the hull, yet not increase the weight. As one premier naval armaments expert exclaimed in 1886, "Steel and iron! To which of these should be confided the trust of defense?"[14]

Naval armor had advanced between Sir William Congreve's 1805 proposal, the famous Stevens floating battery of the fifties, to the four- and five-inch wrought iron plating (backed by three feet of timber) mounted by the French *Gloire*, British *Warrior*, and many Civil War ironclads at mid-century. But laminated plates had to be used during the Civil War due to American inability to fabricate single plates of desired thickness. True, a twelve-inch iron armor was actually made during the conflict, but the *Monitor's* turret was built up from eight one-inch iron plates bolted together.[15]

Everyone seemed to sense that metallurgy was unequal to the task. The Bessemer steel process using a converter had been developed before the war, and the Siemens-Martin acid open hearth process emerged shortly thereafter. But it took time to perfect the systems, transfer them to the United States, and implement their usage. Cast iron might be fine for European frontier fortifications where weight was no problem. But admiralties searched in vain as, by 1876, it required nearly twenty-two inches of iron to blunt the heaviest cannon shell.

A trial at Spezia in Italy that year revolutionized armor manufacture and effected a reduction in thickness. The Spezia trial unveiled a twenty-two-inch mild steel, oil-quenched plate manufactured by the French firm of Schneider et Cie. Naturally the manufacturing process was secret. Yet, for all its ballistic resistance, this steel plate broke up as renewed efforts were directed toward marrying a hard steel face with a tough iron back to achieve a superior plate. The Siemens-Martin method offered promise in this regard. From the all-steel plate deficiencies evolved two varieties of compound armor, the Wilson-Cammel type (open hearth steel cast atop a hot wrought iron back), and the Ellis-Brown type (steel face cemented to an iron back by pouring molten Bessemer steel between the two). Both types used plate rolling following compounding; both were British responses to French developments; and both proved so popular and successful that the admiralty adopted compound armor universally for new ships of the Royal Navy.[16]

While French naval authorities followed suit, Schneider officials continued to search for a perfect all-steel armor. By the mid-eighties additional trials at Spezia pitted Brown and Cammell plates against a Schneider product with complete superiority accorded the French brand. The Italian government immediately adopted the Schneider armor and established its own plant for production. American naval authorities watched these developments from afar. Ad hoc arrangements with American contractors like John Roach of Chester, Pennsylvania for repairs to moth-balled monitors permitted private rolling mills to supply iron armor, but no permanent arrangements or facilities were effected. The Navy Department in the Grant-Hayes era was too involved with politics to provide for the technological future. Eventually, the US Navy had to contract abroad with Brown and Company in England for plate with which to refurbish the monitor *Miantonomah*. This unsatisfactory condition of matériel procurement became a major headache for American naval officials by 1883.[17]

Actually, during the time when Washington policymakers were busy reconstructing the south and pacifying the west, American steelmakers had little interest or concern for the tools of war. They didn't have to. Domestic production for peaceful activities provided sufficient markets. Furthermore, it was also a period for experimentation and flux in the steel industry itself. Men like Andrew Carnegie, Abram S. Hewitt, and others were involved with discovery of the relative merits of mild versus blister steel, Bessemer converters versus open hearth methods, and the trickiness of obtaining a finite product which might be produced quickly, cheaply, and in large quantities. Busy with organizational and fiscal development, the steelmongers learned by trial and error that each new process possessed disadvantages. The entire American blister steel production only stood at seventy-five thousand tons in 1880; the Bessemer process had contributed 1.1 million tons by that date. If Hewitt's open hearth method was to become the dominant manufacture (particularly for naval purposes), by the turn of the century, its uses remained confined to extremely high quality but expensive products in 1880.[18]

Although the United States steel industry had laid its foundations by 1880, its steel products remained tied to a single market. Ranking second in production to Great Britain in mild steel (1,175,000 tons with 90 percent by the Bessemer process), the main market lay with steel rails. True, open hearth products included bridge and steam boiler material. But when Carnegie's Edgar Thomson works were constructed in 1875 and named for a distinguished president of the Pennsylvania Railroad, a shrewd observer might think the steel industry was merely an adjunct of the railroad expansion of the age.

Except for this special field, the United States continued to live essentially in an "Iron Age." Almost twice as much iron (2,134,000 tons), was used as steel in this country. The manufacturers remained cold to steel mainly because of a large-scale iron manufacturing infrastructure as well as the continued unpredictability of the metal. People on both sides of the Atlantic looked askance at American steel in particular. American rails were regarded by Europeans as the poorest and least dependable, and even Cornelius Vanderbilt went abroad for his needs. In 1881, the greatest of all Bessemer supporters in America, Captain Bill Jones of the Edgar Thomson mill, debunked American inferiority in rails before a British audience. The previous annual statistic showed that almost 1,356,000 tons of iron and steel, or 30 percent of American production, still came from abroad.

Post-Civil War economic conditions largely determined the strength of the domestic steel industry. On the one hand, qualitative inferiority was offset by a protective tariff. Free traders claimed that American buyers thus paid more for inferior products than if they had been able to buy abroad. Protectionists countered that the infancy of the domestic steel industry and high labor costs deservedly dictated a price differential between American and European products. Both sides agreed, however, that without a tariff, the development of a domestic steel industry would have been greatly retarded in the United States.

The classic and chronic overexpansion of manufacturing facilities as well as frequent recessions from 1870 to 1890 affected steelmaking. Lacking a really diversified market, too many steelmen ended their optimistic expansion in economic disaster. The steel industry was in a depressed state by the late seventies, due largely to a dull market and technological change. A brief recovery took place from 1879 to 1882 when the railroads enjoyed a renewed, if temporary expansion. Then, the cycle turned downward once more. Obviously overcommitted to a single market and badly in need of product diversification, America's steelmen seemed unconcerned about naval armor and ordnance at the very time such products seemed to offer an option out of the economic straitjacket.

It seems that the rivalry between Bessemer and open hearth methods of production became sharper at the very moment that birth of a "new American steel navy" presented more opportunities for structural shapes, sheets, and appurtenances as well as armor and ordnance. Therefore, fortuitous linkages between government and industry became possible. By 1880, both Congress and the public shared a growing interest in foreign policy and rearmament to protect the nation's expanding trade. It helped, undoubtedly, that $100 million lay idle in the Treasury. Use of this surplus for naval purposes appealed to tariff protectionists as well as to other legislators seeking a larger slice of the world's carrying trade.

The House Naval Affairs committee was most receptive. Long desirous of seriously limiting repairs of old ships, it had sought unsuccessfully to establish a naval construction fund from the sale of obsolete vessels. Leaders like Chairman W.C. Whitthorne of Tennessee and Benjamin W. Harris of Massachusetts admitted the unreadiness of American manufacturers for naval rearmament, but they went on record in favor of mobilizing the country's resources as soon as possible for the task. However, efforts to pass positive legislation in that direction always fell prey to lobbies seeking to maintain profits for constituents engaged in ship repair activities.[19]

The November elections of 1880 continued Republican domination with majorities in both congressional houses and President James A. Garfield in the White House. Constructive work on the naval problem might now be possible. Garfield, seeking to placate the south, appointed William H. Hunt of New

Orleans as secretary of the navy. Hunt, with Garfield's bless-
ing, promptly established a special advisory board of the ablest
naval officers. Chaired by Admiral John Rodgers, the fifteen-
member panel was to study the idea of building a new navy.

Rodgers' board (also called the First Advisory Board),
according to one of its contemporaries, "was fairly representative of the naval service, containing as it did old and young
officers from the different corps that deal with naval material
. . . ." As it studied the petty details of size and displacement,
machinery and rigging, ordnance and armor, and boiler and
engine design, at first glance there was little to set it apart from
other such military study groups. Dutifully pondering the
marine ram ideas of Rear Admiral Daniel Ammen, as well as
numerous proposals from naval dilettantes and shipbuilders
such as Pusey and Jones or Harlan and Hollingsworth of
Wilmington, Delaware, Rodgers and his board took five months
to prepare a final report for the secretary.[20]

Several things were clear by the time this report reached
Hunt's desk in early November 1881. For one thing, the overly
enthusiastic naval officers proposed a peacetime establishment
far in excess of anything acceptable to the U.S. Congress. True,
the vessel types fit the accepted tenets of naval policy of the
day. To sustain the country's naval requirements "for survey-
ing, deep-sea sounding, the protection of American life and
property endangered by wars between foreign countries, and
service in support of American policy where foreign governments are concerned," board members wanted a fleet of
seventy active and reserve vessels. Since only thirty-two of the
sixty-one unarmored cruising vessels were available from the
Navy List of 1881, the board thought primary focus should be
placed on more of that type of vessel. An additional thirty rams
and torpedo boats would round out the program.[21]

Playing a statistical game not unlike those of today's Pen-
tagon planners, Rodgers' professionals envisioned that the
number and types of vessels available for naval service at the
expiration of eight years (their program plus existing ships),
would amount to 120 warships including 21 ironclads, 70
unarmored cruisers, 5 rams, 5 torpedo gunboats, and 20
torpedo boats. But the size and cost of the program was

shocking. Congress probably shuddered at the $29,607,000 price tag until it saw the endorsements of Hunt and President Chester A. Arthur, who succeeded the assassinated Garfield. Legislation to commence the effort with two steel cruisers was approved but not funded by Congress. Yet, the Rodgers board work stood as an example of technical progressivism on the part of the U.S. Navy, an institution often seen as the bulwark of reaction in this era.

A major example of such progressivism might be seen in the board's recommendation that steel should be the construction material for the new navy. This metal had been proposed before, but always the traditionalists like Chief Engineer Benjamin Isherwood and naval constructors John Lenthall, T.D. Wilson, and Philip Hichborn vetoed the idea. While European navies turned increasingly to steel, these American conservatives objected on the grounds that not a single all-steel ship had ever been made on this side of the Atlantic.

This was not quite true, for Pusey and Jones Company had built three steel vessels for the Colombian government utilizing plates purchased through an agent abroad. However, as Wilson contended later, he personally opted for iron over steel because he doubted the ability of American steelmakers to furnish their own steel plates and structural shapes. Hichborn agreed, but decided to go along with steel if the government assumed complete responsibility. In general, the traditionalist, conservative officers fretted about the "treacherous" nature of steel, and cited the quality and lower cost of wrought iron.[22]

Such opinions had some cogency at the time. Still, as the Rodgers board deliberations progressed, more and more members were persuaded by their colleague Commander Robley D. Evans that the country's honor as well as the prestige of American manufacturing demanded only the best for the new fleet. Evans had more firsthand knowledge of mild steel and its superiority than did the others. While accepting the conservative position that domestic industry was yet incapable of fabricating steel, the majority of the board decided to turn an acute problem into a challenge. They pointed to "the impetus that such a step [as deciding on steel warships] taken by the Government, would give to the general development of steel manufacture in this country."[23]

Yet the Rodgers board could go no farther. They rejected imaginative ideas for armored warships since their mandate did not cover consideration of such vessels, especially when "in times of peace iron-clads were not necessary for carrying on the work of the United States Navy." Moreover, Congress surely would oppose ironclads costing $3 or $4 million apiece. Too many Civil War monitors were still available; the U.S. Army was lobbying for its coastal defense role, and foreign ironclads only had an active service span of about ten years before obsolescence set in. Why invest in such craft?

Finally, the Rodgers board claimed that "no type of iron-clad vessel could be developed intelligently without knowing what weight and calibre of ordnance was to form her armament." Six- and eight-inch guns for cruisers were one thing, but the group remained convinced that the ten-inch guns necessary for iron clads could not be made in the United States. The country lacked both the skills and the plant to make such heavy ordnance. That was simple enough. The U.S. Navy could not have ironclads without proper guns, and proper guns could not be made because of the state of the nation's steel industry. The only recourse was congressional funding to underwrite the enterprise.[24]

The buck was clearly being passed to Congress. Meanwhile, the army's Getty board studied more ordnance designs, a Senate Select Committee under John A. Logan repeated the usual arguments, and finally, the House Naval Affairs Committee got down to determining what firms in America could or did produce steel plates for hulls, frames, and other structural shapes with maritime purposes. The picture was better than most people thought. Committee testimony disclosed that steel ships had been built at several yards on the Delaware River, and the firm of Andrew Carnegie in Pittsburgh had successfully rolled steel girders 49.5 feet long and 12 inches thick. Better to rely on the private steelmen, said the witnesses, government yards could not duplicate their feats without a massive overhaul of obsolete facilities.[25]

The upshot of the whole affair was the important naval appropriations bill of 1882. After Congress finished massaging the provisions and wording, the U.S. Navy was authorized to complete five monitors, conduct extensive repairs to existing wooden warships, and apply any leftover funds toward construction of two steel cruisers as recommended by the Rodgers board. Moreover there was to be a permanent advisory board to the secretary and one hundred thousand dollars for Ordnance Bureau development of steel rifled breechloading guns. Domestic steel construction was decreed for the ships, but made optional for the guns.[26]

Thus, the period of inertia in naval rearmament seemed to be passing to one of gestation and fermentation by 1882. Congress was beginning to scurry about in its own fashion, tempering some members' enthusiasm with negotiated response to budget and vested interest issues. Inside the sea service, although some sensed victory, the internecine fight between reactionaries and modernists was far from over. U.S. Naval Institute discussions at least began to explore the question of iron and steel in naval architecture, and even some steel company board rooms echoed with comments about new markets and profits in the armaments trade.[27]

The question remained, how could the matériel be manufactured? Few officials would have disagreed with Admiral Rodgers' statement to the Naval Institute in June 1881 that "Above all things, it seems to me, we need gun makers, and that we should not buy our guns abroad, but should make them ourselves."[28] Midvale Steel outside Philadelphia had successfully forged a six-inch steel gun tube in 1881. Montgomery Sicard's ordnance clerks had a more sophisticated version on their drawing boards the next year. But manufacture of a heavy steel gun in quantity required more than drawing boards and one test product. Nobody could forge the parts necessary for larger calibers, or at least so thought most high officials in government and industry. In 1882, a naval revolution in American armament had scarcely begun.

Chapter 2

The Day of the *Dolphin*

The next stage of American naval rearmament began with the succession of William E. Chandler to the post of Secretary of the Navy on 12 April 1882. He would be responsible for implementing the hesitant steps taken by Congress to date. An unabashed Republican lobbyist, politician, and spoilsman from New Hampshire, whose principal interests lay with party politics, tariff, and Southern reconstruction, Chandler nonetheless proved to be an energetic administrator. He sought to improve the morale of the service, to persuade legislators to build new ships, and to encourage the latent technological expertise in the navy itself. Although tainted in the eyes of some Democratic colleagues, he contended pragmatically, "if the naval establishment is not to be made effective it should be discontinued, and the fifteen millions annually expended should be preserved to procure in national emergencies, the assistance of foreign ships and guns."[1]

It took awhile for Chandler to gain his "sea legs" in the department. He listened to the latest importunings of shipbuilder John Roach, who astutely opined that postwar demagogues on Capitol Hill had been too willing to play partisan politics with the navy while some naval bureau chiefs had been all too willing to build obsolescent ships but "were not willing to admit that they were failures and insisted that they must be preserved as evidences of their wonderful engineering skill. . . ." With admirable hindsight, Roach pronounced: "The great mistake that was made regarding the navy was that we did not do as was done in the Army with old guns and carriages, mules, tents and horses, sell them all out, they served their purpose and were not worth preserving."[2]

Chandler quickly moved to set up a second advisory board, under the enigmatic Commodore Robert W. Shufeldt, whose diplomatic missions far outshone claims to technological proficiency or innovative thinking. Still, he became something of a spokesman for change and a propagandist for reform; a relatively unsung precursor to Alfred Thayer Mahan. Moreover, he presided over a board comprising experienced officers from marine engineering, construction, ordnance, and torpedo development. Such professionals were not advocates of any "big gun-big ship" fleet. Yet none of them could be dismissed as a mediocrity, and attached civilian naval architects and engineers like Henry Steers and Miers Coryell were expected to supply most of the modern technical expertise. Still, carping criticism from navy bureaus, charges of political favoritism for old cronies of John Roach, and the inability of the board itself to decide between repairs to old monitors and the immediate start on construction of the two steel warships authorized by Congress all delayed initiation of the board's efforts until mid-November.[3]

Actually, the board's mandate was very specific—to advise the secretary concerning the plans and construction of the two new steel warships and to examine material, inspect the work, and supervise the whole program from drawing board to operational vessel. Elegant and impractical designs poured into the board from shipbuilders and naval enthusiasts. Only the piqued navy bureaus remained silent, angered by a competitor in their sacred domains of naval construction and engineering. Undaunted, the Shufeldt group emitted an air of confidence. As the influential *Army and Navy Journal* noted: "It will be thus seen that few boards (indeed we are aware of none) have had such an amount of labor to undertake or such responsibility to assume, and the position is no sinecure. Practically speaking, the success or failure of this first effort to revive the Navy will rest entirely on them."[4]

Meanwhile, nobody was prepared to actually start construction. The navy itself failed to agree on the type of warship required—the old harbor defense monitor versus cruiser controversy continued to plague spokesmen from Secretary Chandler, senior admiral David Porter, the Shufeldt board, and even naval supporters on Capitol Hill. Most of the debate revolved around dimly perceived strategic notions, opposition from western legislators to maritime expenditures, and political feuding concerning who would get the largest portion of the spoils. Very few comments could be heard concerning the technological ramifications of any naval program. In Congress, for example, few legislators really comprehended Tennessee congressman J.D.C. Atkins' perceptive comment: "We have no artisans competent to make guns! If that is true, we have no artisans competent to make ships."[5] All the other arguments were academic in comparison.

As finally enacted on 3 March 1883, the first appropriation for the "new navy" allotted $1.3 million for the construction of the smaller of the two cruisers authorized (but not funded) the previous August, two of the three 2,500-ton cruisers recommended by the Shufeldt board, and a dispatch boat. Wooden ship repairs would now be reduced to twenty percent of the cost of a comparable new warship. While the act's phraseology would not prevent new warship construction in government facilities, it was quite obvious that those facilities lacked the requisite machinery and equipment. The United States Navy would have to go to the private sector for its new warships.[6]

Once committed, the navy moved quickly to secure the necessary materials for the new ships. Shufeldt sent a circular letter to most of the major American steel firms on 21 March, asking about their ability to produce steel plates and structural shapes of the weights and dimensions prescribed by Congress. Such plates were to be of domestic steel having "as near as may be possible" a tensile strength of sixty thousand pounds per square inch and a ductility of twenty-five percent in eight inches. The response from the steelmen was unexpectedly encouraging.[7]

Only one firm admitted its inability to make at least some of the desired material. Carnegie Brothers, already a leading name in the field, stated that it was prepared to fabricate nearly all the structural plates. It did admit that it was unable to meet specific breadth requirements. Midvale Steel proclaimed a special interest in structural shapes because of its recent contract for the Brooklyn Bridge, and suggested that it was the first American company to fill a sizable order for such shapes. Midvale managers foresaw no problem in supplying the navy. They were thinking of turning their production almost exclusively to structural steel anyway, they claimed. Even when their plant seemed ill-equipped for ship plates, the Midvale people claimed to know other steelmakers who could be contacted for subcontracting operations.

H.R. Whitney and Company as well as Schoenberger and Company represented other concerns known for steel rolling capabilities. Midvale had also used Cambria Iron Works plates, but the Schoenberger firm had in fact pioneered in American plate production at its Juniata, Pennsylvania works. Company spokesmen claimed that they could roll plates which would considerably exceed Shufeldt's requirements. Four additional companies including Nashua Iron and Steel; Park Brothers; Pusey, Jones; and Oliver and Philips, also announced varying abilities to support naval programs.

Similar response was not immediately forthcoming from the nation's shipbuilders, however, Shufeldt's board also solicited comments concerning ship and machinery design from twenty-one members of the maritime construction industry. Most of the private entrepreneurs remained aloof. William G. Gibbons, president of Pusey, Jones, hinted at the reason. His firm's naval architects were simply too busy with commercial designs to worry about the U.S. Navy. Besides, he suggested, the service's own experts were better qualified to design warships than were private designers.

Chandler was having trouble with his own bureau chiefs over designs. Institutional inertia threatened to ossify the naval rearmament. Quite simply, old line bureaucrats like T.D. Wilson (Construction and Repair), W.H. Shock (Steam Engineering), and even Montgomery Sicard (Ordnance), actively sought to reduce the Shufeldt board to a cipher. Feeling threatened by such competition, the bureau chiefs procrastinated in designing the ships. The blueprints on file in the department remained quite incomplete when the new navy went on to the bidding stage on 2 July 1883.[8]

Scarcely eight of the country's shipbuilders responded to the public announcement soliciting bids that summer. All eight represented well-respected concerns, but they labored under certain handicaps, not the least of which was the matter of incomplete blueprints. Then too, bidders were not pleased with technical matters like tensile strength, completion time requirements, and bond posting. Within weeks pessimism replaced the optimistic tenor of the March correspondence between Shufeldt and the industrialists. This new note resulted from an advisory board circular asking the manufacturers for their views on matériel testing requirements.

Replies from Pusey, Jones; Midvale; Otis Iron and Steel; Harlan and Hollingsworth; Park Brothers; and Schoenberger unanimously condemned the impractically high government technical standards for steel. The Shufeldt board had decided upon an average ductility of 25 percent (with 23 percent absolute minimum) when the British admiralty, Lloyds Insurance Registry, and Liverpool Underwriters required only 20 percent. American naval authorities and Congress demanded superiority, not parity. They had already expected this of the domestic iron industry and saw no reason to make any exception for the steel trade. The steelmen did not agree. Finally Chandler and key shipbuilders like John Roach and

TABLE 1

First Advisory (Rodgers) Board Recommendations (1881)

No.	Class	Material	Speed	Tonnage	Type	Complete Cost Each
2	1st	steel	15 knots	5,873	Unarmored Cruiser	$1,780,000
6	1st	steel	14 knots	4,560	Unarmored Cruiser	1,422,000
10	2d	steel	13 knots	3,043	Unarmored Cruiser	930,000
20	4th	wood	10 knots	793	Cruiser	218,000
5		steel	13 knots	2,000	Ram	500,000
5			13 knots	450	Torpedo Gunboat	145,000
10		steel	21 knots	100	Cruising Torpedo Boat	38,000
10		steel	17 knots	70	Harbor Torpedo Boat	25,000

SOURCE: Report, Naval Advisory Board, *Annual Report, SN*, 1881, 37–38.

William Cramp from the Delaware River group hit upon a compromise of 21 percent. One hurdle was overcome only to give way to yet another when the bids were actually opened on 2 July.[9]

TABLE 2

PROPOSALS FOR CONSTRUCTION OF STEEL STEAM CRUISERS AND DISPATCH BOAT

CHICAGO

1.	The Harlan & Hollingsworth Company, Wilmington, Delaware	$1,120,000
2.	The William Cramp & Son's Ship and Engine Building Company, Philadelphia, Pennsylvania	1,080,000
3.	C.H. Delamater, Delamater Iron Works, New York, New York	1,163,000
4.	John Roach, Morgan Iron Works, New York, New York	80,000

ATLANTA

5.	The Harlan & Hollingsworth Company, Wilmington, Delaware	775,000
6.	The William Cramp & Son's Ship and Engine Building Company, Philadelphia, Pennsylvania	650,000
7.	John Roach, Morgan Iron Works, New York, New York	617,000
8.	H.F. Palmer, Jr., & Co., Quintard Iron Works, New York, New York	763,400

BOSTON

9.	The Harlan & Hollingsworth Company, Wilmington, Delaware	777,000
10.	The William Cramp & Son's Ship and Engine Building Company, Philadelphia, Pennsylvania	650,000
11.	John Roach, Morgan Iron Works, New York, New York	619,000
12.	Harrison Loring, Boston, Massachusetts	748,000

DOLPHIN

13.	The William Cramp & Son's Ship and Engine Building Company, Philadelphia, Pennsylvania	375,000
14.	John Roach, Morgan Iron Works, New York, New York	315,000
15.	Theodore Allen and Anthony H. Blaisdell, St. Louis, Missouri	380,000
16.	Henry Ashton Ramsay, Baltimore, Maryland	420,000

SOURCE: Secretary of the Navy, *Annual Report, 1883*, 56.

Much to the consternation of seven of the eight bidders, the Navy department awarded all four warship contracts to John Roach of Chester, Pennsylvania. William Cramp groused about it on the train ride all the way back to Philadelphia. He felt he had been taken in by a naval secretary in collusion with Roach. Other naval officials, the press, and many politicians agreed, but in retrospect, it was Roach's shrewdness and business acumen that won him the first prizes of the new fleet. The Chester builder had an edge because of his coordination of raw material sources, subcontractors, and suppliers as well as his political pull in Washington. Other competitors like J. Taylor Gause of Harlan and Hollingsworth could admire success, and Gause, for one, praised Chandler's fairness throughout the negotiations.[10]

In the end, Roach based his low bid on his "perfectly integrated complex from the mine to the shipyard," which meant that his costs were lower than his competitors. Only Roach possessed steel works and a rolling mill plus construction ways, and he had actually experimented with the manufacture of structural material required for steel cruisers. Thus, his production cost amounted to only five cents per pound compared with the seven or eight cents quoted by steelmakers to the other shipbuilders—an advantage of $270,000 in the price of steel alone.

Furthermore, Roach had convinced other steelmen of the favorable results of his planning and experiment. Thus, he could augment his own supply sources through subcontracts with Norway Iron and Steel Company of South Boston, Massachusetts, the Phoenix Iron Company of Philadelphia, and Park Brothers of Pittsburgh. Roach boasted of his ability to "build the ship in my own yard, from the coal and iron up to the finished ship, making every part of the ship in my own yard, if I gave any work to others to do they must do it for me at a small profit, otherwise I would do it myself." Although he was described as an "illiterate, elderly, infirm ironmonger," with a "somewhat senile mind," Roach seemed shrewd enough to solve the most vexing problem of his era—the production and organizational structure necessary for translating plans and programs into instruments for national policy.[11]

Roach's subsequent tribulations with the ABCD ships (as they were styled from their names—*Atlanta, Boston, Charleston,* and *Dolphin*), are well known. Staggering cost overruns, substitution of iron shafts for steel with resultant breakdowns during sea trials, naval officials' increasing dissatisfaction with the results, carping criticism from outside politicians, competitors, and the press all accompanied the first efforts to

refurbish the U.S. Navy. Meanwhile Chandler and the department reevaluated the direction of naval policy and by the end of
1884 solemnly declared, "It is not now, and never has been, a
part of that policy to maintain a fleet able at any time to cope
on equal terms with the foremost European armaments." The
U.S. Navy remained uncommitted to maritime supremacy. The
immediate object, said its chief civilian, "should be at moderate expense to replace our worn-out cruisers with modern
constructions fitted for general service, and for this reason the
reconstruction should for the present be continued on the lines
already begun."[12]

Translated into specifics, this meant more unarmored
cruisers and gunboats, a few torpedo boats and rams, and little
else. Frankly, the question of armor and armament development was so thorny that nobody could safely propose bigger
programs. In fact, Chandler readily admitted the navy's inability to find a domestic source for supplying armor to the monitor
Miantonomah. He had been forced to contract with the English
firms of John Brown and Charles Cammell for 2,240 tons of
steel turret and pilot house plates for $118,000. He bluntly told
the public, "In view of the large amount of compound armor or
of steel armor which will be required for the completion of the
four other monitors, it is desirable that Congress should in
some way encourage its manufacture in this country."[13]

It was no different with gun forgings. While Chandler harped
on the need to do something, the question remained, how?
Several American steel works had the furnace capacity, but
nobody seemed ready to produce cannon from forging to
finished tube. Despite slow progress under the tutelage of R.W.
Davenport at Midvale Steel, that firm still had no apparatus for
rough-boring and turning even six-inch ordnance. The Washington Navy Yard, designated site for a naval ordnance factory,
still had to be fitted for machining the parts and assembling the
gun.

Events began to gel by the mid-eighties just as the ABCD
ships needed their ordnance. Once Midvale finally demon-
strated an ability to produce the required steel forgings, the
navy's Ordnance Bureau contracted with the South Boston Iron
Works and West Point Foundry for finishing part of the order

for twenty guns. The rest were finished at the Washington yard, with the first pieces finally emerging from production lines in February 1884. An ad hoc but prophetic arrangement had been set up involving both private industry and government shop. Spawned by an emergency situation, it proved to be the pattern for ordnance production in the future.[14]

For the present, however, the U.S. Navy still searched for a way to end its dependency on foreign sources for any ordnance above a six-inch caliber. True, Midvale could make nine-inch hoops by hammering them on a mandrel. But it could not forge such tubes, and other steelmakers sought to avoid the heavy investment of capital for machinery when orders still appeared to depend upon the budgetary whims of Congress. Charles Cammell and Sir Joseph Whitworth executed U.S. Navy eight-inch contracts and, ironically, the parts left England only after long delay, reaching America nearly a year overdue. Such were the early difficulties in constructing the new navy. Technological and production delays in turn affected policy planning, new construction programs, and the whole evolutionary pace of naval power in the late nineteenth century.[15]

In the eyes of many naval officials and politicians, the situation was untenable. As a remedy, a clause in the 1883 naval appropriations bill established a joint army and navy board to decide which of the navy yards and government arsenals had the requisite capacity and location for adaption to heavy ordnance manufacture. Questions of private alternatives, costs, types of equipment, and machinery for such plants were also to come within the purview of this so-called "Gun Foundry Board." The results of such investigation were to mark "the beginning of American production of modern heavy ordnance."[16]

Secretary Chandler instructed Commodore Edward Simpson on 2 April 1883 to form a six member group to report to Congress on the best means for ordnance manufacture. Naval members included Simpson as president, Captain Edmund O. Matthews and Lieutenant William H. Jaques (secretary), while Colonel Thomas G. Baylor, Ordnance; Lieutenant H.L. Abbot, Engineers; and Major Samuel S. Edler, Artillery reflected the army's interest in coastal armament. Together they requested their respective services to provide all information on file regarding European arsenals and procedures while at the same time soliciting American steelmakers for their views on the government inducements needed to institute domestic production.

The board had gathered supplemental information with greatest difficulty, however. James M. Swank, secretary of the American Iron and Steel Association had actually facilitated contacts with key manufacturers like Joseph R. Anderson of Tredeger Iron Company, Samuel L. Felton and Major L.S. Bent of Pennsylvania Steel, Edward Y. Townsend and Powell Stackhouse of Cambria, William Sellers and R.W. Davenport of Midvale, John Fritz and Joseph Wharton of Bethlehem Iron, or Chester Griswold of Albany and Rensselaer Iron and Steel. While others such as Louisville Board of Trade representative A.S. Willis expressed interest in the naval board's activities, little was heard from many key firms like Carnegie. Still, Simpson's group could conclude on Christmas Eve, 1884 that while a two-year lead time was required to begin production at two government gun factories, "the total estimate of $17,000,000 will complete the steel-producing plant, establish and equip the steel gun factories, supply the guns for six and one-half years, and inaugurate the manufacture of steel in large masses in the United States."[32]

The question was, how would Congress react? That body seemed perfectly content to enter the new year with a continued blockage of naval funds. The bill which finally received President Arthur's signature on 3 March 1885 included $25,000 for "testing American armor made of American material;" $10,000 "for completion and public test of two breechloading rifle cannon of the large calibers now in course of construction for the Navy"; and authorized construction of two cruisers (three to five thousand tons) costing $1 million each; one heavily armored gunboat of sixteen hundred tons, costing $520,000; and a light gunboat of eight hundred tons, to cost at the most $285,000.[33]

1, "If you recollect during our conversation in London I endeavored to clearly point out to you that it was hardly to be expected that the process of manufacturing artillery upon my system could be shown to you, a process only arrived at by an immense expenditure of time and money, while on your side no compensation would be guaranteed, and that we should thus be upon unequal terms; and from your favor of 15th ultimo I can now gather that a simple walk through the Essen shops would even not be all that you would require, but that the system of construction should be made clear to you—an amount of information scarcely to be expected."[18]

While the Americans might have been disappointed, they had seen enough to make definite recommendations upon their return home. After a final swing to Rock Island and Frankford arsenals the board laid out its preliminary findings on 21 November. They then adjourned to await price lists from Europe before notifying American steelmen of probable costs for plant, tools, and other items required for cannon production. At least one member of the board, William H. Jaques, used the time to solidify negotiations with Joseph Whitworth to act as the Englishman's exclusive commerical agent in the United States. Whitworth was possibly the leading European manufacturer of heavy forgings. This arrangement with the American naval officer gave him entry not only to the American market, but to inner governmental circles of procurement and contracting.

The Simpson board trip meant more than personal gain, however. It could be viewed as a landmark in American technological development. Together with the domestic inquiries of the group, the trip led to the first systematic infusion of technical information into American industry regarding modern procedures for heavy forging. Therefore, the board's investigations impinged upon the larger and more sensitive matter of a proper relationship between government and private business when it came to questions of national defense.[19]

The final report of the Simpson board propounded four alternatives. First, board members pondered a government foundry and factory owned and operated solely by the federal government. Second, they considered a partnership between government and private interests whereby the former would supply one or more private plants with such additional tools and equipment as would enable them to turn out finished steel cannon. Third, the board thought about letting enough contracts to private concerns to supply guns without direct subsidy. Finally, another alternative suggested erection of a government owned and operated factory, and the granting of private contracts large enough to supply the forged and tempered materials ready for final manufacturing.

The Simpson board relied in all cases upon what it had learned in Europe. The French had used the first method before 1870, and it was quickly dismissed by the Americans since it excluded native talent and ingenuity, and prevented helpful criticism from the private sector. Moreover, declared the board, "The result is well known; a great crisis came; the Government works were inadequate to meet the additional demands made upon them, and the patriotic efforts of private establishments were inadequate to produce all the material that was needed."

The second or partnership method had been found untenable by both British and Russian governments. The British had been forced to pay very high prices for a time, and the government had finally sold its share at great loss. The Russians had also paid exorbitant prices and had become involved in a joint-stock company from which it could free itself only by buying up shares and operating the plant as a government establishment. Even the third method of large contracts had entrapped Germany in the coils of a single supplier, Krupp, said the Simpson group. This tended to place the government at the mercy of a single entrepreneur, who then dominated national policy.

The joint board of American officers decided that the fourth method was best. It had been practised in France after 1870. "Her Government establishments are still retained," said the board, "but as *gun factories* [their emphasis] simply, in which the parts are machined and assembled, but for *foundry* [their emphasis] work she depends upon the private industries of the country, and many of these works have found it to their profit to establish gun factories which supplement the Government factories to a great extent." Therefore the Simpson board recommended "that in inaugurating the manufacture of war material in our country a conformity as close as circumstances will admit to the plans which have proved so successful in France should be observed."[20]

The Simpson board sought to enable the government to avoid complete dependency upon self-aggrandizing private interests. Artificial competition might be introduced between government-finished and some private-finished ordnance. From a strictly practical standpoint the necessarily large investments involved in establishing a complete forged-to-finished gun works might be borne, at least initially, by both industry and government. How then to induce private steelmakers to even initially invest heavy capital outlays for a plant capable of producing heavy forgings but not finishing them?

There were two possibilities. In the British and Russian "partnership" idea, the government granted outright subsidies or bought the necessary machinery for private enterprise. The alternative was a stipulated, annual appropriation from Congress for ordnance procurement. Simpson and company rejected the former plan since it led to a lack of clear-cut responsibility between private maker and government as well as high prices and often shoddy products. Rather, they viewed stipulated annual appropriations as the best method. The private manufacturer might then expect a promise of steady, reasonable remuneration for his heavy investment.

The Gun Foundry Board concluded:

> It would not be necessary for the Government to be associated with a large number of firms for the supply of its material, for it is probable that the private establishments that would take up the subject would only be those with large available funds which they would be willing to put into a special plant, and for remuneration on which they would be willing to wait a reasonable time. The permanent appropriation would give them surety of ultimate profit, the only condition being success in providing the material that would be indicated in their contracts. From personal intercourse with some of the leading manufacturers the Board is led to believe that the plan will have the effect of guiding the private industries of the country to

the aid of the Government in developing this work of
national importance.[21]

Indeed, communications from companies like Cambria Iron
sustained this conclusion. E.Y. Townsend of that firm stated
very bluntly, ". . . if the United States Government will make a
sufficiently large contract or give other positive guarantee
which shall insure the Cambria Company adequate employment or sufficient profit to reimburse this large expenditure, the company on its part [will undertake] to meet the
required tests." Simpson and his board must have felt reassured by the first of the year, when suddenly American
manufacturers showed greater interest in cooperation with the
Navy Department. Not only Townsend, but Powell Stackhouse
of Cambria, William P. Hunt of South Boston, and representatives of the West Point Foundry Association appeared before
the board to deliver final statements in response to the original
interrogatory circular of 1 May 1883. Suddenly there was a
spirit of comraderie.[22]

The Gun Foundry Board conclusions accurately reflected
circumstances. Private industry—superior in efficiency and
product due to competition—was for that very reason un-
trustworthy when it came to matériel vital to the national
interest. Might not competitors combine in order to protect
their heavy investments from ruthless price wars? The government as sole customer would be caught in between and the
resulting absence of competition would introduce shoddy
material and high costs. Government officials of the era saw the
introduction of some type of artifical competition as a solution.
Yet everything depended upon the maintenance of good health
in both private and public sectors. If the boundary crumbled
between them and a "partnership" developed, then the
artificial state of emulation and competition might be destroyed.[23]

The Simpson board recommended two gun factories, with
the army's plant located at the Watervliet Arsenal, Troy, New
York while the Washington Navy Yard would provide the
setting for the naval facility. Again, the model was France, not
England. A single British establishment had produced years of

parliamentary bickering due to Admiralty dissatisfaction with production directed more toward the army's needs. Despite space limitations on available Federal properties, America's Gun Foundry Board did not recommend purchase of any new sites. But it did stress the need to set annual appropriations from Congress, citing the 1808 militia arms act as proof for such a contention.

Simpson's group felt that the cost of constructing a plant to temper gun parts up to one hundred tons in weight would vary from $660,000 to $835,000. An additional $900,000 would be required for a gun factory. While admitting that it would take as much as three years to complete the tools, construct the shops, and establish the plant, the navy analysts added that such a factory could conceivably produce fifty six-inch, seventeen twelve-inch, and twelve sixteen-inch guns (or a proportionately larger number of smaller calibers), at an annual expenditure of about $2 million.

Simpson later told a Naval Institute audience that his board had relied upon a production prediction of two thousand tons per year. They had estimated steel prices at twenty-five cents per pound or an average of $559 per ton, thereby reaching a yearly production cost of $1,118,000 for the two thousand tons. Simpson had then calculated 15 percent of this amount as a fair business profit, which after six years would accrue $1,090,050, "a little more than the original outlay." He figured that the lump sum required by congressional appropriation would be six and one-half times the amount of the yearly production cost, or $7,367,000 (roughly corresponding to the army-navy split in the Gun Foundry Board report figure of $15,000,000). Nobody knew at this time how controversial steel statistics would be in a decade or so.

The Gun Foundry Board president told the institute that bidders had to be prepared to supply guns in all calibers. Each manufacturer should realize that "it is all important to the country as a means of national defence that these large plants should be erected, and all means should be taken by the Government to encourage the work; thus, by requiring all parts of the gun material to be included in a lot, an advantage is given to those establishments which propose to make their plants complete." Cottage industries did not interest the Gun Foundry Board. An expanding navy required a corresponding industrial base, and naval ordnance was one part of such large plant expansion.[24]

Asking for an immediate appropriation of $1.8 million for this project, the Simpson board noted the strategic implications of continued dependency on foreign suppliers. But even the stark opinion that "the United States is destitute of the means of fabricating the modern guns so urgently needed," failed to provoke immediate congressional action. Men on the hill wanted to ponder the matter still further. Several months later a Senate Select Committee on Ordnance and Warships, as well as a House Commission on Ordnance and Gunnery began their own investigations. No one seemed anxious to proceed further in an election year.[25]

Few, if any, of the senators and representatives denied the necessity of doing something about the state of the navy. But controversy raged over the administration's latest proposals for a large, mixed package of eleven new cruisers, gunboats, torpedo boats, dispatch boat, and ram. All too few members of Congress really knew what was most cost-effective, much less politically acceptable. They filled the pages of the *Congressional Record* with loquacious speeches about national destiny, protection of commerce and citizenry, and navy yard patronage. They displayed little appreciation of the best naval policy for the future.

Much of this was understandable. Even the U.S. Navy failed to project a clear-cut policy in 1884. But the Forty-eighth Congress was quite adept at bitter partisanship, constantly harping on whether Republicans or Democrats poured more money into wooden ship repairs and pursuing the witch-hunt against John Roach. They agonized about Roach's cruisers and how their obsolete machinery, inadequate sailpower, private yard construction, and pork-barrel contracting would eventually make them worthless. It seemed the legislators always had time to quibble about monitor repairs, uncooperative bureau chiefs like ultraconvervative Wilson, even unpopular Benjamin Isherwood, and the obstinate senior admiral, David Porter. Behind it all, said the critics, lay the crafty

machine of Republican President Chester A. Arthur, with his
puppets Chandler and Roach manipulating the new navy.

TABLE 3

NAVIES OF OTHER COUNTRIES, 1883–84

	Armored ships.	Unarmored ships.	Transports.	Torpedo-boats.	Guns mounted.	Officers.	Men.	Marines.	Total personnel.
England	61	186	12	100	1,861	4,798	58,800	12,000	75,998
France	58	159	42	70	1,541	5,824	42,126	25,370	73,320
Germany	27	36	2	19	471	1,012	7,400	...	8,412
Spain	5	81	4	3	424	2,367	14,000	7,033	23,400
Italy	18	23	11	17	311	1,014	15,055	3,638	19,707
Argentine Republic	4	28	...	9	24	160	800	2,000	2,960
Chile	3	10	3	10	63	250	1,500	...	1,750
Brazil	21	15	5	5	100	776	4,000	...	4,776

SOURCE: *Congressional Record*, 15, pt. 2: 1391

A patient reader of the *Record* can find some sound data and
reasoning interspersed with the amateurish rhetoric about the
sea service. Men like Senator M.C. Butler of South Carolina
and congressman William D. Hill of Ohio might not understand
technological problems, but they regaled their colleagues in the
winter of 1884 with arguments concerning international naval
strengths, and how foreign navies possessed better guns,
manpower, and ship reserves. By comparison, Congressman
Hill pointed out that the American navy comprised:

> 91 ships; of these 91, 38 are wooden vessels, and generally
> unfit for service. Thirteen are serviceable monitors. Five
> are unfinished monitors requiring expensive additions. We
> have some vessels of wood and 1 torpedo boat. Of the 38
> mentioned as serviceable, 1, the *Mohican*, is finished, 1 is on
> the lakes, and 8 are dispatch and freight boats. The
> *personnel* of our Navy is but 8,000, and a large number are
> officers.[26]

Such statistics led some legislators to consider larger national defense issues by 1884. It was not merely a question of
commercial protection for House members Abram S. Hewitt of

New York, Samuel Randall of Pennsylvania, or Senator John F. Miller of California. They worried more about the defense of waterways leading to commercial centers like New York or San Francisco. They fretted not only about European ironclads but even about Chile's European-built warships. Leaders like Senators Butler, Eugene Hale of Maine, and Congressman Charles Boutelle realized there was more to the whole question of annual appropriations and new construction than the old issues of partisanship and contractor favoritism. Everyone agreed with Senator Miller's oratorical flourish, "I am in favor of constructing American men-of-war from American material, by American workmen, to be manned by American seamen, and to be used in the service of the Government of the United States, whatever that service may call for, and I am in favor of constructing just such ships as will be effective and useful and economical and will serve the purpose for which a navy is intended."[27]

Everybody favored domestication of tools and processes for constructing the navy. At this point, naval ordnance chief Sicard disrupted the debate by telling the Senate Naval Affairs Committee that not only was the department unprepared to produce eight-inch guns at home (although they could finish Whitworth, Krupp, or French forgings), but the U.S. Navy simply couldn't use any more money than the basic request for approximately six hundred thousand dollars in ordnance procurement funding. Facilities simply could not handle a larger program. Suddenly the Senate's dander was up. Morgan of Alabama said the country should feel ashamed; Hale and Democratic senator Thomas E. Bayard of Delaware both wanted to get European ordnance and armor immediately to resolve the impasse. Citing a much vaunted one-hundred-ton French hammer which was ideal for naval steel, Senator James E. Beck of Kentucky proclaimed, "The largest hammer in the world is for sale, I presume, no matter where it is, and if we need it it can be had." A riptide of support for a government gun factory and construction of a domestic armaments industry swept the Senate chamber.[28]

It was short lived. Impasse continued in the House. Although it remains difficult to pinpoint the cause, various technical questions, congressional prerogatives, political maneuvering, procedural questions all entwined to the detriment of naval rearmament. Unfortunately the saga of Roach's difficulties at building the first steel ships was continually debated in the press and in Congress. Sloppy blueprint preparation by the navy, various seasonal and man-made disasters at the Chester yard, and eventually a snapped propeller shaft on the *Dolphin* led to Roach's bankruptcy, political scandal, and four incomplete warships when the Republicans left office the following March.

The navy and its rigid steel requirements created much of Roach's problem. The 25 percent ductility provision proved difficult for the steel manufacturers. Roach had contracted with Norway Iron and Steel, Park Brothers, Phoenix Iron, and Carnegie for hull and boiler plates, angle bars, deck beams and the like. When the Naval Advisory Board's rolling mill inspectors rejected 146 out of 880 heats (16.6 percent), they threw the work schedule months behind. Roach was caught off guard, apparently thinking his friendship with Secretary Chandler would give him some leverage on such matters.

When the subcontractors frankly refused to honor original supply arrangements with Roach, the Chester builder had to run his own facilities at full capacity sixteen hours a day. He never caught up. The navy bent slightly on the number but not the quality of its tests. This helped Roach very little. He failed to meet crucial time constraints and steelmakers and shipbuilders alike grew increasingly suspicious of navy methods and procedures. The test standard issue was to remain a sore point in naval-industrial relations for many decades.[29]

Chandler attempted to soothe industrialists' feelings in his final annual report as he boasted of the eight thousand tons of mild steel examined by the advisory board for the new fleet. "It has been shown," he claimed, "that our steelmakers can readily furnish this excellent structural material in large quantities, and its high quality has been assured by the tests adopted." He counseled "Patience, forbearance, and liberal treatment of the manufacturers are necessary in order to encourage them to undertake the development of the production in this country of steel plate and armor for naval vessels and ingots for heavy cannon."[30]

The 1884 report was a perfect summation of the state of naval rearmament and modernization at the end of the Arthur administration. Chandler's policy recommendations pointed toward continuation of the hoary cruiser-coastal defense monitor type of program. If the monitors cost almost $1.6 million each, noted Chandler, "It has never been claimed for the monitors that they would be a match for the enormous iron-clad battle-ships of Europe, costing $4,000,000 each." When the secretary complained about continuing deficiencies of guns and armor, the reader might discern the real problems at that stage of program development. Midvale might be turning out six-inch guns, but lengthy delays at the Cammell and Whitworth works in England made it uncertain when larger tubes would appear. The navy was at the mercy of the "convenience of foreign manufacturers," and Chandler cautioned "it should be borne in mind that the manufacture of modern high-power guns, such as are required for the new cruisers, being wholly new in this country, is slow and difficult, and the cost here is necessarily higher than if they were procured abroad."[31]

Chandler was more sure that the navy should continue to buy armor abroad for the monitors. Rejection of English armor plate from the Brown and Cammell companies had produced delays similar to those in the ordnance field. But the monitors required 2,960 tons of armor—too small an amount to spawn domestic manufacture as yet. "If, however, additional armored vessels are to be built, it is desirable that active measures should be taken by the Government to encourage the manufacture of armor in this country, in connection with the production of steel ingots for guns," said the secretary, thus signaling an appreciation for the future direction of naval policy that has gone largely unnoticed by modern naval historians.

Meanwhile, Simpson's Gun Foundry Board had received additional instructions to investigate what annual installments would economically provide modern ordnance, and it was specifically charged with preparing detailed plans and estimates "for the preparation and purchase of plant for gun factories to complete guns for the Army and Navy, from 6-inch to 16-inch caliber, including buildings and shrinking-pits." In the process of such investigation, the board had discovered a number of steelmen ready to "supply the requisite material for the heaviest guns adapted to modern warfare, if a guaranteed order of sufficient magnitude, accompanied by a positive appropriation extending over a series of years, should be made by Congress." Chandler urged early action on that proposition in his final report.

The board had gathered supplemental information with greatest difficulty, however. James M. Swank, secretary of the American Iron and Steel Association had actually facilitated contacts with key manufacturers like Joseph R. Anderson of Tredeger Iron Company, Samuel L. Felton and Major L.S. Bent of Pennsylvania Steel, Edward Y. Townsend and Powell Stackhouse of Cambria, William Sellers and R.W. Davenport of Midvale, John Fritz and Joseph Wharton of Bethlehem Iron, or Chester Griswold of Albany and Rensselaer Iron and Steel. While others such as Louisville Board of Trade representative A.S. Willis expressed interest in the naval board's activities, little was heard from many key firms like Canegie. Still, Simpson's group could conclude on Christman Eve, 1884 that while a two-year lead time was required to begin production at two government gun factories, "the total estimate of $17,000,000 will complete the steel-producing plant, establish and equip the steel gun factories, supply the guns for six and one-half years, and inaugurate the manufacture of steel in large masses in the United States."[32]

The question was, how would Congress react? That body seemed perfectly content to enter the new year with a continued blockage of naval funds. The bill which finally received President Arthur's signature on 3 March 1885 included $25,000 for "testing American armor made of American material;" $10,000 "for completion and public test of two breechloading rifle cannon of the large calibers now in course of construction for the Navy"; and authorized construction of two cruisers (three to five thousand tons) costing $1 million each; one heavily armored gunboat of sixteen hundred tons, costing $520,000; and a light gunboat of eight hundred tons, to cost at the most $285,000.[33]

Chandler's final days in office were hectic. Aging Admiral Porter wrote petulantly about the Senate's omitting his favorite gunboat from the construction authorization ("as I desire to leave it as my monument to the Navy"), and Commodore J.E. Walker, chief of navigation, called attention to the supposed need for new compass stations since the new steel ships would undoubtedly throw those delicate instruments off course. Even Commodore Simpson showed signs of wear. Writing from a vacation retreat later in August, he noted having "come to repair damages to nerves and mind produced by unfair treatment that has been received by the Advisory Board." Building the new navy was taking its toll of officials of the old fleet.[34]

Simpson told Chandler that he had refrained from countering every point of criticism, but he complained bitterly about being "ostracized, relegated to New London & League Island" for advocating construction of the very guns then being made at the Washington Navy Yard and Woolwich, England. Betraying the prima donna attitude of most naval professionals of the era, Simpson's tone was deeply wounded as he told his former boss, "I have lived that down, I shall hope to live to see the cruisers vindicated, but the last year of my official life has been embittered by this effort at humiliation, but I know my reputation is on a solid basis (not won by cruises at Washington) and I await the prevailing spirit of justice which will assert itself only when politics (improperly so called) is banished from the Navy Department." Simpson thus joined John Roach on the back bench of new navy malcontents.

The publicity which accompanied the turbulence of those years was not always detrimental to the navy. Both Lieutenants W.H. Jaques and Edwin Very published detailed and highly informative articles on armor and ordnance in the influential *Proceedings* of the United States Naval Institute. Probably too technical for most American citizens—and few read that journal anyway—these articles alerted professional peers to technical advances. Extensive diagrams, charts, and photographs stimulated the emerging breed of technocratic naval personnel. Jaques and Very certainly personified the type of professional naval man oriented towards the scientific, technical, and mechanical demands of the Age of Steel.[35]

The Republican years ended temporarily in early March 1885. Criticism and controversy had surrounded their halting, erratic attempts at naval rearmament. Partisan politics, corruption, power, and payoff all accompanied the administrations of men like Hunt and Chandler, and it would take years to salvage battered reputations and gain any balanced perspective. Chandler's contemporaries, like many later historians, concluded that the navy improved very little during this time. Yet most observers missed key elements in the painfully slow process of naval modernization.

The transition from wooden to steel ships, from Gilded Age political administration to streamlined techniques of management and procurement, from politically appointed cabinet official to managerial expert in a modern bureaucracy was evolutionary, not revolutionary. The new ties between industry and national defense in peacetime were imperfectly perceived by an early generation of participants and observers. There seemed nothing ominous about linkages established by Lieutenants Jaques and Very with arms makers Whitworth and Hotchkiss while still in American naval dress. In fact, Very was quite critical in his complaints to Secretary Chandler concerning the department's arrangements with the French firm in 1884. Very stood high in Commodore Simpson's esteem, and Simpson told Chandler that the lieutenant, with twenty-one years of service, was more likely to get important information from European ordnance makers than any other naval officer.[36]

The political deals, favoritism and corruption portrayed in the newspapers actually existed in the naval establishment. The statutory requirements for low bidders on government contracts sometimes were slighted, and the intentions of top reformers in Washngton often fell apart when translated into actual daily operations at Mare Island, Norfolk, or Boston navy yards. Chandler was notorious for his political use of the yards while in Congress, and Henry Cabot Lodge considered the Boston facility his own fiefdom. All of the so-called "ills" of the modern industrial-military interlock—kickbacks, cost overruns, favored contractors, political interest in defense-related industries—may be traced to the time of the ABCD cruisers,

John Roach, William Chandler, and the Forty-ninth Congress.

The pattern had begun. The U.S. Navy had become a technical prod and a demanding advisor for the industrialists. The Advisory Board's persistence in procuring quality naval steel in the 1880s led to a phenomenon even more important than instant profit for the steel industry. This was the assemblage of a body of skilled labor and management capable of producing steel plates and shapes with relative ease and a quality hitherto unknown in the United States.[37]

Nevertheless, the Gun Foundry Board had raised an issue which was by no means resolved by 1885. This issue concerned management and institutional arrangements, and whether an armaments industry in America would be under the direct control of the central government or be vested with private enterprise. As the Democrats began to grapple with the problems of naval rearmament, Congress, the executive branch, and American industry would all be put to the test.

Chapter 3

Lion, Cock, and Eagle,
The First Commercial Contracts

For years the Democrats had blamed the Republicans for corruption, naval degeneration, political favoritism, and the general state of the nation. Now it was their turn to correct such problems. President Grover Cleveland selected wealthy corporation lawyer William C. Whitney of New York to "clean up" the Navy Department. Trained at Yale and Harvard Law School, Whitney had joined his brother in practice in New York City. He had married into the prosperous Payne family of Cleveland, Ohio, and first encountered his predecessor, William E. Chandler, while serving as corporation counsel in New York. Whitney was determined to use his tenure in the State, War, and Navy Building to reform military-industrial relations.[1]

This boded ill for Republican favorites such as John Roach. Whitney wasted little time in coming to grips with the builder of the ABCD ships. At the same time he used the Roach contracts as the basis for a probe of departmental affairs both in Washington and in the shore facilities around the country. The ensuing storm of controversy lasted beyond Roach's bankruptcy announcement in July 1885, his death two years later, and the final naval acceptance of the warships. In fact, the political crossfire about the first ships and their builder provided grist for Republican-Democratic campaigns beyond the close of the century.[2]

The Navy Department eventually had to complete the warships itself. Settlement of Roach's estate took years and the whole business must have amused foreign ministries with all the hoopla and tumult. *Atlanta, Boston, Chicago,* and *Dolphin* were miniscule by world naval standards. They graphically reflected the experimental nature of naval rearmament in the Chandler-Whitney era. But, when finally banded together as a "Squadron of Evolution" by Whitney's Republican successor, Benjamin F. Tracy, the ABCD warships surpassed expectations at home and compared with foreign vessels of similar class. Meanwhile, the ABCD episode was merely the most controversial of the armaments matters addressed by Whitney.[3]

The country's general disappointment with Roach's "navy" might be seen in the oft-quoted phrase that the new steel vessels were too weak to fight and too slow to run. Whitney was mindful of such criticism. As he suggested in his 1886 annual report, "The inexperience of the Department in its first attempt at the creation of modern vessels of war has been such as to excite greatest concern and disappointment." Yet he showed little inclination to rush blindly ahead during the initial months of his administration. He listened to civilian naval architects dispense free advice while seeking favors. He quietly set out to secure more facts before awarding contracts or committing the navy to a particular policy. He left the March appropriations untouched until mid-July, and he avoided altogether the Naval Advisory Board recommendations on an 8,500-ton armored vessel. In fact, Whitney later thought his greatest contribution was not new shipping at all, nor any new policy. Ships might soon become obsolete and the country was unready for policy shifts. Rather, he considered his major achievement to be the development of domestic facilities which freed the United States Navy from foreign armor, guns, and ships.[4]

Naturally, some people disagreed with Whitney. Shipbuilding and armament competition from Europe could provide stimulants to domestic self-improvement. Congress and the armed services wanted to get more information, the easiest recourse when institutions are not ready to seize the initiative. Both houses appointed additional committees to investigate naval technical problems, and the U.S. Army established yet another board to study coastal defenses. The Senate Select Committee on Ordnance and War Ships, under chairman J.R. Hawley of Connecticut; the House Commission on Ordnance and Gunnery, under Congressman Samuel J. Randall of Pennsylvania, as well as the so-called Endicott board on fortifications and other defenses all provided an appropriate capstone to years of inconclusive investigations of national defense.[5]

Naturally there were many parallels between the conclusions of the three groups. Both Senate and House groups reflected their member's constituent interests. They opposed large-scale government entry into industrial production via ordnance and armor plants. Yet the Endicott board plan for a "fortress America" to protect harbors and coastal cities envisioned over twenty-five thousand tons of armor plate for forts and warships. Someone would have to produce it, and Randall later told Whitney it should come exclusively from private industry. The only trouble was that his committee could transmit only one concrete proposal from an American firm to do the work. Benjamin Atha and Company of Newark, New Jersey proposed to deliver planed edge armor plate, with bore bolt holes, and bent to specified pattern, if a contract could be guaranteed for five thousand tons per year for five years at five hundred dollars per ton.[6]

The one connecting thread in all the deliberations on ordnance and armor seemed to be the whims of private steel manufacturers. They conveyed to government officials a phlegmatic interest in possible contracts, and repeatedly told Congress that prices of five hundred dollars and more per ton would be necessary in any formal arrangement. After all, they said, foreign 20-inch armor, completely finished and ready for installation, cost nearly that much, and 12.5-inch compound armor stood at three hundred dollars. In short, the initial spurt of industrial interest after the Gun Foundry Board's study faded with the disappointing failure of Congress to take specific action.

The next two years of activity in Washington rekindled private interest and the powerful Iron and Steel Association *Bulletin* swung in behind the Gun Foundry Board proposals for heavy forging appropriations. Faced with harsher economic times as plants operated below capacity and prices sagged to their lowest in years, the steel magnates turned their thoughts to the largely unused surplus in the federal treasury. The executive committee of the association, possibly pushed by its leader, Robert Swank, addressed a memorial to Congress urging support for armor and ordnance. By the end of 1885 venerable Simon Cameron of Pennsylvania (always ready to reflect his senatorial constituents' best interests) had introduced bills calling for a total of ten thousand tons of rough forgings from industry.[7]

At the same time, the U.S. Navy had insufficient shore facilities and trained technicians to bring off rapid naval rearmament even if the American industrialists had been able to provide the proper tools. Whitney's first annual report highlighted the problems, from inadequate ordnance proving grounds, obsolete departmental organization and procurement policies, to the dearth of training and educational programs to equip professional specialists in modern naval design, fabrication, and management. "It must be evident that there is something radically wrong with the Department," he claimed. His prescribed reorganization addressed policy development, managerial problems, and the relations between scientific development and government in one of the most perceptive statements on institutional modernization submitted by any of the cabinet officials of the period.[8]

What especially disturbed Whitney was the great independence enjoyed by the navy's bureaus in procurement matters. Each bureau appeared to deal with "regular dealers" without concern for one another or the needs of the service. They consequently stockpiled vast amounts of matériel, most of which was never used. He saw a lack of centralized fiscal or managerial accountability— possibly a natural ingredient of the nascent stages of any military-industrial complex. Citing British, French, and German experience, Whitney wanted a change in bureau structure, not merely personnel. He envisioned three subdivisions—personnel and the fleet, material and construction, finance and accounts—supplanting the seven existing bureaus.

Whitney sensed that European admiralties were far ahead of the United States in developing naval corps of specialists, trained professionals to deal with ordnance and armor, engineering and machinery, naval architecture, matériel, and supply. Indeed, they were also ahead in exploiting civilian maritime expertise. It was to private enterprise that the art of naval warfare was indebted for most if its improvements, he said, "iron or steel used for her hull and for her armor; her power and the engines by which it is controlled and directed; her revolving turrets; her guns; her projectiles; her explosives; her torpedoes; her search-lights; her steering gears; her wire cordage, are almost exclusively the invention of private individuals, and are manufactured and supplied by industrial agencies operated mainly by private capital." Whitney pressed for private enterprise to team up with the navy.

The policy of enlisting the private sector tended to create and develop new branches of industry. Since 1868, said Whitney, the government had easily wasted $75 million on its naval arm instead of sponsoring the inventive genius of the country and stimulating "competition among our people in the production of modern ships of war." The Hotchkiss gun, an American invention, had been ignored or rejected by U.S. government agencies while finding its true field of development abroad. Similarly, the famous inventor John Ericsson was working at age eighty-three "without encouragement or notice" at the great problems of naval warfare, and "is receiving more attention and greater encouragement from other Governments than from our own."

Whitney sensed that business, naval administration, technology, and policy were inextricably linked in the modern world. "After you have freed your technical, scientific men from unnecessary burdens, put the finances where they will be handled in a business way, freed your designers largely from the executive work, so that they are enabled to put the

Department in the way of producing advanced products (appropriating, adapting, and inventing new and improved methods in their various lines), it is of the first importance that the system should center in a wise and judicious and capable directing power, for there is necessarily the daily decision to be made of what shall be done in any particular line," declared Whitney. The winds of change and centralization were blowing, and he knew it. Men like Porter, Sicard, and Chief Constructor Wilson could sympathize with Whitney's position. Evolving technology meant changes in public administration and institutional relationships.

If these issues kept Whitney from suggesting immediate construction of an armored battlefleet in his first annual report, others in the U.S. Navy were less hestitant. Rear Admiral Edward Simpson, for one, was preaching this doctrine to all who might listen. He told both Whitney and the Washington branch of the Naval Institute in December 1885 that "there should be no delay in commencing construction of armored vessels." Notwithstanding inadequate harbor depths or drydocks, according to him, seven-thousand ton armored vessels mounting ten-inch turret guns for main batteries would form "the outer line of defence of the coast in war, always available for operating abroad either in peace or war, and affording a school of practice and instruction in peace to prepare us for war."[9]

While Simpson advocated the building of America's first high seas battlefleet, he also told his audience of the problems coincident with acquisition of such a weapons system. Delivery dates for gun forgings were key elements in the equation since "it is manifest that the delivery of the tempered material for guns, rough-bored and turned, is of no avail unless the gun factories are prepared to take the parts as they arrive, and to smooth-finish and assemble them." The Gun Foundry Board had estimated a lead time of three years for completing the tools, constructing the ships, and finishing the plant. Thus, the two operations were part of one transaction. To Simpson, "the time for the delivery of the material and the time when the factory would be ready to receive it synchronize, and if the authority to erect the factory be given at the same time as the contract for the manufacture of material the work will go on harmoniously from the commencement."

Even if the next Congress would enact all legislation required to equip the two arms of the service with modern ordnance, and the steel manufacturers would respond favorably to government proposals, said Simpson, it would still be impossible to begin fabrication of even the smallest guns before 1888. The largest ordnance could not be started until 1890. To Simpson, between guns and ships, "the ships are the more readily attainable"—shipyards existed, but cannon fabrication awaited plant construction. It was no different with armor, and he concluded "It is well that we familiarize ourselves with the ideas of large masses of material and large expenditures of money; the rehabilitation of the Navy is a work of magnitude, and Congress and the people must be approached without disguise."

Since large-scale educational efforts for public, Congress, and the sea service itself were impeded by Whitney's basic desire to move slowly and deliberately on ships, armor, and armament, there was no American naval revolution in the eighties. But even Whitney appeared to quicken his pace by the early part of 1886. Lieutenant Jaques, Commander F.E. Chadwick, London naval attache, and naval constructor Philip Hichborn received instructions to secure the lowest terms for English and Japanese warship plans from British architects. The U.S. Navy eventually paid twenty-five hundred dollars for such plans. Roundly condemned in the press for going abroad in this manner, Whitney unabashedly observed that "our true policy is to borrow the ideas of our neighbors so far as they are thought to be in advance of our own."[10]

Whitney hoped to get Congress upset enough to grant appropriations to domesticate shipbuilding, ordnance, and armor procurement for the navy. While House Naval Affairs Committee Chairman Hilary Herbert of Alabama went along, other congressmen were not so positive in their response. The first session of the Forty-ninth Congress was nearly as conservative about the navy as its predecessor. Spurred by Cleveland and party manipulators like Herbert, the new legislation for two six-thousand ton armored cruisers and four torpedo boats moved slowly. Now the roles were reversed. The Democrats pushed rehabilitation and the Grand Old Party battled on the old ground of monitor completion, Roach cruisers, and rebuilding wooden ships. But the ABCD ships had awakened a spirit of chauvinism, and calls for the sole use of American designs, American inventions, and American workmanship crowded the record of the deliberations. Legislators from Pennsylvania, Virginia, and California saw navy yards in home districts as logical construction sites for the warships.[11]

The major issues of armor and ordnance slowly crystallized as the principal roadblocks to completing programs authorized by Congress. An important provision of the proposed legislation demanded that the armor "shall be of the best obtainable quality and of domestic manufacture, provided contracts for furnishing the same in a reasonable time, at a reasonable price, and of the required quality can be made with responsible parties." At first, Democrats wanted an escape clause to permit the naval secretary to buy abroad if the material was unobtainable at home. But Republican debators like Samuel Randall and Andrew Curtin of Pennsylvania, Charles Boutelle of Maine, and Frank Hiscock of New York immediately proclaimed grandiloquent possibilities for American industry and labor. Many politicians simply ignored the facts, for both they and the U.S. Navy knew well that few, if any, American industrialists could give credence to such claims.

Whitney and Herbert were especially anxious to stress the "reasonable price" clause so as to avoid "any combination on the part of the iron men or anybody else so that the Department or the Government shall not be placed in their power." They also underscored a steel quality amendment to the basic legislation. Navy experts like Jaques wrote former secretary William Chandler, destined to join the Senate the following year, warning that the question of domestic ore was a serious one. Claiming "the report of the Gun Foundry Board seems now to be a sort of Holy Writ," Jaques observed that "no bill should pass requiring the manufacturing to be restricted to domestic material. The tariff should take care of the ore. The *manufacture* should be domestic and restricted to reasonable manufacturers both financially and technically." In the end,

Republican protectionists in Congress prevailed. They held sufficient votes to prevent passage of the bill unless the Democrats relented on the steel armor clause.

The legislators finally sent the bill to President Cleveland in early August. Whitney was delighted that it authorized two armored cruisers (*Maine* and *Texas*), one protected cruiser (*Baltimore*), and a first-class torpedo-boat (*Cushing*). One unique feature held that the material for all the new vessels (except shafting) had to be of domestic manufacture, and at least one of the warships was to be built in a navy yard. Apparently Congress not only wanted domestication, but also feared that private shipbuilders might make extortionate demands upon the government if given exclusive rights to construction.

In addition, the legislation provided $1,000,000 for ordnance and $3,178,046 to complete the monitors. Whitney was directed to apply portions of this sum "to the manufacture or purchase of such tools and machinery or the erection of such structures as may be required for use in the manufacture of such armament . . ." or to contract with domestic manufacturers for the construction of such heavy ordnance as the government could not fabricate. This made possible the implementation of a gun factory and contracting with steelmen for armor. It may have been the most important clause of any naval legislation in the decade.[12]

It was an attractive package handed to Secretary Whitney. The armor and gun forging problems had been partially resolved. Legislation for moving ahead with the gun factory and procurement of armor and forgings led the navy immediately to the contractual stage. The secretary had already approached shipbuilders like Pusey and Jones as well as William Cramp and Sons seeking advice on warship plans. When the navy issued a specific circular on 21 August 1886 soliciting bids for 1,310 tons of gun forgings and 4,500 tons of armored steel, it was proceeding mainly on Whitney's faith that a block order would surface interested steelmakers.

The block order scheme had been a continuous thread throughout previous navy-steelmaker correspondence as well as in recent congressional testimony. It was further enhanced by private messages to legislators like S.J. Randall which made their way to Whitney's desk through government "back channel" sources. One such message involved Joseph Wharton, Philadelphia businessman and entrepreneur, proprietor of the American Nickel Works, founding father and major stockholder in Bethlehem Iron, as well as one of Randall's constituents. Wharton obviously possessed an interest in any negotiations which might benefit his commercial portfolio.[13]

Wharton went to Europe in the late spring of 1886 with the blessings of Whitney. His mission was to inspect foreign steel mills. It was well known from Gun Foundry Board findings and congressional hearings that Whitney not only leaned toward importation of ideas and techniques, but preferred the type of armor and gun forgings which could be provided only by Henri Schneider of Creusot, France and Joseph Whitworth of Sheffield, England. Therefore Wharton sought to corner the American market for the Bethlehem firm by making commercial arrangements with the Europeans for patent rights, technical assistance, and even machinery. Bethlehem would then domesticate the foreign products for the broader American market—both military and civilian.[14]

Bethlehem was suffering from a dull rail market in 1885 and 1886. The firm's managers had been forced to take a $1. million mortgage in order to continue operations. They understandably sought product diversification, largely at the wise enjoinder of the company's general superintendent and chief engineer, John Fritz. Fritz had earlier suggested unsuccessfully that the business turn toward structural steel, and his engineering instincts convinced him that it was a national disgrace that the United States could not make heavy forgings. His commercial philosophy was: "Put the forging plant up and let the engineers know what they can get and then wants will soon grow up to it."

Fritz's sentiments undoubtedly led Wharton to tell Randall on 12 June that

> I am thus with my knowledge of American establishments, better able than any other person (with a very few exceptions) to form a clear and unbiased opinion as to the

probability of American works being with any reasonable time [able] to produce large gun parts and armor, or either, and I feel bound to state to you in the most emphatic manner that, except for the preparations made by the Bethlehem Iron Co as you know for the production of steel forgings suitable for shafts and gun parts, there is nothing in America and no beginning or preparation of anything that can turn out such shafts, weapons, and armor as are being made every day in Europe for all the important nations. [15]

Wharton told Randall that large quantities of forged steel had never been considered in America. Lacking the proper artisans and tools, Wharton thought an alliance between an American company like Bethlehem and a European tutor like Schneider was the quickest and cheapest way to reach "within a few years, independence for America in those great arts." He admitted some reluctance to venture the great additional capital required for such a project. Yet he opposed any government prohibition to going abroad, contending "the condition that of the 5,000 tons or thereabout of armor needed for the monitors and for the new armored vessels, such part as cannot be made early enough at home may be imported, is a condition that ought to remain and become law."

What Wharton did not tell Randall was that it was Schneider who had first approached the Bethlehem company in November 1885 seeking inroads into the American market. The Frenchman admitted "that the only chance for him to get any order from America is to offer to form an alliance with an American establishment, by which he would agree, in consideration of having say half of the first 4 or 5,000 ton order, to impart all information and give all assistance to enable the American establishment to produce the remaining or last half of that order in America," as well as a cut of future orders. Prices would stand at current rates and Creusot would guarantee the product.

Wharton had countered by presuming to speak for the U.S. government on the domestication of armor and on international prices. Schneider in turn asked for a very large sum of money, that the first several thousand tons of armor plate be produced in France, as well as the proviso that Bethlehem would agree to produce solely for the American market with Creusot getting a slice of future orders. Wharton abruptly executed a *tour de force* by urging Secretary Whitney to press for the "domestic only" clause in the next appropriation act. Whitney agreed, however, to buy American armor only if he could get a reasonable bid. Whitney obviously wanted to manipulate the steelmen, seeking to gain congressional permission to buy foreign armor in the absence of a reasonable bid, while recognizing that only Bethlehem could really produce superior Schneider armor. The Navy Department's main concern was to avoid exhorbitant prices.

The department was prepared to issue steel and warship bid advertisements by mid-August. Some 1,360 tons of steel gun forgings and 4,070 tons of armor plating were needed and delivery projections ranged from one to two and one-half years. Ordnance chief Sicard had specific information for bidders concerning navy chemical, physical, and ballistic test requirements. The circular for the new ships was even more complicated, and snags developed almost immediately on both.[16]

The actual advertisements were not published until a month later. Naval bureaucrats worried about whether any manufacturer could meet their rigid specifications. They were reassured when Joseph Wharton wrote to Whitney on 7 September from his Newport vacation home, conveying information from his nephew, Robert Thurston, vice president at Bethlehem, to the effect that the firm had purchased a Whitworth plant in England. It would be shipped to the Pennsylvania facility immediately. Wharton noted that the navy might have to compromise some of its standards, but he assured Whitney that European standards would be surpassed, albeit at high cost. Said Wharton, "if by paying double the cost that Europeans pay you could get guns or plates ten per cent better than Europeans get, you could better afford to do that than to get guns or plates ten per cent worse for half cost."[17]

Wharton seemed entirely confident that his organization would ultimately win the contracts, perhaps because Whitney and his advisers were secretly leaning toward preferential treatment of Bethlehem. Later that same month he told the secretary of progress in erecting the Whitworth plant and importuned him to visit Bethlehem. He also noted that he and the Creusot agent, Commander F.M. Barber, planned to spend time together before Barber went to France for consultation. Barber apparently thought 6,900, not 4,500 tons would be required for steel orders. All of these links—Wharton (Bethlehem) and Barber (Schneider-Creusot)—were known to Whitney and the Navy Department. The secretary was possibly less concerned with combinations, corners on the market, or even a certain winking at the domestication clause, so long as an ordnance establishment was able to keep the ship construction program on an even keel.[18]

By the autumn the first criticism concerning these machinations began to surface. Publicity in Great Britain threatened the backchannel information sharing and professional linkages between British and American shipbuilders and naval officers. London naval attache French E. Chadwick complained to Whitney that "every sentiment of honor demands of course that we should refrain from publishing that which is given us by foreign governments as confidential documents, and every sentiment of self interest demands the same, in the case of documents obtained otherwise." But departmental bureaucrats like Philip Hichborn wrote openly of such matters, thinking, one supposes, to impress the American public as well as foreign governments with naval progress and technical development in the United States Navy.[19]

At the same time, unfavorable publicity also began to attend the liaison roles played by naval officers in the dealings between government and private steelmen. Whitelaw Reid's *New York Tribune* of 5 November 1886 rebuked Commander Barber for suspicious activities on behalf of the Schneider firm with regard to foreign shafting and influence in naval procurement matters. Barber quickly wrote his old patron, former secretary Chandler, declaring "the affair of the shafts is trifling for it will be known that no hollow shafts such as are required can be made in this country even of iron; but as you are aware, I am on the point of closing arrangements with prominent steel men in this country [France] for establishing the fabrication of

Creusot Steel Armor in the U.S. and it is vitally necessary that I should be let alone for it is one of the conditions of my leave that I should not resign at the end of it and I am not ready yet to give it up.'' Such pleas failed to silence the criticism.[20]

W.E. Church, editor of the influential *Army and Navy Journal*, joined the controversy by writing directly to Whitney by November and December about ''Barber's relations to the Schneiders because of the demoralizing effect upon the service of recognizing such employment as legitimate.'' ''In a certain sense they take the vow of poverty,'' claimed the editor, ''if not of chastity, and to have them brought under the influence of the ordinary commercial greed for money is demoralizing and lowers the tone of the service.'' Citing examples of Army engineer officers similarly compromised, Church thought that no military professional should allow himself to fall under the influence of personal interest in matters concerning his service judgment. ''Whatever Lieuts. Barber and Jaques may say to the contrary the question of compound versus steel armor is still an open one and it will not do to allow the opinion of officers concerning it to be subsidized,'' he trumpeted.[21]

In Church's opinion none of the officers knew as much about steel as they claimed. Manuafacturers themselves were still experimenting, and he cited his own brother, a mining engineer, as one who contended that the Rodman method of casting guns could be applied also to steel. The editor felt that the steelmen believed in compound armor with a fervor, but were willing to furnish any kind ''if you ask it.'' Church said that he was no stranger to controversy with ''officers as a class'' during his quarter-century stewardship of the journal.

Altruism may have governed Church's concern, but crass political motives lay behind Reid's moves. His attacks upon the Cleveland administration were well known, and in late 1886 he seized upon a new editorial weapon—Whitney's supposed hostility to American industry. Such an interpretation was possible in light of Whitney's desire to secure armor and guns from any available source, foreign or domestic. Still, Whitney's record with Congress indicated active sponsorship of American manufacturing. He had written to the Senate naval affairs committee in late July, for example, stating that he sought to offer a large enough contract to induce American steelmakers to create a plant for gun forgings and armor since "it is un-business like not to utilize the necessary purchases to encourage the establishment of the required plant in this country." Reid eventually backtracked under a withering counter-assault from the administration. But he fired one final salvo at Whitney who, said Reid, had destroyed Roach, discredited the Advisory Board, discarded Chandler's ship plans, ignored American engineers, and "raided" American industries. This was pure partisan journalism, although it surely caused some anxious moments for the energetic Whitney.[22]

Whitney's record spoke for itself when his annual report appeared in December. Although the report was hardly a high point of optimism, the secretary used this device to prod Congress, warn of waste and inefficiency, and congratulate industry spokesmen who had bid for various new warships. He noted that the department was taking great care to "enlist the contractors pecuniarily in the attainment of a successful result," and by lumping all armor needs into one contract would "offer the same to the competition of steel manufacturers in the United States, and allow a sufficient time for the successful bidder, if one or more should appear, to take the necessary steps in the way of creation of plant and initiating the manufacture." The same would hold for gun forgings, which "is, of course, an experiment."[23]

The secretary admitted to a three-year delay in finishing the warships due to lack of material and the withholding of contracts. "But at the end of five years," he suggested, "the country would by pursuing it, be independent and in a much stronger position in every respect than would result from any other course." In the meantime, the ship list of the U.S. Navy still consisted of fourteen single-turreted monitors (none in commission or serviceable); five small fourth-rate auxiliary vessels; and twenty-seven cruisers, three of which were iron with the wooden remainder in an advanced state of decay. As even Whitney's own biographer later concluded, "The country still had a rump fleet of antiquated wooden vessels."[24]

Cleveland strongly supported his secretary's findings in his own message for the year. Even as he did so, Whitney was already signing contracts for the new warships *Charleston*,

Petrel, Yorktown, and *Newark,* and actively wooing the elusive steelmen. Writing to the president of Midvale Steel, he urged them to get together on armored steel, adding enticingly "I am quite certain that we shall have a fair bid and one that we can accept but I should be glad if you were that person."[25]

The secretary also wrote imploringly to the Carnegie steel interests. He received several rather interesting replies to earlier queries, beginning with an 8 December 1886 note from Andrew Carnegie—the first in which the steel mogul alluded to any naval matters. Praising him for naval reform and re-organization, Carnegie admitted that Whitney's centralizing tendency fell right in line with his own view of the world. "I attribute the success of our concern to the firm stand I have always taken upon this point—one central authority, all others subordinate," he declared.[26]

Carnegie's real reason for writing, however, was to deliver a diatribe on the armor matter. The steelman claimed that recent illness would interfere with his company's entry into armor manufacture, something which he claimed to have discussed only briefly with his partners. Bragging that "of course we have the largest and best plant and best position to make it, and machinery which we are now about to erect for other purposes our managers assure me would make armour." Carnegie claimed that further testing and an additional three to four hundred thousand dollars would enable the firm to complete plates of the finest quality.

Then Carnegie introduced the clincher. He told the secretary, "Our present business is ever growing and to tell the truth I am more and ever opposed to every dollar spent by our Republic upon instruments of any kind for destructive purposes." Betraying a remarkable naiveté, Carnegie did not think that any foreign nation would attack the United States directly; the navy made "a bad nursery" for young men; and American ships around the world "are so many challenges—chips on our shoulders which we go round the world asking people to do us a favor to knock off." He lectured Whitney that were he in public life, the only issue "I would make against your party today is that you are fast transforming a peaceful republic into a warlike power, degrading it to the level of monarchs of the old world." In conclusion he proclaimed "that if Carnegie Bros. & Co. cannot earn a living by making instruments of peace they will conclude to starve rather than make those of war." He added hastily, however, that he would not override the views of all his partners should they decide to enter the armor business even though he held a majority of the company's stock!

Ironically, that was precisely what transpired as by 24 December the *Pittsburgh Times* announced that Carnegie, Phipps and Company Ltd. "are now preparing plans for a new open hearth mill to be built at their Homestead works, which will be capable of rolling the largest sized armor plates named in Secretary Whitney's advertisement for bids." Designed by Julian Kennedy, the firm's general superintendent, and his assistant, Henry Aiken, they received the hearty approval of Captain W.R. Jones of the Edgar Thomson works. Carnegie temporarily capitulated when three days later he wrote the naval secretary:

> You need not be afraid that you will have to go abroad for armour plate. I am now fully satisfied that the mill we are building will roll the heaviest sizes you require, with the greatest ease. I also find that our people have already contracted for the armour plate for one of the ships you have let and are negotiating for the plates for the others. [27]

Carnegie was trying to keep open his options since by 28 February 1887 he told Whitney that his partners were coming to Washington for consultation because he held strong feelings on the question of government inspection. He was especially agitated over navy inspectors who, he declared, were often "martinets" insisting upon "technical points to an absurd degree." The steelman wanted to deal with "practical men" who realized that armor had variables and who might be prepared to allow for them. But Whitney had heard all this before. He declined to lower the navy's traditionally high standards. Carnegie in the end declined to submit any bid, claiming excessive costs, little rewards, and too many headaches. Unlike Midvale leaders who eventually submitted a bid, Whitney's courting of the Carnegie firm proved abortive.

All of this may only have been the secretary's attempt to gain extra insurance. All during the winter his primary negotiations lay with Bethlehem and Joseph Wharton kept him thoroughly conversant with his own negotiations at Creusot. Whitney urged Wharton to make an immediate arrangement with the French firm if he had any real hope of submitting a successful bid. By December, when Carnegie and Whitney were corresponding Henri Schneider had agreed to let Bethlehem produce his brand of armor, and Wharton had some idea of the price which would be involved in the deal. Despite difficulties in the latter vein, Wharton had discussed everything with Whitney and had virtual assurance that, providing his bid was a reasonable one, the armor contract would go to Bethlehem since the secretary had made it abundantly clear that only Schneider armor would meet the necessary requirements of the United States Navy.

Feeling that he had given the steelmakers enough time to meditate on the contracts, Whitney issued a second circular on 12 February 1887 setting the minimum figure for successful bidders at three hundred tons of heavy steel per month. By this time Congress was also becoming restive as the issue of armor and ordnance was again part of the new naval appropriation bill. They finally appropriated $4,000,000 for domestic armor and $20,400 for experimental ordnance (with one cannon to be made of Bessemer steel, one of open-hearth steel, and a third from crucible steel to see which was best). All of this added to the insurance necessary to get Whitney's armor and armament program off the ground.

By late January, Wharton told Whitney that prospects appeared good for a satisfactory arrangement with the French; a final understanding was reached by mid-March (only a few days before bid opening), but final agreement was not signed until August. The Americans wanted the French to guarantee the steel projectiles against any government-imposed test. Creusot refused politely. Many Americans viewed the French plant and technology with disgust, especially since Schneider demanded part of Bethlehem's profits in return for technical information and patent rights. But, in the end, Wharton, Schneider, and Whitney had all secured their goal.

Lieutenant Commander Barber was present as intermediary throughout the negotiations. Paying no heed to criticism from Reid, Church, or even the influential *Bulletin* of the American Iron and Steel Association, which also termed Barber's role as "shameful," Whitney set the pattern for later national defense officials by winking at indiscretion in order to assure the best possible material and equipment for the armed services. Barber might have preferred to see Schneider construct his own plant in America, but he shared Whitney's primary interest in securing the best armament no matter the national source.[28]

The story was quite similar for Lieutenant Jaques, Bethlehem, and the English connection, Joseph Whitworth. Jaques approached John Fritz of the Pennsylvania firm in 1885 regarding authorization to deal with Whitworth. Fritz immediately seized the bait in apparent anticipation of winning the gun forging contract as well as that for armor. The subsequent Bethlehem-Whitworth contract called for the same technical and patent rights which Schneider had yielded on armor, and additionally, the right to buy large amounts of Whitworth machinery. Financial details never surfaced, but one company official termed them "very great." Whitney naturally knew all of this and approved completely, just as he had the Schneider machinations.[29]

Such maneuvers remained unknown to other steelmakers. Robert H. Sayre, Bethlehem's general manager, informed Whitney on 18 March of progress with the new plant which had seven blast furnaces in operation and 4,500 tons of special steel coming off production lines each week. Navy bureaucrats were probably quite prejudiced when armor and ordnance bids were opened four days later. Surprisingly, they discovered that four companies had made concrete proposals.

Original advertisement provisions allowed bidders to seek either the gun forgings or the armor contracts, although preference would be shown to bidders on both. E.Y. Towsend's Cambria Iron and C.J. Harrah's financially troubled Midvale Steel bid solely on ordnance forgings. William Chisolm's Cleveland Rolling Mills bid for armor alone, and naturally, Bethlehem proved to be the only company bidding on both types of work. Admittedly, the latter's bid on armor was much less than its competitor, but Cambria underbid Bethlehem on gun forgings. Consternation pervaded the bid opening. Wharton might have awarded the gun contract to Bethlehem anyway, due to the dual bid. But Cambria pressed for its lower bid. The shrewd Whitney confidently threatened to give the bid to Cambria unless Bethlehem lowered its orginal forging bid.

TABLE 4

SCHEDULE OF PROPOSALS FOR GUN STEEL AND ARMOR, 22 MARCH 1887

Name of Bidder	Proposed Plant	Gun Steel Price	Armor Price	Total
Cambria Iron Co.	Johnstown, Pa.	$851,513.90		$851,513.90
Midvale Steel Co.	Philadelphia, Pa.	1,397,240.00		1,397,240.00
Bethlehem Iron Co.	Bethlehem, Pa.	902,230.79	$3,610,707.50	4,512,938.29
Cleveland Rolling Mill Co.	Cleveland, Ohio		4,021,560.00	4,021.560.00

SOURCE: Secretary of the Navy, *Annual Report, 1887*, 460.

Wharton reluctantly agreed. He reduced the Bethlehem figure to that of Cambria but, in turn, asked the navy for a promise that the contract would include additional forgings. Then, at the last moment, he felt a twinge of conscience. He told the secretary to disregard this suggestion since if other bidders got wind of it, the navy "might be subjected to most annoying urgency and clamour." Bethlehem and the U.S. Navy had finalized the $4. million contracts by June. The company agreed to deliver 6,703 tons of armor and about 1,310 tons of gun forgings at prices ranging from $500 to $650 per ton.[30]

Whitney later recorded that the bid openings "caused a feeling of quite universal congratulation throughout the country," since "it marked a most important step in the progress toward national independence" from foreign suppliers of ordnance matériel. Reid's *New York Tribune* of 23 March praised both Whitney and the Republican-controlled Senate for the blessed event, and the secretary rejoiced that the cost of armor and gun steel was within 20 percent of European prices, a difference attributable to labor costs. Moreover, Whitney thought that American shipbuilders would also profit, since they had been prevented from filling orders for foreign warships because neither armor, gun forgings, nor even lighter secondary batteries were available in the United States. Later in the year, Whitney "repatriated" the Hotchkiss Company from France, requiring it to establish a Connecticut factory in return for a contract for ninety guns. Superior tools permitted that company to manufacture lighter cannon more cheaply in New England than in Paris, and the firm also acquired the right to construct the Howell torpedo used to some extent by the U.S. Navy.

Beginning in May, Washington Navy Yard buildings were altered from forge and anchor fabrication, cranes were erected, and preparations were made for a naval gun factory to finish the gun forgings into polished tubes. The national capital now became a manufacturing seat as the factory was to finalize twenty-five five-inch, four eight-inch, six ten-inch, and four twelve-inch guns (or portionate numbers of each) annually. The string of successes led the Bureau of Ordnance to suggest encouragement of domestic gun cotton manufacture on both seaboards. By the end of 1887 Whitney could look proudly toward growing self-sufficiency for the American fleet.[31]

All of this was timely. On 3 March 1887, the second session of the Forty-ninth Congress had authorized President Cleveland to again enlarge the navy. Two steel gunboats and two steel cruisers were among the provisions as well as money for rams, monitor completion, ordnance, and armor. The legislators were still wedded to cruisers as opposed to armored ships for battle, repair of wooden ships, and coastal forts, but the winter sessions of the year seemed to provide less shrill and partisan debate than before. Then too, national elections were in the offing for 1888, so the legislators may have had their eyes set on other goals.[32]

The pace was beginning to tell on Secretary Whitney's health. Worrying about "insurgents" among naval personnel, the minute details of establishing the gun factory, quick trips to the Cramp shipyards and other industrial facilities, and coping with the daily grind of bureaucracy, the secretary completely collapsed in October. The solicitous Joseph Wharton offered Whitney the use of his Batsto, New Jersey hideaway, but doctors confined the secretary to a New York sickroom, Yet, by late November Whitney was back in time to pen a solid annual

report. Praising steelmakers and other domestic manufacturers, the secretary and his bureau chiefs devoted much space
to discussion of the implements and tools for the new fleet.
Arguing for two more heavy armor-clads plus more cruisers,
the naval officials were setting the stage for the advent of
Mahanite sea power upon the scene.[33]

Election year 1888 dictated that Whitney and the navy
contribute in some manner to the reelection of the Democratic
party. Naval progress held political dividends in influential
coastal states, and so it was a banner day in April when two of
the first Whitney-era ships were launched before five hundred
people at the Cramp shipyard on the Delaware. The gunboat
Yorktown and dynamite cruiser *Vesuvius* brought praise from
both parties as Pennsylvania legislators Samuel G. Randall and
Thomas Bayne expressed pleasure that the administration was
boosting that state's steel and shipbuilding industries. Kansas
representative Bishop M. Perkins wished that *Vesuvius* had
been named for Whitney himself, and even an archetypical
Republican like Joseph Cannon of Illinois admitted, "It's a big
thing." Given the gusto of the occasion, little wonder that
voices were also heard shouting "Whitney for president!"[34]

The secretary had little time for the hoopla, however. He was
more worried about the pace of naval construction. The year's
record showed mainly an extension of previous activities—
plans gathering abroad, maintenance of a tight leash on
contractors like the Herreshoff and Columbian Iron Works
companies working on gunboats and torpedo boats, as well as
listening patiently to Joseph Wharton complain about problems
in Bethlehem's continuing programs for relocating an entire
English steel plant in Pennsylvania. The British Admiralty was
still upset about American pirating of plans; Sicard and his
ordnance officers were too cliquish and slow about their
business, thereby incurring needless delays in matériel deliveries. Norfolk and New York navy yard supervisors as well
as the private shipbuilders were constantly carping on naval
inspection and Bethlehem armor delivery delays. Soon Whitney
found it impossible even to recruit a civilian to fill the vital
superintendent's job at the gun factory.[35]

Timing was everything that year. Whitney wanted a tight

schedule, and the constructors basically agreed. Yet many private contractors were beginning to find drawbacks in working for the government. When Congress threatened to rush through a fortification bill dictating domestic procurement of all tools, machinery, and ordnance, Wharton, R.H. Sayre, and other Bethlehem officials immediately petitioned Whitney for intercession. They could not comply without English material, and loss of Bethlehem expertise would affect industrial-government relations. As Wharton put it, "As the matter stands I apprehend that parties having inferior applicances will claim, when the time for bidding comes, that the government is debarred from the use of Bethlehem Co.'s plant." Such a disaster to the natal military-industrial complex was averted narrowly.[36]

Indeed, the pace quickened in Congress on the eve of the elections. Legislators passed a naval appropriation bill on 7 September which provided for two 3,000-ton cruisers, a 5,300-ton steel cruiser, a 7,500-ton armored cruiser, and three gunboats. Premiums were to be paid for speeds bettering eighteen to twenty knots. Five million dollars was appropriated "towards armor and armament of domestic manufacture," and the congressmen officially recognized America's growing technological independence of Europe by decreeing that the authorized shipping should be built in accordance with provisions of the 1886 "save in all their parts shall be of domestic manufacture."[37]

Two weeks later Congress gave the U.S. Army its share of the 1888 version of strategic deterrence with a coastal fort rebuilding bill, establishment of an army gun factory at Watervliet, New York, as well as $1.5 million for purchase of rough-finished gun steel for eight-, ten- and twelve-inch cannon. The prepassage debate was as discursive and verbose as that surrounding battles for the new navy. Many legislators like Senator Joseph Dolph of Oregon drew graphic pictures of American cities mercilessly pounded by the heavy battleships of the Royal Navy of Great Britain. But the matter of gun production was central to the discussion, and Senator Joseph Hawley of Connecticut thundered, "I hope this contract will not go to the Bethlehem Steel Works simply because I want another establishment set up, and I would not care if there were three of them in the country, who [sic] while answering such stray commercial demand as might come along for steel shafting, would be ready all the while to enter into the manufacture of heavy guns for us, for a considerable number of them we must absolutely have."[38]

Advertisements for the army's gun steel contracts appeared just after the elections and $90 million was eventually lavished on static brick, concrete, and steel systems which never fired a shot in anger. The election itself delivered national power back to the Republicans. Whitney sat down to write his last report as a lame duck administrator. He proclaimed that when he had taken office in 1885, "the United States had no vessel of war which could have kept the seas for one week as against any first-rate naval power, and was dependent upon English manufacturers for the forgings of guns, for armor, and for secondary batteries." He then proceeded to tell how his administration had attempted to domesticate such industry, notwithstanding an accompanying three-year production and construction delay.[39]

Contracts in March 1885 for English armor and gun steel had totaled $227,365.29, said Whitney, and final payments on those contracts added another $100,000.00 to the figure. "No further purchases of either armor or gun steel have been made abroad since March 1885," claimed the official. Stockpiling of orders and funds had induced American steelmakers to begin production and, said Whitney with some inaccuracy, "at the present time the conditions are such that everything necessary to a first-class fighting ship can be produced and furnished to the Department in this country as soon as in the course of construction any element or feature is required." All of this still suggested a postponement of embarking upon armored ship construction, however.

Whitney felt that his policy had enabled the American Navy to develop a superb unarmored fleet. "When the ships in course of construction and those authorized shall have been completed, the United States will rank second among the nations in the possession of unarmored cruisers, or 'commerce destroyers,' having the highest characteristics, viz., of a size 3,000 tons and upward, and possessing speed of 19 knots and upward," he declared. Yet the secretary realized the weakness of *la guerre de course* strategy. "We can not at present protect our coast," he cautioned, "but we can return blow for blow, for we shall soon be in condition to launch a fleet of large and fast cruisers against the commerce of an enemy, able to inflict the most serious and lasting injury thereon."

Just before the Cleveland administration left office, Congress handed the navy a final present. A steel cruising monitor, another dynamite-gun cruiser, two light cruisers or gunboats, a harbor defense ram, and miscellaneous funds for the old monitors, armament, and $625,000 "to complete the construction and equipment of the ordnance shops, offices, and gun plant at the Washington Navy Yard." If nothing more, the incoming Republicans would have plenty of work to do.[40]

In the final analysis, Whitney contributed measurably to a growing bond between military and industrial sectors in late nineteenth-century America. The proto-battleships *Maine* and *Texas* were the first craft constructed in government yards. The *Texas* was built on prizewinning plans from the Barrow Shipbuilding Company in Great Britain; the engines for both ships came from private American industry—the H.F. Palmer Jr. Company of New York and the Richmond (Va.) Locomotive and Iron Works. The absence of facilities for steel plate fabrication at the yards led to links with Park Brothers and Carnegie, Phipps for fittings; Standard Steel of Thurlow, Pennsylvania for castings; and Bethlehem Iron for armor. When the latter fell behind contract delivery specifications of 1 June 1887, it became necesary to have Linden Steel finish the work.[41]

Controversy, changes in plans, material delivery delays, all the later trappings of military-industrial relations became apparent with the *Maine* and *Texas*. The latter ship was laid down in October 1888, her launching did not occur until two years later. Nondelivery of armor was blamed for delays to both ships and neither ship was actually commissioned until late 1895. Privately built warships fared better and spawned an immediate controversy as to the better method. The tentacles of a naval-industrial interlock were growing. Government and private yards engaged in construction; there was a host of subcontractors for ordnance, machinery, equipment, armor. The Whitney period added more statistical tonnage to the navy (93,951) than did that of William Chandler (11,986). Such statistics looked good but were largely academic. If the Democrats launched the first ships of a real fighting fleet, all were virtually obsolescent upon launching. Such was not the case with the launching of the ties with industry.[42]

Government-industrial solution of the problem of procuring armor and ordnance was possibly the more important achievement, and Whitney took pride in that accomplishment. The peculiar position of a civilian secretary facilitated delicate negotiations with private industrialists, although Whitney knew little of the technical details of tactics or command of men and ships. The diplomatic maneuvers in Whitney's relationship with Wharton resulted in a contract with good chances for success. In fact, there was no doubt that the contract led to immediate success in heavy gun forgings production. The shipment of an entire English plant to Bethlehem combined with provision of a retired naval officer (former Lieutenant Jaques) as company ordnance officer to produce a product required by the U.S. Navy. By 1888–89 Bethlehem was producing the first high-grade forgings ever made in the United States —ahead of schedule.[43]

The American steel industry similarly profited from Joseph Wharton's "noble gesture" of allowing his hydraulic forging press to be used in operations other than his own. The press proved far superior to the steam hammer technique then generally used in America. Introduction of this single device was important not only for munitions production, but for the whole manufacturing community. While the U.S. Navy had helped pioneer its appearance in the New World for purely military purposes, its greatest application was eventually in commercial forgings.

The Bethlehem Board of Directors ironically fought against much of this, John Fritz having "to make the fight of my life," to overcome corporate opposition. Of course the board had a point—the navy knew nothing about costly steelmaking and the introduction of difficult new processes. Thus, institutional change was difficult for both the navy and the steel industry. In the end, John Fritz won out. Citing the experiences of American manufacturers such as Park Brothers, Carnegie, Phipps, Oliver Brothers and Phillips, Standard Steel, Midvale, Pennsylvania Steel, Phoenix Iron, and Pacific Rolling Mills—all involved with steel production (but not armor) for the navy—Commander Robley D. Evans concluded in 1887:

> With all these practical results it can be said that the Government has done much for metallurgical production in the United States. Better material is being put into the new vessels for the Navy than has ever been put in any ship in the United States, and, as far as the records in our possession show, better than has been put in ships abroad. I think Mr. Cramp and Chief Engineer Melville will agree. . . . [44]

The dealings between Bethlehem and the navy created an atmosphere of partnership—the very thing feared by the Gun Foundry Board. Whitney, Jaques, and Barber, among others, had all played key roles, and the steelmen blamed the navy when Schneider methods later proved discouraging. Also, the government had allowed a system wherein slack periods in warship construction automatically led to cutbacks in orders for armor and ordnance forgings. Thus, Bethlehem spokesmen complained that it had been understood from the beginning that their heavy initial investment was to be repaid by a steady flow of orders.

Still, little of this discontent was apparent when Whitney left office. Naval professionals congratulated themselves on the special interest they had in the model ordnance plant in northeastern Pennsylvania. They listen attentively during various technical symposia which focused on steelmaking arts and ordnance manufacture as the Naval Institute undertook to study such phenomena. Nobody at the time thought the price for armor and gun forgings as excessive; after all, Bethlehem had invested $3.5 million in its plants and the contract prices at the onset seemed absolutely necessary to realize a fair return on their investment. It remained for later scholars to view these high prices as a virtual surcharge or government subsidy (also an anathema to the Gun Foundry Board). As one modern student of the government-industrial arrangement concluded:

> Take it all together then, and it appears that the classic laissez faire theories expressed by the Gun Foundry Board and others, regarding the desirability of a complete separation between business and Government, had been rather completely disregarded by Wharton and Whitney. But, without this close partnership, which was really the Navy's technique of encouragement, it is doubtful whether a responsible American manufacturer would have been found to undertake the production of high-grade forgings.[45]

This was the legacy bequeathed by Whitney to his Republican successor. There was every hope for the success of the navy-steel relationship as political change took place on a blustery March day in Washington. But, as both parties were beginning to discover, implementation of contracts, plans, programs, and partnerships in armor, armament, and shipbuilding often proved thornier than initial bargaining between cabinet officials and the captains of industry.

Chapter 4

A Military-Industrial Complex
Is Born

The Republican administration of Benjamin Harrison began on a rainy Inauguration Day in March 1889 with the sentiment that "the construction of a sufficient number of modern warships should progress as rapidly as is consistent with care and perfection in plans and workmanship." The president's speech also called for acquisition of overseas naval bases. Sensing that the nation stood at a crossroads, Harrison's administration was faced with the revival of European colonial expansion, as well as domestic business desires to share in global markets and foreign spheres of influence. Further stimulation of maritime interests would require a larger, modernized fleet. Thus, the Republicans returned to national power committed to more extensive programs and strategies designed to surpass Democratic achievements. Whitney's energy during the Cleveland period was a gauntlet thrown before Harrison and his new cabinet. [1]

Neither Harrison nor the machine politician whom he chose for his naval secretary knew much about maritime affairs. Secretary of the Navy Benjamin Franklin Tracy was a New Yorker like Whitney. A Civil War brigadier general, well known as a Brooklyn lawyer and judge following the war, Tracy was also a dedicated henchman of Boss Thomas Platt's Empire State machine. Yet, like Whitney before him, Tracy combined energy, a willingness to listen to professional advice, and a streak of individuality and purpose which marked his administration as a quantum jump forward in the naval renaissance.

Tracy's four-year tenure continued Whitney's administrative reforms. Moreover, Tracy sought to remove naval shore installations from political patronage. He gave strong support to the Naval War College of Stephen B. Luce and Alfred Thayer Mahan. A belligerent saber rattling marked his approach to international issues concerning trade and national power. All of this placed Tracy in the forefront of the American expansionist and imperialist spirit in the nineties. Still, of primary importance were his efforts in the field of naval construction. His negotiations with armor and armament manufacturers led to a second stage in the development of a modern military-industrial complex.[2]

Tracy spent the spring studying the results of previous naval rebuilding. He continued the steel inspection board of Whitney, realizing that his initial efforts would be to complete the authorized ships of his predecessor. As he told a Brooklyn reporter at the end of his first week in office, "Within sixty days we shall advertise for proposals for contracts for several new vessels." Yet Tracy surely realized that the U.S. Navy's construction program could hardly match those of potential European enemies. Britain's Royal Navy numbered some sixteen first-class and seventeen second-class "battleships" mounting main batteries of 12- and 16-inch guns. The Americans simply had nothing to counter the 18-inch armor and 13.5-inch breechloading rifles of H.M.S. *Anson, Camperdown, Howe,* and *Rodney,* or French warships like *Admiral Duperre* with her 22-inch armor and 13.4-inch guns. Together, or separately, British and French seapower more than matched American warships, either those in the water or under construction.[3]

By this stage the naval secretary had come under the influence of persuasive navalists in Washington and elsewhere. His own bureau chiefs and departmental professionals argued for particular programs and concepts. They included Chief Constructor Theodore D. Wilson (construction and repair),

Rear Admiral George W. Melville (steam engineering), Commodore Montgomery Sicard (ordnance), Commodore Winfield Scott Schley, soon to be succeeded by Commander George Dewey (equipment), and Commodore J.C. Walker (navigation). Elsewhere, theorists like Luce and Mahan at Newport, and Professor James R. Soley at the naval academy provided advice and counsel. All became important to shaping Tracy's ideas of seapower and the need for a battlefleet.

The secretary was preeminent as a politician. He felt most comfortable among civilians. Over brandy and cigars in influential Washington salons, Tracy met Speaker Thomas Reed and Charles Boutelle, chairman of the House Naval Affairs Committee, as well as Henry Cabot Lodge, Boutelle's chief lieutenant. There were also pro-navy voices in Democrats Hilary Herbert and William G. McAdoo as well as Republican senators Eugene Hale and Nelson Aldrich. Then, too, Theodore Roosevelt from the Civil Service Commission, Charles Dana for the *New York Sun*, and numerous correspondents added their thinking to the growing chorus of navalists seeking to add not only to the fleet, but to the glory of the nation.

This support, plus Tracy's own eye for a good idea, prompted him to appoint a so-called "Policy Board" under Commodore W.P. McCann, and a "Board on the Designs of Ships," or Board of Construction, under Montgomery Sicard. Neither of these boards, nor the questions posed to them by Tracy, reflected any break with traditional policy. Still, taken together they represented a corpus of expertise and theory which provided systematic measurement of the evolutionary progress in naval rearmament. Meanwhile, Tracy ordered the chief of navigation to form and command the navy's first "Squadron of Evolution," the germ of a concentrated peacetime fleet. The steel crusiers *Atlanta*, *Boston*, and *Chicago*, as well as the newly commissioned gunboat *Yorktown* would apply in practice strategic and tactical principles then under study at Newport and Washington.[4]

Tracy was not content, however. His first annual report in November 1889 estimated that future naval wars would be short, and fought with forces-in-being. He suggested that "to strike the first blow will gain an advantage and inflict an injury from which [an enemy] can never recover." To do so he wanted the creation of a fighting force—a balanced battlefleet of twenty "sea-going battle-ships," twenty coast defense vessels, sixty fast, armored cruisers, a line of swift torpedo boats and merchantmen for coaling and transport service. He wanted this force organized into two fleets for service on either coast. Basically they would not be tied to coastal defense, but would strike enemy fleets at sea or even in their own home waters.[5]

Naval historians subsequently focused upon the battleship clauses of Tracy's message as something new and unique. Actually, there had been previous murmurs, and Tracy himself had been talking about such warships with Hale and other navalists since the previous summer. Nobody at the time or since has caught the subtle implications of these clauses. While Tracy warned that construction of his fleet would take fifteen years due to limited production facilities, even he failed to appreciate the inability of domestic American industry to supply steel armor and armament for such a project.

The battlefleet plan was really a vast public works project designed to further stimulate the business community. It was a shift in naval policy, true, but one which had vast implications in terms of economic pump priming, jobs and votes, government-industrial alliance, and cost for future generations of Americans. Only one St. Louis daily caught the trend, claiming that it was poor economy for farmers and working men to pay for huge capitalist weapons of war. By Christmas, Tracy himself was locked into selling his program to Congress.[6]

Tracy quickly learned, as had his predecessor, that while custom dictated that he supply estimates on and judgment of future navy needs, this did not guarantee his plans' acceptance on Capitol Hill. Neither the Senate nor the House responded automatically to the desires of the administration. Tracy's naval advisor, Rear Admiral Stephen B. Luce, told him three years later, "These two branches of government continue to this day, as they have in the past, to play at cross-purposes." It did not take long for Tracy to grasp the significance of Congressman Boutelle's comment: "The record shows that in two years and nine months a Republican administration put afloat 12,363 tons of modern steel warships, while a Democratic administration, with nearly $30,000,000 at its command, in four years time succeeded in getting afloat, simply launching the hulls, of [only] 11,466 tons of similar vessels." Tracy could expect a continuing partisan political battle over the "new navy."[7]

In the late fall, Hale asked Tracy to draw up four bills relevant to his plans for the next stage of naval rearmament. Almost immediately after Hale introduced the navy bills in Congress, ex-secretary and now Senator William E. Chandler announced his opposition to battleships. Chandler and others were wedded to the traditional monitor-coastal defense strategy as more economical and would oppose "any bill for 8 armor-clads on the ground that sufficient armor cannot be immediately produced in the U.S.," according to ordnance expert Commander F.M. Folger. He also told the secretary that these legislators opposed foreign steel imports and that American shipbuilders wanted unarmored vessels which could be produced quicker and more profitably.[8]

Folger also noted that no matter who manufactured armor in America, the government had to pay the cost of final product and plant plus the price of the manufacturing process as well. If English, French, or German firms owned the process, "they would undoubtedly prefer to receive their pay in an order for armor to be made at their own works," while at the same time guaranteeing the work of their American connections. The government might also own any patented process, by that means, and permit as many American manufacturers to use it as it chose. Folger advised that some multinational sharing of armor contracts would allow consideration of more ironclads on Capitol Hill. He contended that the House had been receptive four years before, but the Senate had killed the idea. American senators had opposed the threat of foreign intervention on a purely American market at that time. Now, Bethlehem existed as a viable production facility and foreign intervention posed no real threat.

Then, late in January, McCann's Naval Policy Board delivered a bomb on Tracy's desk. Somebody in the department leaked the controversial document to the public, and a noticeable chill crept over the House and Senate. The naval professionals had recommended far too radical a construction program, and Tracy knew it. McCann's people wanted a navy at least equal to the most powerful navy in the world—in case we had to fight that nation. They wanted tactically offensive battleships if only to fight a strategically defensive war. Ten "offensive" battleships with fifteen-thousand mile cruising range would be supplemented by twenty-five "defensive" capital ships having a three-thousand mile range. A supporting force would include twenty-four armored cruisers, fifteen light torpedo cruisers, five China station gunboats, ten rams, three depot ships, and one hundred torpedo boats. This 497,000-ton program would cost $281,550,000 and at the end of its development, the U.S. Navy would rank second only to the Royal Navy of Great Britain.[9]

Tracy realized that this ambitious program was out of step with public reality. He probably hoped to suppress it until he had personally smoothed its path at the other end of Pennsylvania Avenue. Now, as Senator Hale declared, it would be difficult to find anyone in the administration willing to support the McCann program, so Tracy had to simply repudiate his subordinate's views. Family tragedy fortuitously took the secretary out of the limelight for the moment, while congressional allies like Hale and Herbert attempted to dampen the effect of the McCann report and rally support for annual naval appropriations at a more realistic level. Based on Tracy's and McCann's schemes, the House Naval Affairs Committee went along with "three sea-going coastline battle-ships designed to carry the heaviest armor and most powerful ordnance upon a displacement of about eight thousand five hundred tons," and a steaming range in excess of five thousand miles.[10]

New as well as traditional objections surfaced in the congressional debate. In the end, however, the smooth talk of Speaker Thomas Reed, Boutelle, and Lodge won the day for Tracy's program. Three battleships, only slightly larger than the *Texas* and *Maine*, were provided in the enacted bill. Displacing over ten thousand tons, they mounted four thirteen-inch and eight eight-inch rifled guns plus numerous rapid-fire weapons and four torpedo tubes. Named for the states of Oregon, Indiana, and Massachusetts, Tracy felt they would compare favorably with anything afloat. Twelve of them would easily equal the twenty battleships noted in his 1889 report, and the secretary also claimed that all monitors might now be retired to use of state naval militia. In fact, the American battleships would compare favorably with England's *Majestic* class, having heavier armor and ordnance although not as much speed or range.[11]

Tracy's enthusiasm was quickly transmitted to subordinate bureaucrats. Employees in construction and steam engineering worked relentlessly on plans and by autumn, Cramp and Sons and the Union Iron Works won contracts for the warships. At this point, holdover construction projects from the Whitney period threatened to create a logjam. Moreover, the U.S. Navy found itself in the summer of 1890 on the brink of a real crisis concerning delivery of armor and ordnance from domestic sources.

Tracy probably became aware of the impending problem as early as May 1889 when he studied Chandler's and Whitney's experiences with domestication. The catalyst was a series of conversations with William Bisphan of the New York firm of William H. Wallace and Company, American representatives for English compound armor concerns. Bisphan told Tracy that Whitney had been wrong in selecting all-steel armor over the compound armor used by the Royal Navy. The homogeneous all-steel plate did not equal the shattering ability of the hard surface/soft back compound plate, said Bisphan, who asked for another hearing for his English clients.[12]

Tracy, however, found that his ordnance experts, headed by Folger, disagreed. They claimed the compound armor was prone to cleaving at the point of welding, thus exposing the soft back. While these experts preferred homogeneous all-steel, they could not tell the secretary how such plate might be produced domestically. Tracy therefore decided that he himself needed to know more about armor, and he devoted much time to examining the various foreign tests. He discovered "that the tests were very ingeniously planned to give the plate the victory over the gun." It did not seem to matter whether the plate was all-steel or compound, since neither was destroyed but merely damaged, and each proponent could advocate his own particular product. Tracy decided to defer a decision on new American armor until definitive tests could take place.[13]

Bisphan had offered a free compound test plate for any American competition, but other competitors refused to do so. Tracy quickly contacted Lieutenant Commander F.M. Barber, former member of the Gun Foundry Board and now attached to Henri Schneider as an American representative during a leave of absence from the service. With irritation, Tracy told Barber that he knew of the links between Creusot and Bethlehem and that "there never will be a contract for a ton of armor let by me until I have had a competitive test." The test would take place whether or not Schneider cooperated with the U.S. Navy. Barber conveyed this blunt news to Schneider. The Frenchman, astonishingly, not only promised cooperation, but insisted upon using nickel armor, with the Americans purchasing the test plate and shells.[14]

In fact, nickel armor added to the munitions puzzle confronting Washington naval experts. It seems that in July 1889, S.J. Ritchie of Akron, Ohio (owner of several Canadian nickel mines) first approached Tracy with news of unusual activity in the international nickel market, centering on nickel matte. Confessing ignorance of the cause, Ritchie promised to investigate the situation, and the secretary sent him as unofficial departmental observer to discover what was going on in Europe. Ritchie suspected that European arms makers were using nickel in armor manufacturing, and he quickly confirmed this in conversations with Henri Schneider—all before the Frenchman surprised Tracy with his response to the armor tests.

Pressure now mounted from yet another quarter. Tracy had begun his independent probes into armor types in the belief that since the Bethlehem people were still working upon their plant, there would be ample time before production began so that additional inquiry and experiment would cause no unnecessary delay. But suddenly it was December. The 1877 Bethlehem contract had called for completion of the plant on or before 1 December 1889. The firm's failure to deliver armor plate soon affected completion of the *Maine* and the armored cruiser *New York*. Tracy reacted by ordering a test plate from Creusot and a progress report from Bethlehem. Joseph Wharton and W.H. Jaques rushed to Washington in late

January, promising Tracy delivery of armor within six months.[15]

The Bethlehem people pointed to the difficulties of purchasing and transporting the British forging plant to the United States, and of conversion of their hydraulic press from making gun forgings to steel hammers for forging armor plate. They promised that fifteen hundred to two thousand tons of armor would be delivered during the last six months of 1890 and that they would maintain an annual eight to ten thousand tons thereafter. Tracy was not to be outmaneuvered. He cited the ease with which Bethlehem had finished initial plant construction and delivery of gun forgings ahead of schedule. He told Wharton and Jaques that he simply failed to understand the armor plate delays.

The issue dragged on until May, when, finding no armor deliveries in the offing, passage of the 1890 appropriation bill pending, and his temper growing short, the secretary sent his chief of ordnance to inspect Bethlehem progress. Sicard reported that nothing would be forthcoming for another fifteen to eighteen months. Bethlehem spokesmen were irate, but Tracy had no choice. All of his building programs faced indefinite delay unless he moved personally to find alternate sources for armor. As he told a Senate panel several years later (neglecting historical accuracy in the process), "having the authorization to build three battle-ships and three large cruisers which would require about 14,000 tons of additional armor . . . I felt it necessary to found a second armor plant, because at 300 tons a month for each establishment they could only furnish armor enough to build about two battle-ships a year." For this reason, Tracy turned to negotiations with Carnegie, Phipps and Company in the summer of 1890.[16]

Andrew Carnegie, the individual who helped the Navy Department past the armor crisis, was himself ambivalent about the tools of war and later served unabashedly in the front rank of the antiimperialists. He said afterward that it was the importuning of his president and the needs of the nation which had caused him to reverse his previous stand against entry into the armor market. Yet the record shows Carnegie, Phipps among earlier suppliers of steel to the navy, suggesting that patriotic motives and Carnegie's fear of naval inspection procedures aside, his admission that "there may be millions for us in armor" more accurately reflected his motives. At any rate, when Tracy asked the steel magnate to "read up" on the subject in late 1889 or early 1890, Carnegie at first remained aloof and adhered to his earlier stance, asking subordinates to study the armor market, but to avoid involvement in the nickel armor scheme.[17]

Carnegie first learned of Tracy's renewed advances towards his company while vacationing in Scotland. The secretary apparently told board chairman William L. Abbott that the navy needed more armor, noting his preference for nickel-steel, but admitting that the final decision awaited results from further tests. At this point Tracy offered Abbott a contract for "a good quantity" of armor which might be either nickel-steel or any other type. Abbott dutifully cabled this information to Carnegie along with the fact that the Bethlehem people opposed the nickel tests but were sending two men abroad to investigate the matter. He wondered if Carnegie shouldn't again approach Le Ferro Nickel in order to gain reduction of the exorbitant French demands for use of the patent rights. Indeed, Carnegie did so and won a concession from the French just as Tracy learned that even the British government had successfully tested a nickel-steel deck plate at Portsmouth.

Negotiations now entered a delicate stage. Both Tracy and Carnegie were shrewd bargainers. The secretary realized that Bethlehem had gained extra incentives under the Whitney contracts because of the huge outlay of money for plant construction. But he also knew that the Bethlehem experience provided future shortcuts to the trial and error method of management. He assumed that the Carnegie people would not hesitate to profit from their competitors' experience, and that the Pittsburgh steelmakers would accept a lower price than that accorded Wharton and the Bethlehem group in 1887. Meanwhile, Carnegie hid his true feelings on the point as he wrote Tracy about his European inquiries, his doubts about the superiority of compound steel plates over all-steel plates, and his intention to provide the U.S. Navy with some type of armor plate in four to six months.[18]

By mid-July Carnegie had Tracy's first price and quantity quotations in hand. In turn, he gave the secretary a taste of the intense bargaining which lay ahead. He flatly told the cabinet official that Carnegie, Phipps could not accept anything less than the Bethlehem price. "If you give us five thousand tons Bethlehem prices shall order necessary tools and go ahead otherwise must decline . . . armour making no childs play," Carnegie cabled on 19 July. Tracy naturally knew nothing of the numerous telegrams Carnegie sent his Pittsburgh chieftains demanding hard bargaining by Abbott and the rest, with no room for compromise over Bethlehem and European prices.[19]

Pittsburgh-Washington negotiations stalled by late July 1890. Carnegie patronizingly told Tracy that he was disappointed that the navy's offer was so low, especially since it was obvious that the department expected his firm to succeed where Bethlehem had not. He referred constantly to European prices, and he noted Bethlehem's fatal miscalculations about lead time for plant erection. He explained the large effort in training men to handle such masses of steel. Since Carnegie, Phipps was well supplied with orders, "it will not disappoint us very much if you decide to drop us as to Armour." But, Carnegie added slyly, "We could no doubt deliver finished plates a year before any other party in the United States. Any one else who tries to deliver in a year will just land where Bethlehem is."[20]

At this point a vague and verbose letter from Robert H. Sayre, Bethlehem's general manager, broke the back of the Carnegie-Tracy impasse. Sayre retreated from his earlier opposition to the Sicard estimate of the fifteen-month delay in delivery of armor. Continuing technical difficulties and unforeseen contingencies had changed his mind, but he predicted no difficulty in exceeding the rate of deliveries as fixed in the contract once things settled down. But Tracy was in no mood for fifteen-month delays. By 27 August, the navy reached a verbal agreement with Carnegie, Phipps calling for manufacture and delivery of some six thousand tons of armor, at precisely the same unit prices promised Bethlehem three years before. Meanwhile, assured of a contract on his terms, Andrew Carnegie left the details to his home office. He once more left to locate and purchase English tools for the new venture.

Carnegie insisted on adding several key provisions to the contract. His sharp bargaining tactics prolonged the final negotiations until autumn. In some ways this haggling placed Carnegie in a better position than Bethlehem. To begin with, the navy, not Carnegie, Phipps had to pay the two cents per pound royalty demanded by Le Ferro Nickel. Carnegie also extracted a second concession, similar to that given Wharton by Whitney, whereby the secretary of the navy implied that Carnegie, Phipps would receive more work than called for in the contract. Finally, the steelman strongly desired to avoid any penalty clauses for specification failures. Meanwhile, there remained the matter of the definitive armor test.[21]

This test finally took place at the Annapolis proving ground between 18 and 22 September 1890. Rear Admiral L. A. Kimberly's board pitted Henri Schneider's nickel-steel armor, treated by the Americans with a new hardening process named for its inventor, Augustus Harvey, against plates made of English compound armor and simple, all-steel armor. Much to the dismay of the steel makers, Tracy insisted upon a test at point-blank range. In place of the usual six-inch projectiles, Tracy demanded eight-inch shells. He wanted complete and final results. And he got them.

The compound armor was demolished completely; the all-steel plate showed alarming cracks. Yet, the "harveyized" nickel-steel plate completely stopped the test rounds. Even prolonged bombardment failed to dispel the impression that the ultimate armor had been discovered at last. This proof astonished international munitions makers and admiralties. Sages quickly pronounced Britain's Royal Navy defenseless. Congress, at Tracy's urging, appropriated one million dollars for the purchase of nickel, scarcely eight days after the Annapolis trials.[22]

These nickel developments paralleled negotiations with Carnegie. While nickel-steel patents could be purchased, the metal itself was in extremely short supply. Demand was great even before the tests because of the very possibilities promised by nickel-steel armor. Prices soared accordingly. Carnegie's representatives knew that S.J. Ritchie was a businessman prone to failure and that the nickel market was fraught with speculative danger. Just before the Annapolis test, Carnegie had warned Tracy again about his misgivings and had lectured the New Yorker on the need for further experimentation. Every type of plate had some weakness, said the steelman, and the technological state of the industry was such that the solid steel plate of one American maker might be unsatisfactory while the solid steel plate of a French or English competitor might be excellent. Carnegie added, "this armour plate business is, so far, all uncertainty."[23]

Be that as it may, Tracy also had some trump cards in reserve. He had prevailed upon Ritchie's patriotism by promising to press congressional leaders to place nickel on the free list of the pending tariff legislation if Ritchie's Canadian Copper Company would retain their supply of the metal until the navy received permission to buy it. This strategy worked as Tracy maneuvered with Congressman William McKinley and Senator Arthur Gorman, citing soaring international prices, Carnegie's reluctance to buy the metal, and the urgency of cornering the supply before Canadian Copper sold it abroad. Congress gave the necessary permission to contract with Ritchie and the protective McKinley tariff completely removed the duty on nickel ore when it passed in October. Once again, Tracy's initiative averted a costly deadlock.[24]

Now that Tracy had an immediate supply of nickel ore, he purchased only fifty thousand dollars' worth for experimental purposes. But he told Carnegie, Phipps board chairman Abbott that the department was prepared to conclude negotiations, and he soon tried to implement his new power over the steel industry. During a mid-October meeting of shipbuilders and steelmen, he planned to expedite all steel armor deliveries for the various construction projects. The *New York Times* speculated that while little change might be expected in the steel inspection procedures due to the law, "it is likely that the Secretary will urge all steel producers taking naval contracts to turn out a fixed amount of steel each day on such contracts, without regard to private work they may have on hand at the same time."[25]

Tracy was unaccountably absent when the conference finally opened on 16 October. The meeting degenerated into a name-calling contest and accomplished little. Shipbuilders blamed the steelmakers for delivery breakdown. The steelmakers complained loudly about the navy's steel inspectors and their high rejection rate. The navy held its ground on the high standards for material. Even the final round of negotiations between Tracy and Carnegie found the latter adamantly opposed to Tracy's "pet nickel." He urged further testing and an open mind. "Yours for all-steel, compound, nickel, aluminum, chrome, or anything that will give us the best results," he concluded.

Best results were foremost in Tracy's mind. A breakthrough finally came on 20 November when the two parties concluded a written contract. Based on the earlier verbal agreement and incorporating the steelmen's demands, Carnegie, Phipps, and Company agreed to deliver six thousand tons of "either ordinary or nickel-steel" at the Bethlehem price beginning in June 1891. This was a bit later than the four to six months originally promised by Carnegie. But Tracy had gained his alternate source of armor supply. True, the navy had to pay French nickel patent royalties but Tracy doubted the validity of that patent and he planned to contest it in a U.S. Court.[26]

Thus, the year ended on an upbeat for the navy and steel industry. Montgomery Sicard reported to Tracy that Bethlehem probably could not deliver anything before late summer of 1892, but encouraging word came from Pittsburgh in December that Carnegie's Homestead works had successfully produced the first nickel-steel plate in the United States. By the time of the publication of Tracy's second annual report, Democrats had wiped out the comfortable Republican margin on Capitol Hill in off-year elections, but cruisers *Baltimore*, *Philadelphia*, and *San Francisco*, gunboat *Cushing*, and dynamite cruiser *Vesuvius* were all newly commissioned. Elsewhere, twenty-one steel vessels, sixteen of them Whitney holdovers, lay in various stages of construction. But, as the secretary told Senator John D. Cameron, "The new ships of the Navy are too complicated structures for each one to be without a mechanic specially acquainted with her requirements." Everybody was beginning to learn that one couldn't revolutionize the U.S. Navy overnight.[27]

Tracy's preoccupation with armored ships cost him a superb opportunity to underwrite a second major breakthrough in naval architecture and programs in the nineties. John P. Holland, inventor of a submersible craft, had long sought the navy's support for his ideas. But Tracy's administration looked elsewhere, although in systematization of ship repair programs, dispatch of young naval constructors to the Ecole d'Application Maritime, University of Glasgow, and Royal Naval College, Greenwich the administration did reflect forward thinking.

Tracy's 1890 report on the navy featured a scenario which pictured an enemy armored fleet sweeping in to lay New York City under tribute. Other Gulf and Pacific coastal cities also lay naked before the onslaught. The secretary's answer was a vast fleet of heavily armored battleships and coastal defense monitors. But now Tracy faced an even more hostile, Democratic-controlled Congress, filled with Populists and Democrats concerned with silver legislation, temperance, and parochial schools, not warships. Despite the written warnings and scenarios from the McCann board to Tracy's latest annual report, American politicians were not altogether receptive to requests for more money for battleships. Even Alfred Thayer Mahan's seminal study on seapower was greeted with more interest abroad than at home when it first appeared that year.[28]

Of course, not all Democrats opposed a stronger navy. But isolationist congressmen from the hinterland reflected their agrarian constituent's restlessness with machines of war. Loud complaints might be heard about the $432,820,762 lavished upon fleet overhaul since the Civil War. On the other hand, the American frontier was closing; the admission of Idaho, Montana, Washington, Wyoming, and the Dakotas to the Union reflected a trend. Commercial expansion on both coastlines, Mahan's maritime theories, and Tracy's battlefleet program seemed at odds with an inward-looking America. Yet cities like New York, San Francisco, New Orleans, Galveston, and Portland were looking outward for markets, trade, and money. Farmers continued to clamor about their plight, but the main plank in the expansionist platform called for overseas outlets for American industrial and agricultural products. Warships and a navy were necessary to protect a national merchant marine carrying such trade.[29]

Tracy plunged ahead somewhat blindly as the new year opened, suggesting the navy needed at least six to nine additional battleships, more armored cruisers, harbor defense craft, torpedo boats, and the like. He apparently disregarded the sagacious party stalwart Eugene Hale who told him, "I do not believe that we need a great extravagant Navy." The secretary's latest package would cost $65 million. Congress agreed with Hale and trimmed the naval appropriation bill in March to only one protected cruiser. Still, Tracy received $4 million for more armor and ordnance.[30]

The secretary's problems were not with Congress alone. Shipbuilders like Charles H. Cramp and T.W. Hyde thought their naval contracts gave them license to dictate policy. Cramp was especially troublesome, since he felt the naval inspectors at his yard reflected the "most pernicious and harassing evils of the Navy Yard system." Tracy might have listened sympathetically if he were not busily pursuing patronage and civil service reform in those very navy yards. Old political friends like Boss Platt were shocked, but Tracy's purpose was to streamline and modernize, to clean out marginal employees and increase efficiency. Speed in construction was paramount, and Tracy fretted at the constant chorus from Cramp, Hyde, Carnegie, and Sayre about extensions, changes, and contractor dalliance. More than once the departmental stationary carried a sharp rebuke for public and private officials alike:

> The Department cannot understand how a delay of this extent on an unimportant item of work should be permitted to occur. The Department also fails to understand why necessary work of this character was not done or reported long ago.[31]

The armor situation continued to plague Tracy more than any other basic construction issue. Congress had looked askance at Tracy's failure to advertise for competitive bids during the 1890 armor crisis. They rapped his knuckles in the 1891 appropriation legislation with a clause that "no contract for the purchase of gun steel or armor for the Navy shall hereafter be made until the subject matter of the same shall have been submitted to public competition by the Department by advertisement." But Tracy was probably too busy to notice.[32]

On 3 March 1891, the Navy Department signed a contract with Augustus Harvey, for his process to harden the surface of steel while retaining body toughness. Tracy and his advisers felt this process improved nickel armor even more. Harvey had approached Commander Folger during the latter's tenure as ordnance inspector at the Washington Navy Yard in 1889. Folger realized immediately the potential of the process, which at the time had been applied only to tool steel by its inventor. Folger provided assistance and encouragement, and he approached Secretary Tracy on the matter. Ironically, Folger later came under congressional censure for accepting employment from the Harvey company during an extended leave of absence from the service. In any event, Tracy accepted Folger's recommendations. Following testing of both Creusot and Linden Steel plates with the Harvey process, Tracy pronounced "If the Harvey process can be applied to nickel steel, we have the ideal armor." William Cramp and Andrew Carnegie concurred and the latter retreated a bit as he wrote Tracy in May 1891, "The favor with which you have regarded [nickel] from the first is now in my opinion, fully justified . . . our nickel steel excelled the Creusot plate which proved even our French competitor is behind us."[33]

The steelmaker loved nothing so much as success. He and Tracy became close friends as Carnegie sent demijohns of refreshment to the secretary's residence as well as offering special trains to carry Tracy to the Pittsburgh steel works. Still, Tracy knew that Carnegie bore close observation. He sent a young naval officer, Lieutenant J.F. Meigs, to western Pennsylvania under the guise of providing departmental advice. In addition, Tracy established an armor inspection board to study design changes and problems associated with the industrial fabrication of armor plate.

In the meantime, Henri Schneider became restive at developments in America. Doubting the validity of the Harvey process, for one thing, Schneider's spokesmen protested Tracy's utilization of Creusot test plates "in direct violation of our rights." But if the secretary had any inkling of possible future litigation on the matter, he took no notice, and proceeded with his experimentation. He toured the Bethlehem facilities in the fall, and additional testing on six armor plates provided by the steel companies validated the superiority of harveyized nickel-steel. Tracy wrote to Lieutenant Commander William Emory in England: "It is strange that England fails where we succeed perfectly. Our manufacturers succeed with almost absolute uniformity. We have hardly had a rejection of a nickel plate since we commenced their production."[34]

The pace of naval rearmament affected Benjamin F. Tracy's emergence as the principal chauvinist of the Harrison administration. This "militarized" civilian not only actively pursued the quest for naval bases in the Caribbean, but thought nothing of twisting the British lion's tail over seal fishing in Arctic waters and interfering in domestic Chilean affairs under the guise of protecting American rights. Moreover, he was a prime mover in attempts to incorporate Hawaii into the American orbit. All of this gave jingoists a chance to flag-wave, pound their chests, and flaunt the newly emerging national power of the United States. Perhaps the assertion of one British diplomatic officer, Cecil Spring-Rice, captured the real intent behind the Harrison-Tracy belligerency when he rather ungraciously suggested their reasons as "one to get re-elected, the other to see his ships fight and get votes for more."[35]

There can be little doubt that "votes" were on both men's minds as they entered the election year of 1892. Tracy was experiencing at best only minor success in pushing his ideas through Congress. The naval act of 1892 showed legislators willing to authorize only one nine-thousand-ton battleship of the "sea-going coast-line" variety plus an eight-thousand-ton armored cruiser. Fuel and cruising restrictions were lifted from the vessels, thus giving them a definite offensive capability. Congress seemed to be moving abreast of naval planners in outlook if not in numbers.[36]

Tracy, like his chief, was also busy deciphering the vote of the national electorate. The equation between naval progress and voter appeal for the GOP was important, and so he spent much time prodding subordinates concerned with repair and shipbuilding as well as armor deliveries from Pittsburgh and Bethlehem. The secretary was unprepared for the "Homestead Strike" which broke out in the summer.[37]

True, as early as January, Tracy had heard of labor-management differences at the Carnegie plant where much of the new armor was made. Armor mill workers demanded, in part, a 100 percent raise in pay for all nickel-steel work. They claimed that this material was much harder to make and that its rejection rate was higher. Actually, worker unrest about wages and working conditions went beyond naval armor work, but local labor union leaders thought they they could win demands because of government pressure upon Carnegie management to complete the armor contract.

Carnegie and his people shrewdly stockpiled unfinished plates well in advance of the summer strike. Together with laborsaving machinery introduced to make armor, this strategem undercut the workers' position. Adding to the unsettled Homestead conditions, Bethlehem managers demanded an additional $150 per ton for turret armor for the *Maine*, *Amphitrite*, *Monadnock*, and *Puritan*. By summer, Tracy and others feared a general strike throughout the steel industry. His real concern was probably related less to the plight of workers than to the impact on armor deliveries.

Tracy told Congress at the end of June that steelmen had supplied 1,100 tons of armor thus far. Then, when the news reached Washington that resumption of casting and rolling work at Homestead could not begin before late September, Tracy even shuffled work, perhaps illegally, between Carnegie and Bethlehem in order to keep his programs moving. To complicate matters, Bethlehem lagged farther and farther behind on their contract. Finally Tracy faced the management with the hard facts that their deliveries had not approached even six hundred tons total, and at the present rate of delivery, three additional years appeared to be required to complete the contract. Writing to Bethlehem officials in October, Tracy noted bluntly: "These promises like many others made by your company have not been kept, and now you ask me to extend your contract. This I cannot do. Any extension of your time must be connected with conditions with adequate penalties attached to be imposed in case of failure on your part."[38]

To Tracy, it appeared that neither steel firm cared whether or not they were behind their contract schedule, and contemporary journalists concluded that he was justified in his position. The secretary discussed the problem with M. Hunsicker and Lieutenant C.A. Stone from the Carnegie plant, receiving more promises of shipment speedup despite the Homestead troubles. But, as the *Philadelphia North American* put it, "Secretary Tracy has about reached the conclusion that he has been played with, and it is the impression that he is about to enforce the penalty clauses to bring the contractors to time." But, recognizing the steel industry's support of the Republican party, Tracy quickly refuted reports that he planned anything as drastic as complete revocation of contracts. He did promise intense review.[39]

Immediate shipment of 350 tons of armor from Bethlehem and personal conversations with Henry Frick of Carnegie in November eased naval-industrial relations. At this point, however, the national elections again changed the picture. Cleveland and the Democrats regained the White House. While Tracy blamed defeat on the tariff issue, his own activities may have contributed to the Republican setback. By pushing civil service reforms in naval shore facilities, he had antagonized many politicians, even in his own home district of Brooklyn. In addition, despite yeoman efforts to launch as many vessels as possible before the elections, that fall newspapers proclaimed a political kickback from the steel industry due mainly to the secretary's controversial decision regarding turret designs for the *New York* and *Monterey*.

Secretary Tracy had agreed to the substitution of vertical for deflective armor plates on the gun turrets, apparently at Folger's suggestion. The *New York Herald* exposed the "scandal" as an opportunity for the Carnegie people to profit from the mistake. Tracy tried to duck reporters, but when finally cornered he admitted only: "We are constantly changing our plans. Ship building is a progressive science. There can be no progress when there is no change." He later contended that the question of armor was one for the experts, and that all but one of the navy's analysts had agreed with the turret decision. Apparently other experts had not, but the 1892 elections made the point rather moot.[40]

Tracy's final annual report may have been his last great contribution to the naval rearmament program. It provided a detailed accounting of progress under the Harrison administration. Tracy pointed out that apart from a few "old ships, long since obsolete and fast going to decay," in 1889 the fleet had comprised three modern steel vessels of 7,863 tons aggregate, mounting thirteen six-inch and four eight-inch guns, forgings for which had all been purchased abroad. By comparison, the Harrison years would bequeath nineteen additional vessels, aggregating 54,832 tons and mounting 106 guns (six- to twelve-inch), all but five of which had been manufactured in the United States. Eighteen other vessels of 93,497 tons were due to be completed within the year "should their armor be delivered." They would mount 168 more cannon (four- to thirteen-inch), all of domestic manufacture. As Tracy saw it, "of all the new ships the construction of which has been begun during the present administration, only two will remain on the stocks on the 4th of March next."[41]

What the secretary really was saying was that his tenure had finished the authorized but incomplete program of his predecessors. It had laid the groundwork for the next phase of construction with wide-ranging implications for policy and military-industrial linkage. In the immediate future, Tracy saw need for another seagoing battleship, several torpedo cruisers, four river craft for the Orient, and thirty small torpedo boats. But, if he subsequently became identified with battleships, in 1892 he personally felt his major contribution lay with the balanced fleet concept enunciated earlier by Luce and others.

As Tracy phrased it: "The policy then advocated, which was a radical departure from any view previously presented in this Country, consisted in the production of the three principal types. First, the armored battleship of 10,000 or more tons; second the armored cruiser of from 8,000 to 9,000 tons; and third, the commerce protecting and destroying cruiser, of extreme speed, of 7,500 tons." The secretary saw no cause to depart from this program in the future. Sources for these tools of war had been diversified, from ordnance production at the

TABLE 5

GUN FORGINGS

Caliber of Gun	Supplier	Date of Contract	Time Required to Complete Contract	Number Required	Number Ordered	Actual Delivery
4-inch	Bethlehem Iron Co.	Mar. 14,1889	July 14, 1889	67	6	Apr. 1891
	Bethlehem Iron Co.	May 3, 1889	April 16, 1890		2	Apr. 16, 1890
	Bethlehem Iron Co.	Aug. 17, 1889	Sept. 15, 1890		2	Sept. 15, 1890
	Midvale Steel Co.	Apr. 30, 1890	Jan. 23, 1892		25	Jan. 1892
	Bethlehem Iron Co.	New contract*	228 days from date of contract		32	None
5-inch	Bethlehem Iron Co.	Aug. 27, 1890	Dec. 27, 1890	54	2	Jan. 1891
	Midvale Steel Co.	Oct. 22, 1890	Jan. 2, 1892		25	Completed
	Bethlehem Iron Co.	New contract*	228 days from date of contract		27	None
6-inch	Bethlehem Iron Co.	May 1, 1887	By Mar. 1, 1891	113	41	Jan. 26, 1891
	Midvale Steel Co.	July 26, 1887	Apr. 26, 1888		10	Mar. 20, 1889
	Midvale Steel Co.	Nov. 30, 1887	Feb. 30, 1889		22	Sept. 19, 1889
	Midvale Steel Co.	July 18, 1889	Jan. 18, 1890		6	Jan. 13, 1890
	Midvale Steel Co.	Oct. 31, 1889	Sept. 4, 1890		14	June 24, 1890
	Bethlehem Iron Co.	May 10, 1890	Early as practicable		1	July 1890
	Midvale Steel Co.	May 29, 1890	Jan. 1, 1891		19	Feb. 1891
8-inch	Bethlehem Iron Co.	May 1, 1887	By Nov. 1, 1890	43	6	Mar. 28, 1890
	Bethlehem Iron Co.	Apr. 4, 1890	Oct. 3, 1890		1	Nov. 21, 1890
	Bethlehem Iron Co.	Apr. 10, 1890	Apr. 28, 1891		6	Apr. 28, 1891
	Midvale Steel Co.	Oct. 22, 1890	May 28, 1892		12	None
	Bethlehem Iron Co.	Nov. 8, 1890	Feb. 8, 1893		14	1
	Midvale Steel Co.	May 7, 1891	Nov. 24, 1891		4	None
10-inch	Bethlehem Iron Co.	May 1, 1887	By Nov. 1, 1891	22	22	Jan. 18–19, 1891
12-inch	Bethlehem Iron Co.	May 1, 1887	By Nov. 1, 1891	8	4	May 30, 1891
	Bethlehem Iron Co.	Nov. 8, 1890	Sept. 8, 1894		4	None
13-inch	Bethlehem Iron Co.	Nov. 8, 1890	Sept. 8, 1894	12	12	None

*Contract not yet executed.
† Earlier deliveries expected that premiums may be earned.

TABLE 5 (continued)

Rate of Delivery	Future Deliveries	Price per Gun	Amount Required to Pay for Current Delivery, per Month	Amount Required to pay for expected Future Delivery, per Month
All delivered	All delivered	$1,646.00		
All delivered	All delivered	1,679.59		
All delivered	All delivered	1,680.00		
All delivered	All delivered	2,110.00		
None	228 days from date of contract	1,408.00	$5,632	$5,632
All delivered	All delivered	3,369.24		
All delivered	All delivered	3,054.81		
None	228 days from date of contract	2,409.00	9,636	9,636
All delivered	All delivered	3,934.00		
All delivered	All delivered	5,342.00		
All delivered	All delivered	4,945.00		
All delivered	All delivered	5,616.00		
All delivered	All delivered	5,060.00		
All delivered	All delivered	4,226.00		
All delivered	All delivered	4,446.72		
All delivered	All delivered	10,643.00		
All delivered	All delivered	8,094.00		
All delivered	All delivered	12,332.59		
None	1 set per month	10,882.00	10,882	10,882
1 set per month	1 set per month	11,908.00	11,908	11,908
1 set per month	1 set per month	35 cal 11,571.00 40 cal 12,960.00	24,531	24,531
1 set per month	1 set per month	22,885.00	22,885	22,885
All delivered	All delivered	41,401.00		
1 set per 2 months	1 set per 2 months	40,656.00	20,328	20,328
1 set per 1½ months	1 set per 1½ months†	56,840.00	37,893	37,893
Total			$143,695	$143,695

West Point Foundry, South Boston Iron Works, Bethlehem Iron Company, and the naval gun factory and gunpowder production by both Du Pont and California powder companies to armor procurement from Carnegie, Phipps and Bethlehem. "The aggressive policy of foreign nations has continued," and "our true naval policy for the future is to construct principally, if not entirely, only first-class cruisers and first-class battleships, with their accessories." Here then, in a few brief statements, were both the philosophy of and the blueprint for a fledging military-industrial complex. (See tables 5 and 6.)

Republican members on Capitol Hill tried desperately to push through one final piece of naval legislation in early 1893. Their task was difficult for the opposition focused on delivery delays for steel, Senator Hale querying Tracy on 21 February "if Senate adds a battle ship when will armor be needed for it, and when can it be furnished by the steel establishments?" Ordnance chief William Sampson predicted 1895 as the final delivery date for all authorized vessels. He concluded slyly "if they had orders, meantime, for armor for another vessel, they could commmence deliveries of the armor of that new vessel immediately thereafter, that is in the month of June 1895." This would be quite timely for any battleship authorized "before the end of the Harrison administration."[42]

Congress remained unpersuaded by such logic, authorizing only three gunboats. But the appropriation bill of 3 March 1893 stipulated that "the Secretary of the Navy shall not receive or consider bids from any party or parties not provided with a plant suitable to do the work." Furthermore, the secretary "shall award the contract at the price of the lowest bid to that one of the parties bidding on any such ship which in his judgment it is in the interest of the Government to have do the work." Finally, all previous appropriation balances were released so that the secretary could apply them to any and all vessels under construction—past, present or future—thus enabling the U.S. Navy to finally begin development of a submarine torpedo boat.[43]

These provisions might be viewed as opening a virtual Pandora's box. Civilians like Tracy, moved by the spirit of crisis management seen in the armor impasse of 1890, could underwrite specific firms in specific industries, all in the name of national defense. As seen from the Tracy experience, the proliferation of defense-related industries became inevitable once American industrial capacity and the needs of security became synonomous in the minds of policymakers and entrepreneurs alike. Each crisis—real or imagined—opened another stage in the process. An armor impasse with Bethlehem added a second firm to the interlock, as Carnegie, Phipps gained a share of the spoils. Also, in time, a third steelmaker gained audience as Midvale Steel joined ordnance production. Hilary Herbert had observed in February that six additional shipbuilding firms had joined the previous three constructing fighting ships for the navy. The process was certainly not complete by 1893, but the first tentacles of a modern military-industrial complex were there.[44]

Contemporaries of Tracy and Herbert saw little threat attending the phenomenon. To them such developments were merely ancilary to American patriotism and determination to have the fighting fleet recognized in its own right by competitive seapowers of the age. Each of these rivals required a solid industrial base, free from dependency upon either foreign sources or monolithic domestic patrons; this was the problem that, in their eyes, Secretary Tracy had solved.

TABLE 6

ARMOR

Contractor	Quantity, Tons	Price per Ton	Time of Delivery, (Contract)	Actual Delivery, Tons	Current Rate of Delivery, per Month, Tons
June 9, 1887 Bethlehem Iron Co.	6,703	average $632.61	Dec. 1894	101	200
September 5, 1890 Bethlehem Iron Co.	171	632.61	Mar. 5, 1891	0 171 presented for test	....
November 20, 1890 Carnegie, Phipps & Co.	6,000	625.00	June 15, 1893	60 230 presented for test	200
September 28, 1891 Carnegie, Phipps & Co.	36	265.00	Dec. 28, 1891	36	....

NOTE: The difference between the amount herein shown to be expended to June 30, 1893, for armor, and the amount given on the table which the chief of bureau left with the chairman of the committee is due to the fact that that table had been prepared on the basis of 500 tons of armor per month and from later information the deliveries would be at the rate of 700 tons per month.

TABLE 6 (continued)

Expected Future Delivery, per Month, Tons	Amount Required to Pay for Current Delivery, per Month	Amount Required to Pay for Expected Future Delivery, per Month	Remarks
350	$126,522	$221,413.00	The average contract price is $538.70 per ton, but it is estimated that this will be increased by $93.91, on account of ballistic tests, test plates, premiums, nickel freight, and handling.
85½	....	$ 54,088.16	171 tons now under test ready for shipment.
350	$125,000	$218,750.00	The average contract price is the same as that of the Bethlehem contract but it is estimated that this will be increased by $625 per ton by the additional cost for ballistic tests, test plates, freight, handling, and use of nickel.
....	....	$ 9,552.00	Delivered, but not paid for.

Chapter 5

MIC, Robber Barons, and
an Alabama Colonel

Benjamin F. Tracy's Democratic successor was more of a navalist than the New York Republican had been. For one thing, Hilary Herbert's long service in Congress had provided him with a thorough grounding in both legislative programs and national defense policy. An ex-Confederate infantry colonel, Herbert accepted Grover Cleveland's naval portfolio without trepidation. The president knew a good executive when he saw one. Furthermore, he sensed the general mood of international affairs when he announced, "If we are to have a Navy for war-like operations, offensive and defensive, we certainly ought to increase both the number of battleships and torpedo boats." Herbert would actively push this program through to fruition.

It did not take long for him to securely grasp the reins of office. A month prior to his swearing in, Herbert requested a full statement of additional funds needed in 1893–94 for ships already authorized. Tracy readily complied. Forced by circumstances to pursue a course of gradualism, Herbert nonetheless declared at the outset that he would continue Whitney-Tracy programs. After all, he had been something of an architect for much of that earlier work.[1]

Herbert, like Tracy, was a thoroughly "militarized civilian." He considered naval officers "a very superior class of men" with wide experience and knowledge of other cultures and world affairs. Still, he had never been impressed with the navy's bureaus and their methods of management. He was perfectly willing to disregard bureaucrats' advice, although he took Rear Admiral F. M. Ramsay, chief of navigation, as his chief of staff. He was quite aware of the internecine rivalry between Philip Hichborn in construction and repair, Melville in steam engineering, and Sampson in ordnance—all vitally concerned with fleet development. Herbert avoided his predecessors' device of settling disputed policy questions through the appointment of special boards. To avoid "old boy networks" and influence, Herbert himself sat as final judge and arbiter— the real role of service secretary anyway. He was an early practicioner of President Harry Truman's later adage, "the buck stops here."

The new secretary had an opportunity to see how American warships compared with foreign vessels during an international naval review in New York harbor. The U.S. performance was admirable, and Herbert envisioned America's emerging as a leader in the imperialist squabbling of the time. But in analyzing the review, he warned that only a nation which was prepared militarily, and which was not afraid to go to war if necessary, could keep her place among world powers. Herbert's sentiments were an anathema to good Democrats like the editor of the *St. Louis Republic*. Liberty would be forever lost if the nation were to go on a permanent war footing, claimed that newspaper. The hinterland had not yet embraced the new internationalist trend.[2]

Still, Herbert plunged ahead. He inquired about armor deliveries and began to sense the frustration of being in the driver's seat at the Navy department. Earlier conservatism and opposition to extensive expansion gave way to a grim determination that lack of domestic facilities would not hold up construction. He began to ask hard statistical questions concerning contracts, penalties, and premiums. It wasn't very long before he "leaked" to the press that he thought the nation warranted at least ten new battleships.

The question of statistics was central as Herbert moved to lay his plan before Congress. Carnegie Steel, née Carnegie, Phipps, had fully satisfied its contracts of 9 September 1890, 28 September 1891, and 12 December 1892. Bethlehem had completed none, and both companies were averaging just over 280 tons of armor per month without penalties. Only Carnegie was earning premiums for *Monterey, New York,* and *Amphitrite* side armor. Millard Hunsicker of Carnegie had complained about novelty of design and lack of technical expertise in fabricating sponson armor. Neither Carnegie nor Bethlehem liked the Harvey process because of the extra trouble and expense.[3]

Given such hopeful signs in the industry, Herbert thought it time to recommend large construction programs once again. Unfortunately, he misjudged the state of the national economy. America was in poor financial shape and Cleveland was frankly worried. The president wanted no massive government spending. So the naval secretary could merely reiterate need, previous accomplishment, and future promise. In his annual report for 1893, he cited the cost "of completed and uncompleted vessels of the Navy up to the beginning of the present fiscal year" at $51,701,488.77, including armor and armament. But improving conditions in the shipbuilding, ordnance, and armor trades suggested savings, and he concluded, "Surveying the whole field, we find much to be proud of in the knowledge that we can now furnish the material for, and build, modern ships of war as quickly and, without any doubt, as well as any country in the world."[4]

Herbert spoke with pride of gun lathes at the Washington gun factory which had reduced labor costs over 30 percent. He noted that other navies were moving to use of harveyized nickel-steel armor and that the Bethlehem company now employed eight furnaces for the process. Yet all his citations pointed toward his avowed aim—to see commencement of the next stage of battleship expansion. The navy was not the cause of the country's economic woes, he declared, but unless Congress appropriated money for more warships, lead time considerations would leave construction ways empty by the time of the next national presidential election.[5]

When President Cleveland submitted Herbert's report to

Congress he suggested that the large number of incompleted ships and the depleted state of the Treasury augured poorly for any new ships that year. Some navalists still hoped that Congress would approve Herbert's modest proposal for one battleship and six torpedo boats. But the May 1894 floor debates once again highlighted the typical feud between coastal state enthusiasts and economy-minded legislators from the hinterland. In the end, the navy act of 26 July provided $4,000,000 for armor and armament on contracts dating to 1886, $450,000 for an additional dynamite cruiser, and $450,000 for three torpedo boats.[6]

Herbert's first year in office was full of difficulties. The secretary spent much of his time trying to determine who was responsible for the deplorable physical condition of the cruiser *Atlanta*. Investigating boards found rusted collision doors carried on regular reports as full operable, and papers like the *New York Times* jestingly questioned the wisdom of building a new navy when its officers planned to ruin it through abuse and neglect. Then, in February 1894, the venerable Civil War veteran *Kearsarge* struck a well-known and charted reef off Nicaragua and was lost. Adding to the navy's embarassment were the first of the major armor scandals which emerged during Herbert's tenure.[7]

Government specifications and regulations on steel inspection were rigidly enforced despite industry's constant pleas for relaxation. It was only a matter of time before contractors attempted to circumvent the system. The first issue had arisen in 1890 when Bethlehem's failures to supply armor under time constraints led the Navy Department to contract with the Linden Steel Works of Linden, Pennsylvania for protective deck plates of the *Maine* and *Texas*. On 1 July, a government inspector at the works discovered that a counterfeit of his stamp had been used at the factory. He immediately stopped inspection, and Chief of Ordnance Sicard was ordered to make a complete investigation. Linden's president claimed that one employee, Robert Ball, had made the illegal stamp, and the company disclaimed responsibility. The issue was dropped when the suspect disappeared and no evidence could be secured from other employees. Sicard cleared the company.[8]

A second case also occurred during the Tracy administration when flaws were discovered in steel castings designed for the machinery of both the *Maine* and *Cincinnati*. Departmental investigators found all twenty-nine Standard Steel Casting Company items showed defects which had been concealed by smoothing over the neighboring steel. The firm's president vehemently denied wrong doing, demanding a reexamination in front of company representatives. Such a procedure again confirmed the defects, but the president claimed that he had never issued orders to any employee leading to such an act. Still, these two incidents alerted naval inspectors and department officials to possible fraudulent activities throughout the steel industry.[9]

Thus it should have been only mildly surprising when Secretary Herbert learned of Carnegie misdeeds in the autumn of 1893. James H. Smith, a Pittsburgh attorney, notified the secretary that four of his clients, former Carnegie employees, had information proving fraud in the manufacture of armor plate. The men were willing to provide this information to the government through their attorney in return for financial reward. The secretary was in a quandry. He disliked the notion of purchasing information in this manner. Still, he found even more distasteful the idea that fraudulent practices might endanger the safety of American warships and their crews. Backed by President Cleveland, he agreed to pay the informants 25 percent of any damages assessed against the company as a result of the investigation.[10]

The four informants had done their work well. They charged the Carnegie company with failing to temper armor evenly and properly. They felt that the firm had allowed the plugging and concealing of blow holes, which would have caused rejection of the plates by naval inspectors. Furthermore, the firm had retreated specific test plates without the knowledge of those inspectors, thus making them better than the entire, original group. Equipped with such information, the Navy department launched an extensive inquiry, headed by ordnance chief, William T. Sampson.

Simple examinations of previously submitted plates substantiated these charges. Sampson and his inspectors recommended that the company be assessed a fine of 15 percent of the value of all armor received by the government during the period that the frauds took place, 2 November 1892 to 16 September 1893. Cleveland himself then evaluated the results of the investigation, confiding to Herbert, " I am convinced that a large portion of the armor supplied was not of the quality which would have been produced if all possible care and skill had been exercised in its construction." Still, the president hesitated taking a harsh line since it was difficult to determine just what damages should be assumed by the company. Finally, in an effort at fairness, Cleveland reduced the fine to 10 percent of the price of armor sold to the government during the fraud period, or $140,489.[11]

Herbert sent a copy of Cleveland's letter, together with his own comments, to Henry Clay Frick, board chairman of Carnegie Steel. The secretary praised the general quality of armor despite individual defects and fraud. But he noted that Carnegie Steel had been fined because it had represented the armor as being of prime quality, thus earning government premiums. Herbert rather condescendingly suggested that both company and the navy might learn from this experience. He told Frick that the navy would "redouble its watchfulness" in the future, and would expect hearty cooperation from the company in preventing further abuses. Herbert also settled the account with the informants by depositing $35,121.23 to their credit in a Pittsburgh bank.[12]

The whole issue simmered on for at least another year. Sampson's group gathered additional data further proving that the Carnegie people had deliberately perpetuated the fraud. At the same time, Andrew Carnegie and Frick proclaimed themselves victims of unscrupulous employees and demanded that the government should refund the fine. The informants claimed in turn that the government was covering up to protect the company. Even the House Naval Affairs Committee jumped into the fray with its own investigation. Over nine hundred pages of testimony led to the conclusion that indeed, "manifold frauds" bordering on criminality had been perpetrated at Homestead. But by this time Herbert and others were sick of the whole matter. He had received word that Carnegie had removed Charles M. Schwab from his position as super-intendent of the armor department. Writing to James McPherson, chairman of the Senate Naval Affairs Committee in January 1895, the secretary declared the issue settled as far as the navy was concerned. Congress also chose to drop the matter.[13]

Still, when viewed from the perspective of history, these three episodes seem symptomatic of a predictable process. Suspicion was bound to enter the relationship at some point as profit-seeking steelmakers sought to cut corners and avoid troublesome government inspections and regulations. Steelmen and others in the industrial sector began to realize by the mid-nineties that armor and gun forgings had other spinoff benefits via the successful manufacture of large high-grade forgings. Nickel-steel also promised broad nonmilitary uses, and the Harvey process held great potential for the users of hard steels. Government subsidies for military purposes could now be used by industry for producing high speed machinery, for example. The commercial significance of technical breakthroughs for munitions production may have been most important as the bleak depression years of 1893 and 1894 descended upon America.

While the rail and structural steel markets remained tight, the navy's need for every possible ton of armor carried both Bethlehem and Carnegie through the depression. In addition, American armor makers were now able to compete on the European market heretofore dominated by Krupp, Schneider, and Whitworth. Carnegie Steel (through its valued agent, C.A. Stone, only lately resigned from active duty), competed with some twenty foreign steelmakers for a Russian heavy armor contract in 1894. Similarly, Bethlehem Iron won another contract with the Russians, largely because of the efforts of its expert, former Lieutenant Meigs. These were commercial triumphs for the companies, with patriotic overtones for American craftsmen. A carefully orchestrated official test of the Carnegie armor for the Russians used U.S. Navy facilities, experts, and equipment to serve notice to the world that American heavy industry—like the U.S. Navy—had come of age.[14]

Still, Herbert was worried. He wrote in late 1894, "I am informed upon authority which I believe to be good that about, or perhaps before, the time of the last contract of the Bethlehem company with Russia there was a meeting in Paris of the representatives of the principal, if not all, of the armor manufacturers of Europe and America. These facts seem to lead to the conclusion that there is at least a friendly understanding or agreement among the principal manufacturers of the world that prices shall be maintained at about the same level." Indeed, by 1897, steel representatives of Krupp, Vickers, Armstrong, Schneider, Carnegie, and Bethlehem had agreed to pool information. Collusion and monopoly were an anathema to a Democrat and public official such as Herbert. He decided to keep alert and await developments.[15]

Government-industrial relations were full of nuance in this period. Through a combination of selfish motives cloaked with patriotism, the manufacturers continually urged larger naval appropriations. Carnegie and others needed business for idle plants and skilled workers during harsh times. On the one hand they appeared to seek international outlets for products made possible by government subsidies. On the other, the U.S. Navy was equally selfish if only because it had to maintain an economic base of technology, labor, and management in the civilian world. Thus, the Navy department welcomed, and may even have assisted the steelmen in securing foreign armor contracts when it appeared that it could not itself supply enough work for Bethlehem and Carnegie.[16]

Whatever contributed to the nation's economic health was not lost upon sharp politicians like Cleveland and Herbert. In 1895, with the depression at its height, the gold drain continuing upon the Treasury despite repeal of the Sherman Act, as well as use of federal troops in the Pullman strike intensifying social unrest and spreading it to industrial centers, both officials saw merit in the resumption of naval construction programs as a device to help alleviate problems. On the international scene, the year witnessed revolutions in Cuba and Turkey as well as the Venezuelan boundary dispute with Great Britain. Originally stymied due to the worsening domestic economy, naval rearmament could now act as a spur to recovery, and a further upgrading of American presence abroad.

Herbert told the president that large construction programs would mean jobs in shipyards and steel plants as well as business for many ancillary industries. Skilled manpower pools would not disperse to other fields, plants would not be permanently idled, and technological impetus would not slacken. U.S. dollars should benefit U.S. business and workers, said the naval secretary, and further delays would only cripple America.

Responding to his cabinet offical's advice, President Cleveland reversed his course and endorsed the idea of three additional ten-thousand-ton battleships and twelve torpedo boats. The House of Representatives also responded quickly to shipyard bankruptcy by authorizing $12,000,000 at the very height of the depression—with no foreign threat in sight. But populists like Benjamin Tillman and Augustus O. Bacon rallied stiffer opposition in the Senate. A compromise navy act of 1895 called for the battleships *Kearsarge* and *Kentucky,* six composite gunboats, and three torpedo boats. Some of the smaller craft were to be built on inland waterways and along the Gulf Coast to stimulate local industry. Congress also appropriated $4,837,670 for armor with $2,000,000 immediately available.[17]

By this time Herbert was increasingly dissatisfied with the actual arrangements between the government and the captains of the steel industry. As the initial Bethlehem and Carnegie contracts reached completion, the Navy Department scrutinized the situation. Most of the original private investment had been recouped by the steelmen. Herbert and his advisors thought that prices should now be lowered. Sharp letters passed back and forth between the secretary and John G.A. Leischman, Carnegie vice chairman, and his assistant Millard Hunsicker who headed the armor plate operation. Habit and profit prevented the industrialists from lowering prices.[18]

The naval secretary was certain that an agreement existed between Carnegie and Bethlehem whereby both arbitrarily maintained high prices. A prearranged figure of approximately six hundred dollars per ton recalled the formative days of

Secretary Whitney when he and Bethlehem had first discussed the matter. Herbert immediately sought a reduction by fifty dollars per ton. But events had moved beyond any quiet internal adjustment between steelmen and the Navy Department.

Announcement of the arbitrary armor prices coincided with the appearance of a full-blown Populist revolt on Capitol Hill. Leaders like "Pitchfork Ben" Tillman of South Carolina rose to do battle with the "trust" in the wake of the Carnegie scandals and the Russian armor contracts. The Senate refused flatly to pay more than $350 per ton for armor. Congress wanted Herbert to investigate the matter of "prices paid for armor plate for the Navy and the prices paid for armor plates by other nations," but the department chose to keep developments at a low key, for fear of alienating the steelmen. Herbert readily admitted ignorance of prices paid American manufacturers "under recent contracts for armor plates for other nations."

Ordnance chief Sampson, however, observed that French and English bids for the foreign trade fell far below "the prices paid them for armor intended for ships of their own nationality." The naval officer attributed that to inferior material supplied to other navies through less stringent inspection and acceptance requirements. But, noted Sampson revealingly, "another reason, and one which may have impelled the Bethlehem Iron Company to acquire its recent contract even at a serious loss, is that a far greater loss would be experienced if it was found necessary to break up the organization, disperse the skilled labor, and close the works through lack of orders."

Then the Navy department learned that Bethlehem had agreed to provide the Russians with armor at $250 per ton, (a subsequent contract raised the price to $524, but no one chose to notice that fact). The fat was in the fire. The difference between $250 for the Russians, and $625 under existing American contracts of 1887, 1890, and 1893, appalled citizens and government officials alike. At Herbert's urging, Congress took an even greater interest in armor prices as well as other problems attendant on the naval-industrial relationship. By December 1895, Senate naval affairs committeemen began to investigate not only armor prices, but also whether the Navy

Department had been guilty of expediting patent applications for processes involved in armor production and whether active duty naval officers had been illegally involved in contract or patent negotiations or other matters favoring industry.

Subsequent testimony by key naval ordnance experts like Commander Horace Elmer, steel inspector at Homestead, and Commander John A. Rodgers, his counterpart at the Bethlehem works, disclosed their own feeling that armor could be manufactured for $250.00 per ton. President Robert Linderman of Bethlehem immediately protested to Herbert that such a figure failed to embrace interest on investment, maintenance and depreciation of plant, and working capital. In sum, claimed the industrialist, those costs drove manufacturing prices to $496.56 per ton, "sufficient to convince you that the prices now being paid by the Government are not excessive" because they did not include "loss on rejected plates, cost of experiments, administration expenses etc." much less a fair profit. Finally, the navy and the steelmen got together and reduced the price of *Kentucky/Kearsarge* armor from $520.00 to $450.00 (excluding $50.00 for harveyizing) per ton. But the agreement was only temporary.

Meanwhile the armor problem festered beneath the surface of congressional discussion of the navy act for 1896. Capital ship and armor prices bothered everyone on the hill, and even the appearance of Andrew Carnegie before the Senate Naval Affairs Committee on 8 February failed to defuse the situation. Carnegie advised:

> If the Government of the United States would give us what the British Government gives its armor-making plants— steady work—we should be all right. If the Government would keep us in work 6,000 tons a year, it would be a highly profitable business; but as it is now, gentlemen, I assure you that many departments of our works are making more money and have made more money on the capital.[19]

Congress listened to such thinking and then negotiated its internal differences. The Senate wanted two battleships and a ceiling of $350 per ton for armor. The House remained wedded to four capital ships but was more flexible on armor price, agreeing to a compromise figure of $425. House managers C.A. Boutelle, Amos Cummings, and John B. Robinson labored tirelessly with their senatorial counterparts, Eugene Hale, Matthew Quay, and A.P. Gorman. But while three battleships suited everyone, a compromise armor price seemed out of the question.

The Naval Appropriation Act of 10 June 1896 provided the battleships, ten torpedo boats, two submarines and $4,371,454 for armor and armament. Moreover, the armor price impasse was reflected in a clause requiring the Secretary of the Navy "to examine into the actual cost of armor plate and the price of the same" and report to Congress by the end of the year. No contract for the three battleships could be let until then. In addition, the Senate naval affairs committee won acceptance for the prohibition of active and retired naval officers working for private firms having business with the government. "No man can well serve two masters" was the way the senators phrased it. [20]

Herbert knew that only company records contained the accurate statistics concerning manufacturing costs and price-fixing. He contacted Linderman and Leischman and asked them to come to Washington with their records or assistants to supply the necessary information. Both steelmen flatly refused to cooperate, despite the Alabamian's warning that use of imperfect records might prejudice their case. He was more successful in getting corporate tax returns from the Pennsylvania auditor general. The secretary of the treasury also supplied reports on imported materials received by Bethlehem and Carnegie from 1887 to 1893. Former navy plant inspectors like Lieutenants Karl Rohrer, Kossuth Niles, A.A. Ackerman, Ensign C.B. McVay, and Commander John A. Rodgers supplied detailed statistics on labor and material costs for producing nickel, harveyized steel armor. Finally, Herbert even traveled personally to Europe in order to determine foreign prices. [21]

The secretary tried to keep his trip secret. He alerted Paris and London naval attachés to his mission and his feeling that American armor makers were part of an international conspiracy. He asked them to gather information. Still, the

Carnegie people gained knowledge of his trip and one of the firm's agents actually traveled on the same steamship with Herbert. The agent alerted his British and Continental contacts, with the result that the naval secretary met only high price quotations and evasive answers. The French minister of marine confirmed the American's suspicion of international collusion, however, and suggested that his counterpart also employ secret agents to gain information. The Frenchman readily supplied information concerning his nation's experience with government armor manufacture at Guerigny.

Eventually Herbert was driven to surreptitious research in England. He returned home declaring:

> During the debate in the Senate upon the armor question at the last session of Congress, one question discussed was whether there was an understanding or agreement among armor manufacturers throughout the world to keep up prices. If there is any such understanding it is of course impossible to prove it, unless some one of those to whom the secret has been confided should betray his trust. My impression is that there is and has been for some time at the least a friendly understanding among armor contractors both in Europe and America as to the prices to be charged for armor. This impression I find prevails abroad, certainly among some of the persons who have inquired into the subject.

Without trying to justify such combinations, the secretary admitted that he understood those reasons leading armor men to charge one price to their own governments and another price to countries which did not manufacture the commodity. Still, he was determined to come up with some equitable price for the U.S. Navy.[22]

Herbert and his subordinates carefully reconstructed the history of American naval-steel negotiations and relations. The technical experts explained the technological difficulties of harveyizing, injection of nickel, and machining plate. Ensign McVay provided precise figures on Carnegie's Homestead operation where 400 to 3,500 laborers worked exclusively on naval armor. He also noted that the greatest daily output of steel was 6,282 tons with an average monthly output of 100,000 tons. Finished average output of naval armor for the period 23 July 1893 to 8 March 1896 only stood at 2,766 tons, only a small proportion of the whole.[23]

Ackerman, Rohrer, and Niles agreed that armor prices seemed exorbitant. But they maintained that the steel companies were faced with matériel losses which reduced profits, sacrificed labor and plant time due to naval contract uncertainties, and led to plant deterioration through disuse or underutilization. Ackerman for one reversed his earlier position and told Herbert that steelmen were not making "anything like the amount of money I first supposed they had made." But the secretary still thought the government should get lower prices in 1896 than those of 1890 or 1892 due to industrial plant maturation and the simpler types of armor plates demanded by newer battleship designs. He simply rejected the idea that industry should get $200 of the $550 per ton as pure profit.

Suddenly the steel officials made their counterattack. Bethlehem spokesmen complained about undertaking "this difficult and vexatious business" in the first place. They contended that obstacles and delays compounded "when the Government gave a private contract on the same terms as ours to a rival concern, which, guided by our sacrifices, was spared the outlay of more than a million dollars." They flatly concluded there was "little prospect of continuous work for these two establishments, if even for one." President Linderman especially wanted the government to buy out the armor plate business and felt "reluctantly obliged to decline to give, in such detail as you request, the cost to us of manufacturing Armor Plate, since to do this would necessarily involve the disclosure to our competitor of business secrets which we have obtained by long and expensive experience and which belong to us alone and which might be used to our disadvantage."

Carnegie Steel officials eventually explained their own position to Herbert by claiming "the cost of making armor is not to be found in the details at the shops, upon which your officers have estimated." Rather, they pointed to a $3 million company investment (including five hundred thousand dollars in company money aside from government subsidies), with no charges made for the ground, railway connections, water, electricity, superintendence, or interest during construction. The Carnegie people added to the price of every ton of armor $81.53 for interest on plant, $67.94 for maintenance of plant, $25.00 as working capital, and $75.49 for loss by abandonment of plant when the navy completed its construction programs. They pointed to the basic unprofitability of armor making, their magnanimous response to government pleas in 1890, and, like Bethlehem, offered to sell the armor plant to the government by either leaving it at Homestead to be run by trained naval officers, or by moving it at cost to a location specified by the U.S. Navy.

The Pittsburgh steelmen concluded:

> We make about 150,000 tons of finished steel per month and the two or three hundred tons of Armor we make per month demand greater attention and give more trouble than all the 150,000 tons. We shall be delighted if the Government will let us out of the Armor business. We can use the Capital in several lines of our business to better advantage.

Hilary Herbert was a lame duck cabinet official by the time he submitted his findings of the armor question to Congress in January 1897. The Republicans had again swept to victory in the fall elections, mainly on domestic promises of a "full dinner pail." Foreign issues and naval buildup received only slight attention. Still, the secretary's report was clear and complete in its findings, despite its author's political status and the fact that he had never secured entry to corporate records and so had been forced to rely upon meager statistics and foreign sources. (See table 7).

With a fairness which even leaned toward the benefit of industry, Herbert's calculations held to a fair price of $400 per ton for armor. He suggested liberal treatment of the uncooperative steelmen, for they had to face rigid government specifications and inspections. This would give the steel industry a fair profit of nearly 50 percent, since the industry's highest estimate for manufacturing and maintenance was approximately $270 per ton, said Herbert. (See table 8).

TABLE 7

INTERNATIONAL ARMOR PRICES

	United States	France
1886		Hache, $357.00, compound or ordinary steel
1887	Bethlehem, $538.60,* ordinary steel	
1889		Brennus, $372.00, compound or ordinary steel
1890	Carnegie, $538.60, ordinary steel	
1892		Bouret, $455.00, nickel-chrome, water-tempered
1893	Carnegie, $559.00†, Bethlehem, $565.60†, both nickel steel	
1894		Charlemagne class $468.00, nickle-chrome not Harveyed, $530.70 Harveyed
1895		thin casemate plates of nickel-chrome, $432.20§
1896	Carnegie, $551.10, Bethlehem, $552.20‡, bolts both $400.00, all Harveyed, nickel-steel	

*Price included deck plates; prices range from $500 to $600. No nickel, no Harvey process: these were added later at increased cost.

† Price was about $500 (plus additional $11 to be added for Harveyed plates besides cost of nickel furnished), also $30 premium per ton if grained. Without these additions, the prices range from $515 to $575.

‡ This includes cost of Harvey process, but perhaps cost of nickel oxide should be added. Prices range from $515.40 to $575.00, with no premiums.

§ No exact prices for heavy plates vary; no Harvey process cost $463 to $473 while for armor using Harvey process the price is $525 to $540. The increased cost due to Harveying, everything included, is about $63.00 per ton.

‖ Orders delivered to Copenhagen.

The Swedish contract with Le Creusot included belt armor at F 1,770 or $342.00; 301 tons casemate at F 1,650 or $318.00; 146 tons of fixed part turret at F 1,750 or $340.00; 125 tons of

TABLE 7 (cont.)

Russia	Denmark and Sweden
3 Saints Vickers, Le Creusot, £ 64 or $312.00 St. Chaumond, £ 68 or $347.00, special steel incl. turrets	(Denmark)‖ Vickers, $355.20, Harveyed, but no nickel Le Creusot, $238.10, surface hardened, no nickel
(December) Bethlehem, $249.00, whether or not Harveyed, with bolts, $299.00	St. Chaumond, $357.00, surface hardened turret, thin plates
(November–December) Bethlehem, $520.70, Carnegie, $529.20, both Harveyed, bolts both $389.30	(May–June) (Sweden): Le Creusot, $342.00 nickel-steel approximate price average, not surface hardened#
(January) Krupp (presumably), $523.60, Dillinger, $542.60 all surface hardened, plus turrets &c., bolts both $380.00	
Prices include, in all cases, delivery in Russia	

movable turret at F 2,015 or $388.90; 26 tons of conning tower including roof and tube at F 1,950 or $376.00; and bolts at F 1,840 or $355.00. The average price is about $330.00 for plane plates to $389.00 per turret and plates. All plates "Harveyed" are paid for at an increased price of $120.00 per ton. For Harveyed plates, the prices would vary from $438.00 to $510.00 per ton.

NOTE: The array of foreign statistics acquired by Herbert's agents surely must have dazzled the Alabamian. In 1894, for example, the British firm of Cammel and Company charged Her Majesty's government prices for Harveyed armor ranging from $333 per ton for the battleship *Magnificent* to $413–38 per ton on the *Centurion*. Yet this same firm offered to supply the Russian government with nickel steel armor at $341 per ton or $307 without nickel. They sought to charge the Italians $457 per ton. In Germany, Krupp's price for nickel-steel armor stood at $386 per ton for ordinary and $468 per ton for superior quality. Even Japanese prices paid to British firms stood at £ 90 to £ 96 per ton. Five French firms supplied armor with four in combination against Schneider of Creusot. The price rise from 1885 to 1893 in France was $450 per ton.

SOURCE: Chart, Naval Attache–Paris to Secretary of the Navy, 11 September 1896, Armor Plate Investigation, 1896; Record Group 37, Records of the Hydrographic Office, NARS.

Herbert admitted that his figures were not infallible. But he challenged Bethlehem and Carnegie to open their books and refute them. He suggested that should Congress accept his estimates and the steel industry reject them, then legislators should give the naval secretary authority to either buy or construct a naval armor plant of its own. As one student of the matter concluded later, Herbert apparently felt it was time to end the very special relationship which had existed between the steel industry and the government since the days of William C. Whitney.[24]

But Capitol Hill proved to be less generous than Secretary Herbert. The Senate Naval Affairs Committee rendered its own report in February. While praising Herbert for his efforts at fairness, they rejected his figures. Noting the anguished cries of Linderman and Leischman in response to the secretary's findings, the committee concluded flatly that "a fair average price of armor will be between $300 and $400 per ton." The senators were in a distinctly ugly mood as they suggested that a government armor factory could be erected for $1.5 million "and that it is expedient to establish such a factory in case the armor manufacturers decline to accept such prices for armor as may be fixed by law.[25]

This Senate report also addressed other aspects of the growing military-industrial linkage. It deplored the procedure whereby a contractor having large dealings with the government could employ officials of the Navy Department and through them learn the secrets and purposes of the government, "and moreover insidiously influence its action," with great injury to the public service. This violated a fundamental principle, they said, whereby each side is represented only by persons wholly devoted to its own interests. Thus, "it is viciously violated by a custom which allows one side to take into its pecuniary employment a representative of the other side."

The committee refused to draw the line (as had full Congressional debate the previous spring), between retired and active duty officers. Officers were officers, said the politicians, and "to permit them to take sides against the Government and to enter into the employ of contractors having dealings with the

TABLE 8

COMPARISON OF ARMOR COST 1893 AND 1896

Contracts	Nickel Steel Armor, not including Harveying			Nickel Steel Armor including Harveying			Average Cost of All Armor		
	Tons	Cost	Average	Tons	Cost	Average	Tons	Cost	Average
1893	6,670	$3,752,785	$562.63	5,634	$3,456,962.58	$613.59	6,763.53	$4,134,008.16	$611.26
1896	5,600	2,795,190	499.14	5,232	2,910,900.00	556.36	5,660.00	3,122,710.00	551.72
Difference			63.49		Difference	57.23		Difference	59.54

The above is the actual price paid to the armor makers.
To obtain the total cost to the government of any kind of armor at any time, apply the arguments of the following table to the price paid the manufacturers.

Contracts	For Harveying per Ton	Introducing Nickel per Ton	Royalty of Harvey Process per Ton	Cost of Nickel*	Total
1887–90	$50.40	$11.20	$11.20	$29.68	$102.48
1893	50.40	. . . . .	11.20	29.68	91.28
1896	. . . . .	. . . . .	11.20†	19.20	30.40

*106 lbs. per ton of armor @ 28¢ per lb.
†96 lbs. @ $20 per lb.

SOURCE: Bureau of Ordance December 19, 1896, Record Group 37, Records of Hydrographic Office, Armor Plate Investigation 1896, NARS.

Government reaching to millions of dollars will certainly, if the custom continues, become most pernicious and injurious to the public interests." A case was noted wherein an officer was declared fit by one naval board in the United States, and the judgment reversed while he was on attaché duty in Japan. Thereupon said officer was placed on the retired list and immediately retained by Carnegie Steel for six thousand dollars per years while in Japan. "To this officer, however," said the committee, "the clause of the law of June 10, 1896 will apply and the armor contractors will soon lose his valuable services unless he surrenders his position as a retired naval officer and becomes a civilian."[26]

"Nearly as objectionable" to the committee was the practice of permitting naval officers to become involved in patent processing by the federal government. The guilty party most often cited was former ordnance chief, Commander William Folger. Folger had not only facilitated the process of obtaining a patent for Augustus Harvey and his supercarbonizing treatment for armor plate, but had gone even further by aiding a military colleague who sought to patent a breech-closing mechanism at the expense of inventor Hiram Maxim who claimed the invention as his own. Folger opposed Maxim's claim because he was "an outsider and free lance who comes in for pelf alone, for mere money-making business." Similar conflicts existed on the so-called Corey reforging process patent (also claimed by William H. Jaques), and the Creusot nickel-steel alloy patents. In all three instances, Folger, former secretary Tracy, and even Hilary Herbert applied unusual pressure on the Patent Office to recognize the American patentee above the foreign one. The Senate committee therefore concluded "that Government officials ought not to promote a monopoly of the business of making armor through patents issued to the use of the combined manufacturers while using the power of the Government to destroy patents held by foreigners."

All of this led the Senate investigators to decide against removal of the statute prohibiting naval officers from "double-dipping." The law of 10 June 1896 would remain, and, furthermore, the government would have the right to use all patents for discoveries made by its naval officers "upon paying therefore a reasonable compensation, to be determined in a manner provided by law." The secretary of the navy should not make any contract or pay for any naval officer's patent, and the latter had to get the department's sanction before even applying for such. Future armor contracts should not be let until the United States had acquired the right to use any patented inventions involved, and in all cases navy officials should be present at Patent Office hearings to determine the proper usuage of any such patents.

This influential committee report was well received by the whole Congress. That body moved to appropriate funds for three more torpedo boats on the eve of the change in administration, tacking on a provision that the U.S. Navy could pay no more than three hundred dollars a ton for armor. This Populist triumph caused one less radical legislator to wonder if the steelmen had not contributed enough to the fall election campaign chests! Still, the government armor factory clause failed to pass, and since the legislation which did pass was toothless, it only further exacerbated the touchy relations between industry and government. When later that year Herbert's successor advertised for more armor at three hundred dollars a ton, both Bethlehem and Carnegie simply refused to bid at all. Just as the Gun Foundry Board had feared years earlier, the manufacturers had established a united front to stymie the navy.[27]

There was reason to speculate that this maneuver had been planned by Ben Tillman and William Chandler to force radical government seizure of the armor facilities long enough to fabricate the necessary armor. Later, Bethlehem and Carnegie actually agreed to provide one hundred tons to complete battleships then under construction. Whatever the back room machinations and maneuvers on Capitol Hill, the final results were not to be seen until long after Herbert left office. Meanwhile, his final annual report of 1896 graphically portrayed the progress made in linking industry and the navy more closely to one another.[28]

One hundred seventeen thousand tons of additional warships had been added to the U.S. Navy during the second Cleveland term, but possibly more impressive were the implications for the domestic economy. No less than fourteen shipbuilding firms now bid on major warship construction projects. Eight companies were under contract to supply naval projectiles, and a proportionately higher number of companies than before provided matériel from foodstuffs to clothing and naval stores for the burgeoning "new navy." Most of the major construction firms were located in major urban centers on the Atlantic or Pacific coasts. Herbert was not altogether pleased with the underrepresentation of Gulf Coast and inland regions. Yet concerns there simply could not underbid the giants like Cramp and Sons, Union Iron Works, or Herreshoff. Still, Colonel Herbert's navy provided some pump priming for a sluggish economy. (See table 9.)

Notwithstanding various contract difficulties with the armor makers, Herbert happily noted in his report that deliveries had risen from 1,949 tons at 286 tons per year prior to March 1893, to 17,334 tons of nickel-steel armor at a rate of 5,000 tons per year. He noted that the department had successfully resisted steelmen's desires to drop the harveyizing process since it "has been adopted by all the great naval powers of the world." In an interesting tour de force, Herbert suggested stopping public armor tests, since the United States had now moved abreast and often ahead of foreign governments. The secretary was afraid of disclosing military secrets—a sign that the country had surely joined the ranks of the superpowers of the day!

Finally, Herbert noted development of contractual arrangements with the American Ordnance Company in Washington for "building 4-inch guns and mounts for auxiliary cruisers." The Bethlehem Iron Company had completed a large portion of an one hundred gun order for the U.S. Army, and, in Herbert's view, "the bringing of the American Ordnance Company into the field of competition will insure, in addition to the Government Plant, two establishments in the country capable of manufacturing high-powered guns."[29]

The philosophy behind Herbert's efforts had been reinforced by domestic depression and international events during the second Cleveland administration. General political turbulence in Latin America, a simmering indepencence movement in Cuba, and the emergence of a formidable Japanese naval

TABLE 9
MAJOR BIDDERS FOR NAVAL CONTRACTS, 1896

Ship Construction

Newport News Shipping and Dry Dock Company, Newport News, Va.
William Cramp & Sons, Philadelphia, Pa.
Union Iron Works, San Francisco, Calif.
Lewis Nixon, Elizabethport, N.J.
Bath Iron Works, Bath, Maine
J.H. Dialogue & Son, Camden, N.J.
Columbian Iron Works, Baltimore, Md.
Herreshoff Manufacturing Company, Bristol, R.I.
Moran Brothers Company, Seattle, Wash.
Wolf & Zwicker Iron Works, Portland, Ore.
Charles Hillman Company, Philadelphia, Pa.
Painton Electrical Steamship and Construction Company
George Lawley & Sons Corporation, South Boston, Mass.
Providence Steam Engine Company, Providence, R.I.

Gun Forgings

Bethlehem Iron Company, South Bethlehem, Pa.
Midvale Steel Company, Philadelphia, Pa.

Torpedoes

E.W. Bliss Company, Brooklyn, N.Y.

Steel Projectiles

United States Projectile Company, Brooklyn, N.Y.
Midvale Steel Company, Philadelphia, Pa.
Carpenter Steel Company, Reading, Pa.
Sterling Steel Co., Pittsburgh, Pa.
Taylor Iron and Steel Co., Highbridge, N.J.
Bethlehem Iron Company, South Bethlehem, Pa.
American Ordnance Company, Washington, D.C.
American Projectile Company, Lynn, Mass.

SOURCE: Secretary of the Navy, *Annual Report, 1896*, 65–67, 278–79, 285

competitor in the Far East all had taught the naval secretary
that the naval races of the world and the shrinking isolation of
all countries dictated the need for greater sea power. "It is not
contended," he said, "that we should attempt to compete in
numbers with the great navies of England and France, but we
ought surely to move up steadily into a higher rank than we
now occupy, and into the pace of nations whose necessities are
far less than ours." Herbert did not like to rank sixth, behind
Great Britain, France, Russia, Italy, Germany, and Spain. (See
table 10.)

TABLE 10

STRENGTH OF SEVEN PRINCIPAL NAVIES 1896

Class	Great Britain			France			Russia			Italy			Germany			U.S.			Spain		
	BUILT	BUILDING	TOTAL	BUILT	BUILDING	TOTAL	BUILT	BUILDING	TOTAL	BUILT	BUILDING	TOTAL	BUILT	BUILDING	TOTAL	BUILT	BUILDING	TOTAL	BUILT	BUILDING	TOTAL
Battle-ships.																					
First Class.	22	12	34	10	8	18	5	6	11	8	2	10	4	2	6	3	6	9	1		1
Second Class.	12		12	11	1	12	5	2	7	2		2	7		7	2		2			
Third Class.	11		11	2		2				5		5	3		3				2		2
Total.	45	12	57	23	9	32	10	8	18	15	2	17	14	2	16	5	6	11	3		3
Coast Defense Ships.	13		13	16		16	10	4	14				17	2	19	6	1	7			
Cruisers.																					
Armored.	16		16	9	1	10	9	1	10	1	5	6		1	1	2		2	3	4	7
First Class.	11	10	21	2	4	6	2		2				1		1	3		3	1		1
Second and Third Class.	51	24	75	10	9	19	3	1	4	16	1	17	3	5	8	13		13	7		7
Lookout ships or gunboats.	19		19	12		12							11	1	12	9	9	18	22		22
Torpedo Gunboats.	34		34	12	3	15	8		8	15	2	17	9	1	10				3	4	7
Torpedo-boat Destroyers.	98		98	3		3	1		1	1		1	11		11	1		1	1	2	3
Torpedo boats.	160		160	241		241	161		161	176		176	145		145	3	15	18	19	4	23

SOURCE: Secretary of the Navy, *Annual Report*, 1896.

Herbert concluded that "nothing will so surely make for peace and give us weight abroad and security at home as a substantial navy constructed of the best materials and manned by the highest intelligence and skill." Construction of a substantial navy now involved a mass of technical details— electrification of heavy gun turrets, experiments with liquid fuel, nickel-steel employment in boilers as well as armor plate, improved business methods in departmental administration, and the outfitting of more ships with torpedoes. Keynoting the increasing American government interest in the Caribbean, the secretary pointed out the lack of a Gulf Coast naval base and retreated from the Tracy emphasis on high seas fleets by advocating lighter draft battleships which might enter the harbors of Savannah, New Brunswick (Georgia), Key West, Mobile, and the mouth of the Mississippi.[30]

Herbert emerged from his turn with the naval portfolio as something of an enigma. An ardent navalist, he was not quite as ready to drop the hoary coastal defense battleship concept as modern historians have thought. "Light-draft battleships, if we had them, could make any of these ports bases of supply, could sally forth from them or retire into them at will, and could therefore almost always offer battle on their own terms," he proclaimed. Yet such craft would also require heavy armor and ordnance. If Herbert wanted equity in business dealings with the steel industry, he was also pragmatic enough to realize that Populist radicalism on armor prices and overly ardent prosecution for fraud might endanger a useful, even necessary relationship.

However, Herbert's administration had witnessed an inescapable change in that relationship. A special trust or bond pointing toward a specific national goal—armor and ordnance for defense—had been broken when industry began to realize commercial profits on the international market using the tools of that trust. The U.S. Navy, however, sought favoritism in the use of the tools it had helped develop, and in fact, had paid for with public money. Equity, fair play, reasonable profit, decent prices all took on new meaning as a result of changes in the naval-industrial complex in the late nineties.

Chapter 6

War, Imperialism, and Another Armor Crisis

Republicans returned to the White House in 1897 amidst turbulent times. Grave economic difficulties included the Populist revolt and a business slump. American businessmen sought intervention against European hegemony in China and Spanish oppression in Cuba. William McKinley committed himself to restoration of "the full dinner pail" as well as American action short of war to resolve the Caribbean unrest. But he also wanted a lid placed on government spending. Naval rearmament, begun nearly two decades before, had to level off.

McKinley chose ex-governor John Davis Long of Massachusetts as his secretary of the navy. Long was an amiable and efficient politician. Harvard-educated and a lawyer by trade, he had served six years in Congress during the eighties. Scholarly and pedestrian, Long contrasted sharply with his assistant secretary, the ebullient Theodore Roosevelt, who had been Benjamin Harrison's commissioner for civil service. Whereas Long anxiously delegated authority to naval subordinates in order to avoid petty details and to preserve internal departmental harmony, Roosevelt actively sought power and influence in naval affairs. One kinsman of former naval secretary William Hunt told Long the day after the new administration took office, "Your life as secretary will, without a doubt, be very gratifying, as it brings you in contact with the rights and duties, and with the privileges and honor of the naval profession." Little did Long know, at that time, of his impending struggles with bureaucrats and industrialists. His tenure was to be anything but staid, dignified, or necessarily gratifying.[1]

Long symbolized McKinley's desired pause in the growth of the navy. Roosevelt represented navalist wishes to continue development at an accelerated pace. He became the big navy spokesman, and the various articles and books by Alfred Thayer Mahan became the navalists' bible. Five battleships and sixteen torpedo boats remained incomplete, and a Republican-controlled Congress went along with administration wishes and limited armor prices to three hundred dollars per ton. It remained to be seen who would win in the end—Big Navy or Long's conservatism.[2]

On one thing Long and Roosevelt could agree. Armor was going to be a vital consideration, especially when advertisements for the battleships *Alabama*, *Illinois*, and *Wisconsin* met absolutely no response from industry. The Navy Department's reaction was the appointment of a five-member board under Captain Charles O'Neil, chief of ordnance, to investigate the cost of building a government armor plant. The O'Neil group approached President Charles Schwab of Carnegie and Bethlehem's principal officer Robert Linderman about a selling price for their armor plants. The industrial response was twice the figure of $1,500,000 quoted by Sampson's earlier naval board before Congress. Assistant Secretary Roosevelt told his friend Henry Cabot Lodge: "I am feeling rather blue over the armor business. I am afraid it will be difficult for us to get them to go on with the building up of the Navy, and if they stop I fear they will never begin again."[3]

Andrew Carnegie and Charles Schwab undoubtedly saw a chance to make a sizable profit at the expense of the government. Forever anxious to jettison the troublesome armor business, Carnegie told his company president to offer the plant to Long at an apparent loss, for $2 million. His idea was to show the country that this price was much below what the government would actually have to pay to construct a new facility. Thus, the U.S. Navy could either buy steel from the industry at higher prices, or buy out the steel company's armor plant. The company would retain certain rights to steel and natural gas, and return a handsome profit. Carnegie knew full well that government subsidies had originally helped build the plant so that nothing approaching $2 million had come from company funds. The navy knew it too. They simply refused to accept the bait.[4]

Communicating these difficulties to Capitol Hill, navy spokesmen sought authority to proceed with "preparations" for a government armor factory. As Eugene Hale told Lodge, he could not have gotten ten votes in the Senate for higher armor prices, and the situation was no different in the House. Led by Senators Tillman and Chandler, Congress enacted a deficiency appropriation bill in July which permitted Long to proceed with full-scale investigations of sites and costs for the armor factory. Refecting last minute industrial offers to supply about one hundred tons of armor at premium prices to keep the battleships moving, Assistant Secretary Roosevelt signed an order establishing a formal, five-member Armor Factory Board on 6 August 1897.[5]

Headed by renowned torpedo expert Commodore John A. Howell, the group comprised civil engineers and ordnance authorities. Its job was to investigate, describe, and design the specifics of land, buildings, and machinery as well as to decide whether the government should buy raw steel or make its own. Roosevelt made it clear from the start that he planned strict supervision of the group. Deadline for the report was the opening of the next congressional session. The group responded quickly by canvassing ideas from informants ranging from lowly steel rollers to inventors and industrialists. By the middle of September an impatient TR was prodding the Howell board for conclusions.[6]

TR took personal charge of a mid-month meeting and told Howell, "I need not say that all we want is the facts and if you find we can make armor for $150 or $1000 a ton all we want is to know the exact facts." But deliberate naval experts protested against time constraints and narrowly-defined orders. They wanted to engage the services of noted Bethlehem steel expert,

John Fritz, then present at the meeting. Roosevelt questioned him about his corporate connections, but admitted the need for a steel expert as consultant. He took the matter to Long, who urged rejection of Fritz, but the Howell group was adamant and the secretary eventually gave in. Still, he demanded the board look at sites in the south and get the report to him by 1 December. He told Roosevelt and Howell: " I cannot believe Congress will build an armor plant. I do not think the act indicates that they intended to do it, but they want the information."[7]

Long got his report on time. The Howell board decided that any government facility should include a plant for production of open-hearth steel ingots as well as armor. Technological changes could always be introduced once naval expertise at armor production had been attained, and they estimated the cost, "exclusive of the land, of a plant capable of making and furnishing ready for the installment on board ship of 6,000 tons per year of nickel steel, face hardened, reforged armor," stood at $3,747,912.11. The group felt that a proving ground should be located with the plant, and they appended a list of seventy-three possible locations for the navy's armor plant.[8]

The naval experts gave Long and Congress many details about specialized product demands, costly investment in equipment and plant, and the need for full-time operation to render the endeavor profitable. It was nothing new, however, and Howell's people went so far as to reiterate the old industrial demand for a "constant yearly appropriation for ships to be provided with armor" and the dangers of labor dispersal in off season. "A resumption of work at a later period would require the training, at a considerable expense, of a new set of men," said the experts, and, "in the meantime the progress of the art would perhaps have been such that difficult and radical changes would be required, which under continuous working might have been gradually and easily made."[9]

The armor issue seemed muted by early December when this document actually reached Congress. Less than a month before, Long had sent a basically conservative annual report to McKinley, and the administration asked for only one battleship and a few torpedo boats and destroyers from the legislators. Of course, costs of the navy had gone up from $15.4 million to $17.5 million, and for that reason, Long and McKinley saw no reason to ask for more from Congress. A dejected Roosevelt told Lodge, "It is too little, but it is a recognition of the principle that we are not to stop."[10]

Long was frankly more interested in bringing order to diverse and frictional naval programs. "A modern man-of-war is a compendium of industrial inventions and appliances," he declared. He saw a chance to improve glamourless but vital areas of shore facilities and organizational management, including relations with private suppliers of matériel. Nobody in the department ardently advocated a government armor factory. Ordnance chief O'Neil reported his bureau was of the opinion that the government "can purchase armor more cheaply than it can manufacture it, and regards the making of armor as a proper adjunct to a great commercial steel plant." Accordingly, Long, TR, and the naval bureaucrats suggested raising price levels to four hundred dollars a ton for armor. It took a national emergency and war to finally resolve the issue.[11]

War clouds were already gathering as congressmen like Charles Boutelle of Maine and Oscar Underwood of Alabama once more worried about armor prices. Anti-Spanish rioting in Havana threatened American citizens and property, and the navy sent the battleship *Maine* to show the flag on the very day that Boutelle and Underwood rose in debate on the armor issue. Within three weeks an ostensible diplomatic slur by Spanish minister Dupuy de Lome, and the mysterious destruction of the *Maine* had fanned the flames of yellow journalism. Despite the suggestion by the captain of the ill-fated warship that public judgment be suspended, newspapers, the general public, and Congress clamored for revenge. War with Spain seemed imminent.

Meanwhile Long and McKinley hoped for reconciliation and tried to back away from confrontation. The secretary earned TR's epithet about a chocolate eclair backbone, but he also shifted fleet elements to cover possible contingencies while his bellicose assistant worked feverishly to complete actual war preparations. Long lost control of Roosevelt completely, but the navy was better prepared for possible eventualities when war finally came on 21 April 1898. Such combat preparations soon encompassed questions of ship construction, armor procurement, and money as Congress reacted to the *Maine* by voting $50 million for national security on 8 March. A crash construction program, procurement of auxiliary craft already afloat, and renewed debate on armor prices all accompanied these events.[12]

This naval buildup, and congressional appropriations in particular, helped to escalate the international crisis. American citizens and leaders became more jingoistic while the Madrid ministry reacted in shock to American war moves. Congressmen marveled that the U.S. government couldn't secure armor for the $250 price paid by the Germans for their own. In retrospect, debate that spring seemed less concerned with the immediate Spanish crisis as much as with the larger issue of possible war with some Continental ally of Spain. In fact, it is quite possible to construe the debates as utilizing the Spanish crisis mainly as a convenient guise to effect still another step forward in permanent naval rearmament.

The House of Representatives, with Underwood in the lead, began debate on regular annual naval appropriations on April Fool's Day. Underwood led the attack on armor prices claiming ''I think I can satisfy the committee that the Government can save from one-half to one-third on the cost of armor plate for a battleship if it will build its own plant instead of letting out contracts to private corporations.'' But it would take $4 million in Treasury funds to do it, based on naval estimates plus inflationary additions. His statistics projected $123 per ton savings ($1,230,000 for ten thousand tons to complete the stalled battleships) from a government plant. Concluding that the Carnegie and Bethlehem facilities had similar capacity, he computed $7,606,881 as the private amount ''on which the Government is required to pay the interest, taxes, insurance, and profits for the manufacture of 6,000 tons of armor plate, whereas the Government plant would only cost $3,747,912 or a difference of $3,858,996. In other words, if the Government erects its own plant, it will save interest charges and insurance on nearly $4,000,000.''[13]

Cries were heard for restoration of the $300 price tag, but few House colleagues shared Underwood's enthusiasm for government armor plants. By the time the Senate took up the measure, war with Spain was fact, not speculation. Tillman and Butler once more asked, "Shall we have an armor plant of our own and save this money to the taxpayers or shall we give these monopolies the benefit, not only of the gift we have already made to them but of future contracts, which would double or treble what we have already spent with them?" Both men decried the defective armor previously supplied by Carnegie and Bethlehem proclaiming it endangered the lives of American sailors. But in the end they probably realized the necessity of paying any price to finish battleships needed in the war effort. Congress finally voted an appropriation bill calling for three new seagoing battleships, four harbor defense monitors, plus numerous smaller craft. Moreover, Secretary Long was empowered to invite armor bids for the three half-completed battleships in a price range of $3,210,000 or $400 per ton.[14]

Everyone from Long to Schwab and Linderman probably breathed a sigh of relief. The navy chiefs needed ships, since Admiral Pascual Cervera y Topete's Spanish squadron was still loose in the Atlantic. The U.S. Navy lost little time in effecting an agreement with industry subject to congressional approval. The June 1898 contracts carried a price average of $400 per ton, with Carnegie and Bethlehem dividing evenly the orders. Schwab told his board of managers that there would probably be enough work to last two years. Thus, wartime exigencies seemed to herald the end of the long struggle to secure good armor at reasonable and equitable prices for all parties.[15]

Eventually American squadrons destroyed both Cervera's ships and the Spanish Philippine squadron. Both Cuba and the Philippines were invaded, occupied, and annexed by an America bent suddenly on becoming an imperial power in its own right. The insular possessions growing out of the 1898 war extended American frontiers beyond the continental coastline of North America. Mahan had been vindicated; the political and strategic isolation of the United States shattered; and the navy had more of a mission than even before. Once an armistice had been concluded in August, the naval heroes could reflect more realistically upon the strategic and technical results of battle and what they meant for the future.

The Spanish war proved several things. A panicky commercial class in the eastern cities nearly wrecked sound naval planning by forcing the dispersal of key fleet units in the face of possible Spanish sorties. Yet the U.S. Navy proved that it could mount overseas expeditionary operations, provide fire support, and, principally, that the Luce-Mahan-Tracy concept of heavily armored and armed high seas battlefleets was essential to modern American naval policy. Of course there were blemishes. Long later declared, "It is a striking fact that the resources of the country to supply war material seem practically limitless, and were lightly taxed in the recent emergency," but American gunnery proved atrocious. Fortunately, Senator Butler's worst fears about losing millions of dollars in ships and many American lives due to inferior armor proved absurd.[16]

In the end, American warships and facilities proved themselves worthy of war. The Spanish war euphoria proved to be short-lived, however, when it came to appropriating the big naval construction program advanced by Long, his board on construction, and other navalists. Congress was quite wary of wartime profiteering and new firms like Midvale Steel and Illinois Steel who wanted to join the armor production business. Then too, Bethlehem and Carnegie were renewing their quest for higher prices. Returning to the insurgent attack upon naval-industrial collaboration were not only Tillman and Butler, but John Rixey (Virginia), John Gaines (Tennessee), Albert Hopkins (Illinois), William Hepburn (Iowa), James Lewis (Washington) and Oscar Underwood in the House.

The congressional debate this time was enlivened by the news that the U.S. Navy now wanted to change the type of armor it was using. A new type of Krupp steel had emerged from Germany. It incorporated 1.3 percent chromium together with 3.5 percent nickel to produce an armor ostensibly 25 percent lighter yet stronger than older types. Krupp wanted $45 per ton royalty for use of the material, and legislators immediately questioned whether the new product had been proven reliable. Furthermore, the new type of armor would cost the navy $545 a ton according to industrial spokesmen.

Ordnance chief O'Neil claimed, "If the harveyized armor is worth $400 and the Krupp is 25 percent better, then it is worth $500, besides the royalty of $45." But Rixey and others on Capitol Hill considered this extortion; a $1 million gift to the steel trust. Within a year's time the steelmen had raised prices despite wartime accord. Acceptance of Krupp armor by British and Russian governments as well as American tests of the brand meant nothing to most politicians. To them, American naval officers always wanted to have the latest gimmicks. They recalled the Russian deal with Bethlehem at $249 a ton. They remembered the subsidized American plants. Suddenly, the ever-fattening monopoly wanted more from a pliant government.[17]

Yet, when Congressman Underwood introduced an amendment to allow Long to build a government plant, administration spokesmen Charles Boutelle and William S. Kirkpatrick, representing the Bethlehem district in Pennsylvania, moved to counterattack. The Pennsylvania legislator suggested the additional $145 really only reflected increased cost of production "by a more complicated and detailed process and the payment of royalties for the secrets held by the establishment at Essen, at which it is universally acknowledged the best face-hardened armor in the world is made." He pleaded the case of the twenty-five thousand people who "gather about [the Bethlehem works] and derive their life, their growth, and their prosperity from its benignant presence." He wondered why so much hatred and prejudice attended "the beneficient work it has done in building up those great communities and giving employment and prosperous homes to the artisan and laborer.[18]

Boutelle further proclaimed the "'bloated monopoly' with which we are dealing today is the 'bloated monopoly' of inventive genius." Amos Cummings of New York explained the Russian contract at $249 reflected a peculiar Russian procedure whereby with "bidder bidding in competition until the lowest price is reached." Bethlehem supposedly lost $40,000 on that contract, but being out of American work, received employment and the satisfaction of seeing its mill continue in operative status during slack time. Still, John Sharp Williams of Mississippi could start with the Russian price and compute Krupp armor allowing interest, plant depreciation, royalties, and profit, and still undercut the industry's asking price by $100 per ton. The House voted out an appropriation bill with $445 per ton for the 1899 armor price. It now remained for the Senate to go along.[19]

Tillman and Butler refused to do so. They haggled for three hundred dollars per ton and $4 million to build a government plant. William Chandler was there too, pointing out that Carnegie and Bethlehem were more anxious to produce obsolescent harveyized armor at four hundred dollars a ton than to undertake a better product requiring the acquisition of new techniques and facilities. The Senate concurred in insurgent views, only to complicate passage on Capitol Hill by striking out some of the warships desired by House members. Three conference calls accomplished little as stalwarts like Eugene Hale admitted, "As I look at the future, if we are going to build a large navy, I am more and more impressed that at a near day both Houses have got to consent to an armor plant, so that the Government may have that hold over the combinations for furnishing armor by private establishments."

The time was not yet right, however. With adjournment imminent, the senators withdrew on the armor plant and permitted three battleships, three armored cruisers, six protected cruisers and several submarines to remain in the bill. House members left the armor price at three hundred dollars per ton. One impasse had been ended; yet another was about to develop.[20]

Tillman, Rixey, and others were correct. Carnegie and Bethlehem were indeed acting in concert to set prices and split the armor market. From May 1898 on, Charles Schwab actively sought to gain a larger slice of the armor market from Bethlehem in return for a hands-off policy regarding gun forging, which the eastern Pennsylvania firm found more lucrative. Some of the Carnegie partners like Henry Clay Frick and Frank Lovejoy wanted Carnegie to enter the forging business, but George Lauder and Henry Phipps backed Schwab's position—$2 million was too much to spend on a gamble. While Lovejoy raised the specter of technological obsolescence as nations replaced heavily armored warships with high speed unarmored craft (thus displaying the business community's complete incompetence to judge international weapons markets), the makeweight in the Carnegie decision proved not to be its board of directors, but the threat of competition from a third, unanticipated source. Small, well-managed Midvale Steel of Philadelphia threatened to enter the armor business and underbid both corporate giants unless Carnegie remained out of the gun forging business wherein Midvale was finding great profit. By July 1898 all three firms were locked in battle to wrest larger shares of armor and gun forgings from competitors. Eventually, Schwab and Carnegie obtained a larger share of the armor market by agreeing to stay out of the ordnance competition.[21]

Schwab and Bethlehem representatives watched congressional and naval manipulations with great care. They felt that even four hundred dollars was unprofitable, since Carnegie auditors showed losses for that side of its business. If fact, company officials claimed a profit decline from 30 percent at the beginning of the Herbert era to 15 percent at the time of the Spanish-American War. Yet they could not cite actual costs without disclosing precise production statistics, thereby tipping off the U.S. Navy, Congress, and competitors. Naval ordnance chief O'Neil had cooperated wholeheartedly in helping the steelmen prepare their case for Congress, since the navy seemed more than willing to pay anything the industry demanded in order to get the necessary steel for naval expansion in 1899. Collusion between O'Neil and Schwab, for example was not out of the question.[22]

In retrospect, Schwab's biographer claims that inadequate data dooms any effort to determine which side was correct on questions of price, extortion, or profit. In any event, the steelmen's desires for $545 per ton, O'Neil's advice that $475 was within the realm of possibility, Congress's return to the $300 figure, as well as the navy's advertisement for bids in April threatened to produce barren issue. Added to this confusion was the possibility of a Vickers and Maxim merger with Midvale, Charles Harrah's threat to enter Midvale in the armor game, and a mysterious bid received by the Navy Department (reported to Carnegie managers by their Washington lackey, retired Lieutenant C.A. Stone), which baffled all the steelmen.

When Long finally opened this mysterious bid, it proved to be just what Schwab had predicted, an unreliable quotation from an obscure western producer. The eastern moguls once again moved freely into negotiations with the U.S. Navy. They flatly refused to provide Krupp steel at the congressionally set price, although Schwab privately expressed willingness to produce harveyized armor for $400 just as Senator Chandler had contended. An interim twelve-thousand-ton order was placed with his Pittsburgh firm and negotiations for an additional thirty-six thousand tons continued into the summer and fall. Long and Schwab met in person after the steelman staved off a late surge from Midvale which undercut the Carnegie position. Long was prepared to go to $450 (under special Congressional dispensation), but Schwab held out for the higher price. Carnegie board members were reluctant to see their plant idle for five years, and so eventually Long and the navy agreed to $460 per ton ($360,000 in profits to the corporation), thinking that the issue might be carried before the next Congress in 1900 for approval.

The new century dawned as an election year. Long told President McKinley that $98,529,511.85 had been expended upon the new navy with over $62,000,000.00 left outstanding on unfinished vessels—"hardly more than the sum paid in a single year for pensions to the soldiers and sailors who served a generation ago in the late civil war." He wanted more cruisers and gunboats but declared armor to be the "most important question pertaining to naval construction at the present time." He especially recommended recession of the price limitations on armor procurement.[23]

Few observers missed the fact that times had changed when naval appropriations hearings began in April. Influential Republicans like Joseph G. Cannon of Illinois, chairman of the House Appropriations Committee, and Eugene Hale, Senate Naval Affairs Committee chairman, both counseled moderation. Oscar Underwood predicted that most members would soon drop out "and attend to their business in town," notwithstanding that "the Naval Committee has never brought a more important question [than armor] before this House, and it is a matter that ought to be settled and settled right." However, rather than being indifferent to naval details, legislators in 1900 proved downright belligerent. A lively session appeared to lie ahead.[24]

A budgetary increase of $13 million caught everyone's eye and there was the usual flurry about $545 for armor. With sixty warships authorized or already under construction and building costs escalating precipitously, the cause for more appropriations seemed self-evident. Even the cost of a government armor factory had gone up to nearly $5 million since 1897. Ordnance chief O'Neil had told congressmen, "It is not likely that armor could or would be more cheaply produced by the Government than it could be bought, unless all consideration of interest on the value of the plant and on working capital is discarded." Estimates for navy yard warship construction had also doubled and shipbuilder Charles Cramp told Secretary Long on 3 March, "Some of your predecessors, notably Mr. Whitney and General Tracy, held the same views but they did not avow them so frankly as you have done, and they also yielded to the navy yard clamor from time to time by causing ships to be built in them." He estimated that both the *Raleigh* and *Cincinnati* cost the government 50 percent more than the Cramp yard would have charged to build them.[25]

In any event, some sort of naval building program had to continue no matter who built the American fleet. An emerging German navy had supplanted the British fleet as the major protagonist. Reflecting the country's preoccupation with pacifying insurgent Filipinos, Congressmen George E. Foss of Illinois bombastically declared, "I say that the American battle ship, that never bore a commission of duty but what it carried a message of hope, will do more to civilize these people that the ten thousand sweeter and gentler influences which mold the minds of more civilized people." The modern verbiage of navalism, imperialism, and commercialism descended like a blanket upon Congress in the spring of 1900. As Amos Cummings told his colleagues: "If we are to have an increased navy, it is time to stop talking and begin work. Authorizing it will not build it; you must provide armor and do it promptly. Either do this or stop the authorization of vessels. Do one thing or the other."[26]

Senator Tillman captured the essence of the problem. He told Senate leadership:

> Mr. President, every time that this armor question comes up, and every time it has come up for the past five years, we have to travel over exactly the same ground that we are traveling today. A reference to the *Congressional Record* will show that this debate is in its main features a repetition of the debate which we have had here for five consecutive years. The proposition has been this, and it is the same today, that these armor plants do not deal fairly by the United States Government; that they are exorbitant in the prices which they charge, and that they have been detected in the past in endeavoring to put off upon us defective armor. From that it has been argued that the proper course to pursue is to build an armor plant by the United States government. On the other hand, the answer during each of these five years has been the same as it is today. . . . 'We need armor now; let us pay the price which they demand and settle the question hereafter as to whether we shall build an armor plant!' and each time these armor factories have forced the payment of these exorbitant prices, and as soon as that has been accomplished the question of the building of an armor plant subsides, and it is heard no more until the next time comes for the procurement of armor, and then the same argument and the same action by Congress are again repeated.[27]

Notwithstanding Tillman's perceptive comment, it proved no different in the first session of the Fifty-sixth Congress. A few more senators and representatives arrayed themselves on either side—Augustus O. Bacon of Georgia with Tillman and the Populists; Bois Penrose of Pennsylvania with the Republicanism of big business. Moderate voices like that of John M. Daniel of Virginia ("after all, it is almost a misnomer to call the great corporate establishments of this day private and individual enterprises in the sense that twenty or thirty or forty years ago we referred to the enterprise of the individual") were drowned out. The Senate finally settled on armor prices at $445 per ton with a limit of $545 if necessary to finish the three battleships, but with the proviso that the secretary of the navy could immediately construct an armor plant should prices rise above $445. They set aside $2 million for the factory and required the Navy Department to tell the next session of Congress about price, site, and delivery prospects.

Colorado Senator Henry M. Teller admitted: "I do not like this bill. I do not know whether it is settled now. I suppose it is. We are in the hands of this great steel combine. The Republicans seem to have set their hearts upon giving to these people practically whatever they ask." House members didn't like the Senate version either, but eventually both sides tired of the struggle and the naval appropriations act of 7 June 1900 appropriated $4 million to procure by contract armor of the best quality at reasonable and equitable prices. Should such prices and contracts be unattainable, then the Navy Department was "hereby authorized and directed to procure a site for and to erect thereon a factory for the manufacture of armor, and the sum of four million dollars is hereby appropriated toward the erection of said factory." The bill also yielded two more battleships, three armored and two protected cruisers, and Charles K. Wheeler of Kentucky breathed relief that Congress had finally burnt itself out concerning the United States Navy.[28]

Congressional action in 1900 came up against the politically charged atmosphere of the fall elections. Some Republicans on the hill thought it might be prudent to delay final action on armor contracts until after Election Day so as to stifle Democratic charges about prices. In fact, Andrew Carnegie's outspoken opposition to Philippine annexation nearly destroyed party unity. But calm returned by August and the Navy invited armor bids. Three respondents included Carnegie, Bethlehem, and Midvale, but apparently at this point Schwab had not gained supremacy over a troublesome Charles Harrah. While Bethlehem and Carnegie demanded one-half the total quantity, Midvale asked for at least twenty thousand tons and based its bidding on a sliding scale for varying quantities and types. Even the navy muddled things by desiring particular types of armor rather than any set standard.

The navy needed 7,250 tons of armor immediately, and Long and his people could not wait the twenty-six months necessary for Midvale to complete its armor mill. The trouble was that Midvale submitted the most attractive bid, at least for the *Maine* class battleships for which the emergency was acute. Other armor was needed, but if an award was made to Midvale, then the Carnegie and Bethlehem resources would be lost to the department. Long and his ordnance experts did not wish to turn their backs on proven and long-standing relationships. Already existing factories with higher prices vied with promises and lower costs. The department was temporarily hamstrung. It could neither award all the armor contracts to the high bidders, Carnegie and Bethlehem, nor could it wait for Midvale to deliver the goods.

A conference was set up for 2 October 1900 in Long's office at the baroque State, War, and Navy Building in Washington. All the companies promised to be present, but when the day of the meeting actually arrived, Midvale representatives were conspicuously absent. The company's attorney sent word that the firm was withdrawing from further competition on armor. Unknown to Long, of course, Charles Schwab had won out. "After prolonged negotiations," Carnegie and Bethlehem met the Navy Department "in a spirit of reasonable adjustment," due largely to O'Neil's efforts. An agreement was made to supply the first-class Krupp armor for $420.00 a ton. The government further agreed to assume any liability for the patent process at $24.32 a ton on Krupp armor and a fee not exceeding $11.20 for the Harvey brand.

In the end, while the bid of the Bethlehem and Carnegie moguls had originally stood at $490.00 (and their first asking price at $545.00), the injection of artificial competition from Midvale had at least enabled the government to secure a competitive maximum price of $455.52 for the coveted and $400.00 for all other armor types needed to finish construction programs. The Navy Department had at long last gained private competition—by default, not by design. Schwab told board directors of their pyrrhic victory on 4 December 1900, "The matter is now definitely closed."[29]

The armor matter settled, Long could now turn to his annual recounting of naval achievements. It had been an eventful year with important construction and organizational accomplishments for business-naval relations. The infrastructure of private warship construction programs was maturing with corresponding influence in Washington. (See table 11.) Moreover institution of a general board, or natal general staff for the navy held important policy and planning ramifications. Long told senior admiral George Dewey, the hero of Manila Bay, that the board was not charged "with the constructing, manning, arming and equipping of the ships . . . but with recommendations as to the proper disposition of the Fleet." Brainchild of Captain Henry Taylor of the Newport War College, among others, this organ eventually injected itself into the very construction process that it was meant to avoid. Thus, by the early part of the new century not only were politically appointed cabinet officials and the president, but also bureau chiefs, the construction board, and now a new General Board part of the planning process for shaping the next stages of American naval development.[30]

Then, too, there was Congress. The second session of the Fifty-sixth Congress drew the line on more ship authorizations. Members questioned the backlog of uncompleted projects, the mission of a big navy, and the fact that each year seemed to mean budgetary escalation by $12 to $13 million. Legislators like Representative Rixey of Virginia pointed to images of interlocking interests, policies, and lobbying by shipbuilders and steelmen. He told his colleagues on 24 January:

> It is charged in the public press, and very generally believed—I do not know as to the truth—that the ship-subsidy bill for nine millions is backed by a great lobby promoted by those who will be interested in the subsidy. If so, is it to be supposed that these shipbuilding and armor-plate concerns, which are interested in the $25,000,000 ship contracts annually authorized, are any the less neglectful of their interests? The pressure to build ships is something enormous. Public opinion is manufactured, and the pressure seems irresistible. A man who expresses doubt as to

TABLE 11

PERCENTAGE OF COMPLETION FOR VESSELS UNDER CONSTRUCTION IN 1900

Name of Vessel	Constructor	Estimates of Superintending Constructors	
		Completion Percentage	Probable Completion
Illinois	Newport News Shipbuilding	86	Aug. 1, 1901
Wisconsin	Union Iron Works	97	Nov. 30, 1900
Maine	Wm. Cramp and Sons	37	Dec. 1902
Missouri	Newport News Shipbuilding	17	Jan. 1, 1903
Ohio	Union Iron Works	32	Mar. 5, 1902
Arkansas	Newport News Shipbuilding	43	Nov. 1, 1901
Monitor no. 8	Bath Iron Works	71	Jan. 1, 1902
Florida	Lewis Nixon	51	Nov. 15, 1901
Wyoming	Union Iron Works	58	Mar. 5, 1901
Denver	Wm. Cramp and Sons	31	June 14, 1902
Des Moines	Fore River Engine Co.	9	June 1, 1902
Chattanooga	The Crescent Shipyard	13	Aug. 15, 1902
Galveston	Wm. R. Trigg Co.	2	June 14, 1902
Tacoma	Union Iron Works	7	June 14, 1902
Cleveland	Bath Iron Works	25	Aug. 14, 1902
Bainbridge	Neafie and Levy	81	July 15, 1901
Barry	Neafie and Levy	79	Sept. 1, 1901
Chauncey	Neafie and Levy	79	Oct. 1, 1901
Dale	William R. Trigg Co.	84	May 10, 1901
Decatur	William R. Trigg Co.	83	May 25, 1901
Hopkins	Harlan and Hollingsworth Co.	68	Apr. 15, 1901
Hull	Harlan and Hollingsworth Co.	68	July 15, 1901
Lawrence	Fore River Engine Co.	98	Jan. 1, 1900
Macdonough	Fore River Engine Co.	97	Dec. 1, 1900
Paul Jones	Union Iron Works	78	Jan. 15, 1901
Perry	Union Iron Works	80	Jan. 1, 1901
Preble	Union Iron Works	78	Feb. 1, 1901
Stewart	Gas Engine and Power Co. and Charles L. Seabury and Co. Consolidated	38	July 15, 1901
Truxton	Maryland Steel Co.	43	Mar. 15, 1901
Whipple	Maryland Steel Co.	43	Mar. 15, 1901
Worden	Maryland Steel Co.	43	Mar. 15, 1901
Stringham	Harlan and Hollingsworth Co.	98	Jan. 1, 1901
Goldsborough	Wolf and Zwicker Iron Works	99	Jan. 1, 1901
Bailey	Gas Engine and Power Co. and Charles L. Seabury and Co. Consolidated	98	Jan. 1, 1901
Bagley	Bath Iron Works	95	Jan. 1, 1901
Barney	Bath Iron Works	97	Dec. 15, 1900
Biddle	Bath Iron Works	85	Jan. 15, 1901
Blakely	George Lawley and Son Corporation	96	Dec. 15, 1900
De Long	George Lawley and Son Corporation	96	Dec. 15, 1900
Nicholson	Lewis Nixon	81	Jan. 1, 1901
O'Brien	Lewis Nixon	84	Jan. 1, 1901
Shubrick	William R. Trigg Co.	96	Jan. 1, 1901
Stockton	William R. Trigg Co.	97	Dec. 15, 1900
Thornton	William R. Trigg Co.	90	Jan. 25, 1901
Tingey	Columbian Iron Works	64	Jan. 1, 1901
Wilkes	Gas Engine and Power Co. and Charles L. Seabury and Co. Consolidated	60	Mar. 15, 1901
Plunger	William R. Trigg Co.	85	In doubt
Adder	Holland Torpedo Boat Co. (Lewis Nixon)	8	Apr. 25, 1901
Grampus	Holland Torpedo Boat Co. (Union Iron Works)	0	Apr. 25, 1901
Moccasin	Holland Torpedo Boat Co. (Lewis Nixon)	7	May 25, 1901
Pike	Holland Torpedo Boat Co. (Union Iron Works)	0	May 25, 1901
Porpoise	Holland Torpedo Boat Co. (Lewis Nixon)	7	June 25, 1901
Shark	Holland Torpedo Boat Co.	7	July 25, 1901

SOURCE: Secretary of the Navy, *Annual Report, 1900*, 10–11.

the propriety of building more ships . . . is regarded not
only as an enemy of the Navy, but of the Government.[31]

For navalists the rationale was to be found in such charts of
international building programs as accompanied Long's annual
report. (See table 12.) Great Britain, Germany, and Japan all
offered growing threats to national security and the protection
of overseas American interests. Thus, by the end of 1900 began
the naval numbers game which steadily increased as the
century matured. The question was, just how many and what
type of warship was required to counter the threat? Conflicting
reports from various elements of the naval bureaucracy added
confusion and controversy to debates on Capitol Hill as well as
to the inner departmental feuds between battleship, submarine,
cruiser, and smaller ship cliques which have been part of the
process to this day.[32]

TABLE 12

INTERNATIONAL NAVAL CONSTRUCTION COMPETITION, 1900

| National Navy | Tonnage Laid Down, 1900 | | | |
	Battleships	Cruisers	Torpedo Vessels	Total
Great Britain	44,000	93,600	3,600	141,200
France		45,100	5,730	50,830
Germany	44,400	15,300	2,100	61,800
Italy	61,500	32,000	1,360	94,860
Japan		8,800	1,750	10,550
Russia	33,200	31,630	4,250	69,080
United States	12,300	12,800	1,070	26,170

	Total Tonnage under Construction			
Great Britain	254,800	235,750	12,950	502,700
France	21,680	143,530	3,300	168,510
Germany	111,000	32,500	2,800	146,300
Italy	75,000	46,800	1,360	123,160
Japan	30,400	17,400	2,240	50,040
Russia	150,220	102,650	10,850	263,720
United States	36,900	19,200	8,700* 12,940	77,740

*Monitors.

SOURCE: Secretary of the Navy, *Annual Report, 1900*, 15.

Congressional navalists were swept along by the arguments. They talked of equaling British and surpassing German fleets. Opponents feared that less costly gunboats or submarines might be more important than battleships in the future. Senator Butler went so far in the Senate as to charge that opposition to submarines came not from naval bureaucrats per se but from those who were under the thumb of big business: "It is some class or commercial interest or some other concern or interest that is fighting it, one that is sordid, coming from men who have regaled us with their patriotic speeches in the past when they were appealing to us to give $5,000,000 or $10,000,000 to the armor trust." Cheaper submarines would not mean large profits for the armor concerns and "they can never make another raid on the Treasury and get $7,000,000 in one haul," shouted Butler. Ironically, Bavarian émigré entrepreneur Isaac Leopold Rice was at that very moment building his own submarine construction empire, The Electric Boat Company, on the foundations of the newly acquired Holland Company. Vertical and horizontal trusts were spending throughout the burgeoning naval-industrial complex.[33]

Generally, though, it was not the year for worry about armor prices. The naval appropriations bill of the session floated through on compromise. Legislators wanted a breather, but they also wanted a larger hand in planning for national defense and the navy. McKinley won reelection in the autumn only to fall victim to an assassin's bullet. "That damned cowboy," Secretary Long's erstwhile assistant—later vice president— found himself the first Roosevelt to enter the White House. Spread eagle spirit now took hold of the government, and a conservative administrator like Long could count his days in office. Americans who voted in 1900 seemed less concerned with cost overruns, armor trusts, and military-industrial trysts. Business growth and national prosperity were the benchmarks; the U.S. Navy the symbol of greatness. The next decade of naval-business relations could have been predicted with the Republican victory at the turn of the century.

By March 1902, Secretary Long had had enough of the new administration. Submitting his resignation on 10 March, Long retired to Massachusetts to write a series of articles for *Outlook* which later appeared as *The New American Navy* and to crusade against his former assistant's role in precipitating the Spanish-American War. Long was worn out and embittered. Two questions remained: Just what had he willed to his successor, the Roosevelt administration, and to the nation? Just what might Americans expect of seapower in the future?[34]

Long did bequeath a battle-tested fleet brimming with confidence and competence. He launched the steel navy on a course of unprecedented expansion based on the spectacular achievements of victory in "the splendid little war." As ordance chief O'Neil told the New York Yacht Club early in 1902, "The Navy list of January 1, 1902 contains the names of 243 completed vessels and of 60 in process of construction a total of 303 vessels, and a very respectable showing, so far as numbers go."[35] Unresolved by such statistics, however, were issues over whether battleships of the *Illinois* and *Maine* classes were really well-conceived, or merely designed for the war just finished. Was America merely following in the wake of European developments, mesmerized by Mahanite concepts, status seeking, and pecking order credibility, thereby neglecting the potential offered by the unsung submarine? What about the naval-industrial linkages which had been so laboriously forged a decade before, severely tested in the wave of Populist outcry, and rose undaunted as a powerful and continuing force after the furor died down? Had the Long period served as a spur to or a brake on such matters?

Congressional insurgency had caused the United States government to temporarily dissolve its close partnership with the private sector. Yet the Navy department consciously steered a middle course. It turned its back on the old Gun Foundry Board philosophy of the government becoming a competing manufacturer which would lead to a natural regulation of prices according to classical economists. For some inexplicable reason the debates never clearly enunciated this approach— perhaps because so few men of the day truly understood it— whereby a true team spirit could exist between industry fabrication and government-run finishing operations, as in the ordnance field at the Washington Navy Yard. Institutional memory was short even then, and clerks on Capitol Hill or at

State, War and Navy never searched their records very far for precedent.[36]

Instead, the U.S. Navy chose to practice something styled "liberal regulation of business prices." Mirroring the coming spirit of Progressivism, the Long period clearly pointed to a moderate position, neither abolishing business connections, nor allowing complete and unchecked freedom. The best results may have been obtained through the mere presence of insurgency in Congress rather than through conscious naval policy. In fact, the regime of John Davis Long aptly reflected pre-Progressive Republicanism in which the party was a distinct byproduct of an industrial-government alliance. Naval officers were willing partners of politicians and industrialists in their ardent desire to build the armored Mahanite battlefleet at any price. They had many avid civilian supporters—Lodge, Boutelle, and Theodore Roosevelt. And, now, in 1902, TR had gone to the White House.

Chapter 7

Armor, Armament, and the Progressive Era

The outset of the Roosevelt presidency seemed to signal an upbeat in the pace of national activity. "Trust busting" and conservation, "Big Stick diplomacy" and Mahanite seapower all dictated new responsibilities and priorities for the United States both at home and abroad. Whether Mahan shaped TR's thinking or vice versa, whether the president sought to "manage" the very big business interests reflected in the Republican party or the opposite, both international imperialism and domestic Progressivism became intimately tied to questions of armor and ordnance in the Roosevelt era.[1]

During this period (which extended beyond TR into the administration of his handpicked successor, William Howard Taft), the U.S. Navy accomplished great strides with technology. Superbattleships of the dreadnought design emerged from drawing boards, thereby revolutionizing fleets around the world. Battle cruisers, destroyers, submarines, and naval aviation began their steady ascendancy from the first decade of this century. Naval ordnance expanded beyond the eight- and thirteen-inch guns of the *Kearsarge* and *Kentucky* class battleships to plans for the *Maryland's* sixteen-inch, forty-five-caliber main battery. Most of the organizational, administrative, and personnel reform of the period related directly or indirectly to issues of controlling, managing, and employing this new technology.

Thanks to Bradley Fiske's range finders and improved target drill ("lessons learned" from Santiago and Manila Bay), improved gunnery gave greater credence to American ships and ordnance. The introduction of naval radio communication (in 1900), water tube boilers, liquid fuel, new compass card divisions by degrees as well as points, and medical cures for diseases like tuberculosis pointed to the modern wedding of science and the sea service in the interest of national defense. Clearly then, America's first line of defense in the Progressive era was a far cry from the fledgling days of John Roach and his cruisers.[2]

Both the navy and the nation were becoming more sophisticated. Naval developments reflected the way the president, his chief civilian policy makers, and military professionals all conceived of national goals and of themselves. Capitol Hill politicians, cabinet advisers, and navy professionals began to seriously systematize "political points of view" and "military points of view" when judging "military problems" of national defense, possibly for the first time. At least in retrospect, these matters crystallized around organizational, technological, and strategic factors of naval policy after 1900.[3]

Much attention was given to the organizational framework of the armed forces. The rest of American society, especially business, was becoming more structured. For the businessmen, at least, this seemed like the most sensible was to provide internal "policing" in the wake of the freewheeling "chaos" of the old Robber Barons. Government too was gradually expanding in scope and size, and provided a pattern for the army and navy. Neither service had performed well administratively in the Spanish war. Nineteenth-century organizational apparatus was no longer viable. Bigger institutions, larger responsibilities, and expanded potential for wartime disaster as the hands of possible European enemies pointed to the need for setting the American house in order. Centralization versus decentralization was the most important issue of the day.

What caused so much trouble for men and institutions was of

course the phenomenon of technology and the question of how to harness it. It was not merely the appearance of new and potentially useful weapons like airplanes or submarines, for battleships still reigned on the high seas, and neither airplanes nor submarines made any distinct impact on military minds until the next decade. Rather it was a question of obsolescence, or of technological life versus service life. It was an issue of fleet composition, and, whatever the nature of the "technological revolution" in naval affairs, there was an ever increasing possibility that newer, more expensive weapons systems would become outdated before they were even operational.[4]

The political and business implications of all this were clear. On the one hand, improving technology provided ever more attractive weapons systems for the navy. In turn, this generated demands for mission clarification as well as the military's proselytization of such missions. On the other hand, to secure the various weapons and to gain the necessary policy direction, Capitol Hill politicians needed persuasion, identification with the navy, and substantial proof of positive benefits to constituency—contracts, jobs, and programs. True, all of it had been emerging since the late 1880s. But by the Roosevelt era everything was far more complex and growing steadily more so.

Finally there was the whole thorny issue of the navy's peacetime purpose. Here emerged the cult of Mahan and the first generation of interpreters (or misinterpreters) of sea power, along with the naval fixation on climactic battle, enemy naval strength, and sea force. Often lost in the welter of Mahanite doctrine was the general picture of maritime strength and national power. Rather, naval officers derived their own strategic dogma, tactical notions, and case for a particular kind of fleet from their own interpretations of Mahan's gospel. "Seapower" became politicized.

This had been brewing since the days of Luce and Tracy, but the stakes were much higher after 1900. Delineation of sacred central territory, friend-foe identification, and professionalization of institutions through formal study and analysis were really responses to the whims of the national political administration, which gave and took away in disturbing budgetary succession. All that the naval professional could really seek was some sense of concrete policy guidance, and most of the time he searched in vain.

Naval leaders should have received that guidance from an arch-navalist president. Somewhat surprisingly, they did not, whether due to the president's proclivity to regard himself as his own secretary of the navy or because nobody quite knew what he was talking about when he referred to "military" and "political" points of view. Neither civilians nor the military gave one another much credit, nor did they regard themselves as the final word on any technical subject. This resulted in a piecemeal naval policy with disparate, often contradictory ingredients. To Naval Constructor J.J. Woodward at least, "The most important question of general interest to the naval service of the United States at the present moment, is that concerning the necessity of the adoption by this country of a definite naval program; and the part of such policy concerned with the determination of a program of naval construction of new vessels to be built for the navy during the next few years."[5]

Actually, Washington bureaucrats of the Roosevelt era could not arrive at "a definite naval program." For one thing there were too many competitors—cabinet officials, naval brass, congressional politicians, press investigators, and influential citizenry—to permit any consensus on programs. Each lobby had its own policy, its own program, its own striving for power and influence. Probably all these groups thought hard policy might be scientifically derived from truisms about the international arena. American idealism had deep roots and a strong constitution at the turn of the century. But neither American society and politics nor the world scene was quite as simplistic as Washington observers thought—then or now.

Part of the problem was that Roosevelt employed too many different secretaries during his seven-year term. Succeeding John Davis Long were William Henry Moody (1902–1904); Paul Morton (1904–1905); Charles Joseph Bonaparte (1905–1906); Victor H. Metcalf (1906–1908), and Truman H. Newberry (1908–1909). The position was merely a way station on the road to the attorney generalship for Moody and Bonaparte, and only Morton was not a lawyer by profession. A railroad executive instead, Morton was appointed to provide a spokesman for the business community. Newberry, possibly the ablest of the lot, parlayed extensive industrial and naval administrative experience into an assistant secretaryship before moving into the front office. All of these officials, however, understood their position as figureheads for TR. Only Metcalf and Newberry made important contributions to the U.S. Navy. Yet all of them fit exactly the image of what the president wanted in the post.[6]

The president separated the navy into two parts—industrial and military. Any "fairly able man" could handle the first role, he told Morton in 1904. But they were apt to place too much importance on the industrial side of the house. "It is this military efficiency of the fleet which needs to receive most attention and as regards which there should be systematic development of policy," he declared. In the final analysis, TR wanted his officials to function as clerks, to worry about administration, or what took place at the gun factory and main department. He might want them to think about something besides industry, but only he would be the arbiter of naval policy, strategy, and force diplomacy. The office was simply another device for manipulating political appointments and favors.

By 1903 the navy's General Board members were calling for a four-point development program including a) a forty-eight-battleship fleet, second only to Great Britain by 1920, b) an American policy to be automatically conditioned by naval development abroad, not by any absolute standard, c) a fleet always stronger than likely enemies, and d) a commensurate increase of personnel as well as matériel. True, the board had no real authority in such matters and the Board of Construction immediately became jealous of its prerogatives, but its program reflected a trend. The shipbuilding trust temporarily replaced the armor clique as the target on Capitol Hill, but there was little dissent as each annual rearmament package passed with battleships, cruisers, and other craft.[7]

The armor trust did not try to raise prices—thirty-seven thousand tons at $420 a ton appeared acceptable to all—and the procurement scene was more peaceful than it had been in years. Armor makers apparently could not keep abreast of the navy's desires. Bethlehem Steel president Eugene C. Grace observed later:

> In 1902, the United States Government launched us on a larger and modern naval program. The armor-plate capacity of the country at the time was not sufficient to meet the needs and requirements of the new naval program. We were specially requested—almost commanded—to increase, or to double, rather, our producing capacity at that time.[8]

Carnegie and Bethlehem together were furnishing ten to twelve thousand tons annually, despite conflicting claims as to the speed of supply. At the moment, nobody was worried. Stable prices, a well-supplied shipbuilding industry, political control of the decision-making process to keep the programs coming out of congressional coffers, and TR's brandishing of the "Big Stick" in support of his corollary to the Monroe Doctrine all marked the period. Secretary Moody told Chicago's Marquette Club on 9 October 1902 that despite the fact that "86 cents per capita of our population" was now going to naval construction (compared with only twenty-four and forty-four cents during the two Cleveland administrations respectively), "We count the cost well spent if it preserves us from war."[9]

Furthermore, said the secretary, creation of great shipyards, development of a pool of skilled labor, and naval apprentice programs were all vital ramifications of the naval buildup. They "have had a remarkable influence upon the development of the gigantic steel industry of the country," he contended. Just the previous year Charles Schwab had told the Society of Naval Architects in New York that the ABCD ships had definitely provided the practical beginnings for the successful manufacture of structural steel in the United States. The steelman had admitted that all those inconvenient naval steel tests "were the real means of producing the quality of material now so universally used in the industry."

Later, in December, Moody's annual report noted 233 new ordnance pieces had jumped the total production from the naval gun factory to 1,210 guns. He cited 7,612 tons of armor delivered that year and a reduction in royalties paid to Krupp. But his main point was a contractor list showing the impact on industry.[10] (See table 13.)

The Venezuelan crisis gave impetus to congressional passage of five new battleships plus $10 million for armor and armament despite Representative John Rixey's usual outcry that half the budget was going to shipbuilders and the other to armor makers. Meanwhile, Secretary Moody was involved with the effects of recent business failures by naval contractors Bethlehem Steel and William R. Trigg of Richmond, Virginia. The Bethlehem situation was the more serious since warship construction as well as ordnance and armor were involved. The firm had been part of an ill-conceived venture by Daniel Leroy Dresser, Lewis Nixon, and Charles Schwab called "the U.S. Shipbuilding Company." Actually, the whole shipbuilding trust suffered "from acute financial anemia," from mid-1902 to mid-1903, and only the subsidiary Bethlehem Steel firm offered any appearance of solvency. Both Schwab, as president of U.S. Steel with a controlling interest in Bethlehem, and the U.S. Navy spent anxious moments waiting for the results of litigation on the collapsing merger. Eventual settlement in 1904 spawned a strengthened Bethlehem Steel incorporating both steel and ship programs under Schwab. He told touring reporters in April, "I shall make the Bethlehem plant the greatest armor plate and gun factory in the world."[11]

When the annual "blood-letting" over naval appropriations commenced again that year, the steel firms had raised their supply figure to 11,493 tons of armor per year and navalists saw to it that $12 million was destined for new armor/ordnance contracts. Yet the bill included a clause that "the Secretary of the Navy, in case he can not secure armor of the best quality for any or all of these ships at a price which in his judgement is reasonable and equitable, is authorized and directed to procure a site and erect thereon an armor-plate factory. . . ." Insurgency was not dead in the Fifty-eighth Congress.[12]

Rixey, William Kitchin, and West Virginia representative Alston G. Dayton all wondered about the direction of naval insanity. "We appropriate $96,000,000 by this bill," observed

TABLE 13

THE MILITARY-INDUSTRIAL COMPLEX, 1902

Armor Plate

Bethlehem Steel Company, South Bethlehem, Pa.
Carnegie Steel Company, Munhall, Pa.

Ordnance

Bethlehem Steel Co., South Bethlehem, Pa.
Gatling Gun Co., Hartford, Conn.
Colt's Patent Fire Arms Manufacturing Co., Hartford, Conn.
American and British Manufacturing Co., Bridgeport, Conn.
U.S. Rapid Fire Gun and Powder Co., Derby, Conn.
Midvale Steel Co., Philadelphia, Pa.

Projectiles

Carpenter Steel Company, Reading, Pa.
Firth-Sterling Steel Co., Demmler, Pa.
I.G. Johnson and Co., Philadelphia, Pa.
Crucible Steel Co. of America, Newark, N.J.
Taylor Iron and Steel Co., High Bridge, N.J.
U.S. Projectile Co. (E.W. Bliss Co.), Brooklyn, N.Y.
Miami Cycle and Manufacturing Co., Middletown, Ohio
American and British Manufacturing Co., Bridgeport, Conn.
U.S. Rapid Fire Gun and Powder Co., Derby, Conn.

Warships

Cramp and Sons, Philadelphia, Pa.
Newport News Shipbuilding Co., Newport News, Va.
Union Iron Works, San Francisco, Calif.
Moran Brothers Co., Seattle, Wash.
Bath Iron Works, Bath, Maine
Fore River Ship and Engine Co., Weymouth, Mass.
Neafie and Levy, Co., Philadelphia, Pa.
Lewis Nixon, Elizabeth, N.J.
William R. Trigg Co., Richmond, Va.
Harlan and Hollingsworth, Wilmington, Del.
Maryland Steel Co., Sparrow Point, Md.
Columbian Iron Works, Baltimore, Md.
Wolf and Zwicker, Portland, Ore.
George Lawley and Son, South Boston, Mass.
Gas Engine and Power Co. and Charles L. Seabury and Co. Consolidated, Morris
    Heights, N.Y.
J.P. Holland Torpedo Boat Co., New York, N.Y.
Electric Boat Co., New York, N.Y.

SOURCE: U.S. Congress, *Congressional Record*, 57th Cong., 1st sess., 25, pt. 6: 5386; Letter, Chief of Ordnance to Secretary of Navy, 4 December 1902, William Moody papers, Box, Miscellaneous Unbound Letters, Library of Congress.

Kitchin, "that means $7 out of the Treasury for every head of a family in the United States—$7 to each family. Where will it end?" All of them thought it time the government built its own armor plant. "We know that these plants do not compete with each other. We know that they have combined in an unlawful conspiracy. We know that they are parts of a trust declared illegal," shouted Dayton. He then displayed a table of armor contracts dating to the Whitney period. Particularly galling was the continued refusal of the U.S. Navy to award a contract to the lowest bidder, Midvale.[13] (See table 14.)

TABLE 14

Armor Contracts, 1887–1904.

	Tons	Cost
Bethlehem Steel Co.:		
Contract of June 1887	6,891	$4,168,000
Contract of Mar. 1893	3,882	2,510,000
Contract of June 1896	2,800	1,534,272
Contract of July 1898 (estimated)	3,965	1,586,000
Contract of Oct. 1899 (estimated)	1,142	456,800
Contract of Nov. 28, 1900 (estimated)	18,588	7,996,575
Contract of Feb. 28, 1903 (estimated)	5,798	2,460,404
Contract of Jan. 1904 (estimated)	5,372	2,369,564
Total	42,433	23,081,615
Carnegie Steel Co.:		
Contract of 1890	6,054	3,475,000
Contract of 1893	3,120	2,094,000
Contract of 1896	3,073	1,697,808
Contract of 1898 (estimated)	3,712	1,484,800
Contract of 1899 (estimated)	1,134	453,000
Contract of Nov. 26, 1900 (estimated)	18,588	7,996,575
Contract of Feb. 28, 1903 (estimated)	5,666	2,407,604
Contract of Jan. 1904	5,258	2,323,964
Total	46,605	21,933,351
Midvale Steel Co.:		
Contract of Dec. 15, 1903	6,180	2,453,422

SOURCE: U.S. Congress, *Congressional Record*, 58th Cong. 2d sess. 38, pt. 3: 2154.

During the latest contract negotiations, in 1903, Moody had actually overlooked Midvale and awarded the predominant contracts to Carnegie and Bethlehem. Moody bared all quite openly before the House Naval Affairs Committee later. What had happened was a repetition of the disintegration of the

Carnegie-Bethlehem corner on the market as Midvale submitted a low bid of $398 and the others refused to go below $455 per ton. Moody sent O'Neil to examine the Midvale plant; the ordnance chief still didn't think Midvale could meet time requirements. For that reason alone, Moody was induced to give Midvale only about one-third of the total armor package that year although it warranted full award. Congressmen Rixey, Hitchcock, and Dayton as well as Senators Spooner and Patterson had a field day with that one!

Patterson and the others quickly used fellow trust members like Charles H. Cramp, the shipbuilder, to support their viewpoint. The Philadelphian had told the Industrial Commission in 1901:

> The profit on armor making is something enormous. The people who make money on their ships are not the persons who design and construct them, nor the persons who take two or three generations to get information enough to design a battle ship. But the gun maker who makes the guns for the Government makes the money, and if we had been gun makers we could have had the guns, too. In Great Britain, and Germany and in France they build the ships complete, guns and all, and we are at a tremendous disadvantage. Why, I would be willing to take a battle ship and build the ship at cost if we got the profit on the armor. That is what these big concerns in England do.[14]

Nevertheless the insurgents met strong resistance when they tried to push through a government armor factory clause. In the House of Representatives it was thrown out on a technicality; the Senate stopped it cold when Patterson tried to make it part of the $13 million armor/ordnance appropriation package. On 27 April 1904, the U.S. Navy was awarded one battleship, two armored cruisers, three scout cruisers, two colliers, submarines for testing, and armor—to be procured at a "just and reasonable" price. Republicanism had triumphed again, and the discretionary price policy continued in effect.[15]

Both congressional testimony and internal departmental conversations betrayed discontent at the slowness of naval construction programs. The whole naval buildup seemed like an adolescent game when Secretary Moody told the New York City Republican Club on Lincoln's birthday in 1904: "We have advanced one step in comparison, [since 1898] having slightly passed Italy, and are now fifth in the rank of naval powers of the world, based upon this comparison. But we have under construction and authorized by the Congress a greater tonnage than has any other nation in the world except Great Britain." Applause greeted his statement, "If that tonnage were completed today, and it will not be for more than four years, we should pass Russia and Germany and be surpassed only by Great Britain and France."[16]

Despite all the enthusiasm and rhetoric there remained a dichotomy between strategy and program. Did the navy exist (in the words of Moody's New York speech), to protect "our own and the property of foreign nations entrusted to our care in the West Indies and in the distant islands of the seas?" Or, was it really there because "we owe an especial duty to Cuba" or the Philippines or the twenty-three thousand miles of ocean in the American sphere of influence? These questions passed beyond Moody's ken on 1 July 1904 when he switched to the attorney generalship. His successor Paul Morton from the Atchison, Topeka, and Santa Fe Railroad was another caretaker secretary. The navy was now talking all big gun battleships— several years ahead of H.M.S. *Dreadnought*—and Morton soon went on record as opposing "certain of the ordnance experts in the opinion that the navy should, under ordinary circumstances, undertake to manufacture all, or even the greater part, of the guns and ammunition required for the service." Populism was to be injected into the ordnance program as "it is better that the nation's chief instruments of warfare, offensive and defensive, should be made by its people rather than by itself."[17]

Morton would have great difficulty differentiating between "the people" and the business community of trusts when it came to armaments work. Still, he argued that the buildup of a military-industrial complex in peacetime "may be of important service in time of war." They would of course "doubtless find markets elsewhere, and will do other work in kindred lines, thus adding to the general wealth and prosperity." Therefore, Morton felt that the nation would profit since "large numbers of skilled American workmen can not be long engaged in such a field without developing improvements in guns and their appurtenances, and in machinery for their manufacturing, which will prove of national advantage."

Morton was parroting his naval advisers. His ordnance chief tersely suggested, "The manufacture of armor during the past year has progressed in a satisfactory manner, the rate of deliveries continuing to show an increase over previous years." The structural progress of certain vessels had passed the armor schedule, but this was always an up and down thing. Greater uniformity among individual plates, satisfactory progress at Midvale (despite departmental unhappiness at nonreceipt of either test or finished plates), all boded well for the future, said Admiral O'Neil.

If the Navy Department was reasonably pleased, however, Midvale Steel was not. Congressmen soon heard about Charles J. Harrah's protests at discrimination in the award of contracts for eight thousand tons of plate for the *New Hampshire*, *Montana*, and *North Carolina*. Harrah seethed that Carnegie and Bethlehem received favored treatment, while his firm suffered from "lack of appreciation and encouragement."[18] His cause led to congressional mandate once more "that the Secretary of the Navy shall cause a thorough inquiry to be made as to the cost of armor plate and of an armor plant, the report of which shall be made to Congress." The insurgents won out while navalists gained two additional sixteen-thousand-ton battle ships and $18 million for armor. Then Roosevelt muddied the issue by switching cabinet members—Morton leaving the administration on 1 July 1905 to be replaced by the Baltimore brahmin reformer Charles Joseph Bonaparte.[19]

Bonaparte did little to reform the armor trust or the navy, but he sharply rejected General Board desires for larger battle ships and he pared appropriation requests. Trumpeting TR's momentary retrenchment schemes, the secretary decided that "the aggregate of our battle ships, armored cruisers, and coast-defense vessels built, building, or authorized would seem, according to present indicators, sufficient to provide for any contingencies within the limits of probability." Too, the naval gun factory was overworked and private finishing had been engaged. Somehow both Bonaparte and his new ordnance chief, Rear Admiral Newton E. Mason, overlooked the congressional request for an official inquiry into the armor and ordnance problem.[20]

This omission might have been either accidental or deliberate but, as Bonaparte told the chairman of the House Naval Affairs Committee in June 1906, "it appears that a short time after the passage of the act making appropriations for the naval service for the fiscal year 1905 the clause therein contained directing an inquiry into the cost of armor plate and armor plant was, by the chief of the Bureau of Ordnance brought to the attention of the then Secretary of the Navy [i.e., Morton], but, for reasons of which the Department is not informed, no further steps were taken in the premises until after the retirement of the Secretary and the subject seems then to have escaped attention." Congressman J.A. Tawney reawakened the department to its responsibilities on 4 April, and Bonaparte and Mason rushed to appoint the necessary inquiry board.

Captain Kossuth Niles, an old hand at naval ordnance, chaired the group, which received and evaluated information from the Office of Naval Intelligence, inspectors of ordnance, state fiscal officials from New Jersey and Pennsylvania, and steel company spokesmen. "Such an investigation, to be valuable, must necessarily take some time," noted Bonaparte, "but every exertion will be made to complete the work at the earliest date practicable." Both in excuses and in focus, the whole business repeated earlier investigations of this type.[21]

The House of Representatives was not particularly pleased by the secretary's answer. The full congress set aside $15,145,000 for armor and armament declaring "that no part of this appropriation shall be expended for armor for vessels except upon contracts for such armor when awarded by the Secretary of the Navy, to the lowest responsible bidder, having in view the best results and most expeditious delivery." By early summer 1906, Bonaparte once more faced the onerous task of soliciting and selecting bids for armor for two battleships, *Michigan* and *South Carolina*.[22]

This time Carnegie and Bethlehem submitted independent bids only to find themselves again undercut by Midvale, which offered to supply the requisite armor at $345 per ton, "a lower price than has ever been paid by this Government for armor plate, and, according to the information of the Department, considerably less than is paid by any foreign government." Once more Bonaparte determined to give the Midvale company one-half of the contract and split the rest evenly between Carnegie and Bethlehem, but only if they dropped to the Midvale price. If they would not, then Midvale would get the whole package, said the secretary. His ploy worked handsomely.[23]

Bethlehem retreated from its bids of $380.00 on Classes A, B, and C, and $350.00 for Class D armor. The mere classifications indicated that the armor game was becoming increasingly complex. Carnegie had bid $370.00 per ton for all classes. The final contracts with the three companies were executed in August, and prices averaged out to $345.95 for Carnegie, $345.84 for Bethlehem, and $345.90 for Midvale. Proportionate tonnage stood at 3,660 for Midvale, 1,794 for Bethlehem, and 1,865 for Carnegie with all royalty responsibilities remaining with the steel firms. As Bonaparte later concluded, "The criticism to which this action of the Department was subjected seemed to rest upon a theory that it was the duty of the Department to injure, and, if possible, break up the business of the two older companies as a punishment for their refusal to compete against each other and alleged combination to keep up the prices of their product in the past."[24]

Indeed, Bonaparte's refusal to play "trust buster" raised a storm of protest in the newspapers. Pressmen around the nation declared it a Midvale, not a Bonaparte, victory. The *Washington Post* noted facetiously: "The only criticism that can be made against this arrangement is that the division of the swag is not exactly equitable. Why should the great Bethlehem and Carnegie companies get only one-fourth each, while the Midvale Company gets one-half." The *Milwaukee Free Press* decided that it was merely a question of armor trust power versus Midvale monopoly, and the *Philadelphia Record* noted,

"One is forced to the conclusion that while the Administration detests trusts in the abstract it is wonderfully fond of them in the concrete."

More informative was the *Baltimore News* comment on 17 July that Midvale's labor practices had produced the tripartite split in contractual award. The eastern Pennsylvania firm had been "raiding" not only other steel firms for skilled workers but had even tapped the U.S. Navy's gun factory staff through better pay inducements. Neither the government, nor nonunion Carnegie and Bethlehem wanted to cope with a labor price war, and the contractual division offered the best method of maintaining the precarious balance. The newspaper observed:

> In this view, the matter of the armor contract becomes a good deal more serious politically than it was before. The labor unionists are determinedly at work against the Administration leaders in Congress, to compass their defeat on the ground of their antagonism to labor legislation. Now the charge will be added that the Government is so manipulating its contracts as to favor the Trust paying the lower wages, as against the independent company paying better wages.[25]

Meanwhile, Kossuth Niles and his committee worked hard to dissect the government armor factory problem. Before submitting their report in mid-November, the Niles board meticulously analyzed previous armor contracts, probed the fluctuations of congressional opinion, and studied progressive improvements in armor manufacture. But they were stopped by the usual fragmentary and insufficient data on company profit and loss despite cooperation from state agencies as well as the Federal Bureau of Corporations. Naturally the three steel firms claimed supply of such information would endanger business secrets. Carnegie and Bethlehem eventually gave in reluctantly. But Midvale gave only general statements on capital investment and the Niles board had to rely on ordnance inspector reports in the fashion of previous inquiries of this type. In fact, the Niles board accepted and adopted the 1897 report of the Armor

Factory Board as to details of plant cost.[26]

The Niles board noted that Midvale claimed to have expended in excess of $3,500,000 for its armor plant; Bethlehem reported $5,625,000, and Carnegie supposedly had invested the largest amount at $5,905,425. But estimates for erection of a similar government plant ranged from a conservative $3,500,000 for a facility producing about ten thousand tons annually, to $4,339,271, which included all costs incidental to the establishment and equipping of the plant. However, the Niles board retained the Armor Factory Board figure of approximately $3,750,000. When it came to costs of armor plate, variables in labor and material costs hampered their computations. But they were able to clarify many technical details of process and procedure and they highlighted the relatively higher production costs for private firms when using only partial plant capacity due to inadequate or sporadic government orders.

The naval officers once again spaded over ground previously uncovered by their predecessors. They chose to merely list all the variations of estimates uncovered, both past and present. They left the reader to draw his own conclusions from raw data gathered in their search. (See table 15.)

Since Bonaparte was scheduled to move to the Justice Department at mid-month, his assistant Truman Newberry sent the Niles report to Congress. The outgoing secretary believed an answer to the armor problem lay with either construction of a government plant or with foreign procurement. In fact, he bluntly suggested the use of eminent domain, of confiscation at an equitable price if the armor trust continued to extort high prices. The chief of naval ordnance was far less belligerent and contradicted his superiors by reporting that restoration of competition in the private sector, while commendable "has so reduced the prices of armor, and the element of profit depends so largely on that of output, that a condition now exists whereby the small prospects for demands for armor in the immediate future may result in seriously reducing the resources in this country for this special material."[27]

Not that Congress was in any hurry to square the issue. When it met soon after the turn of the year it rather dutifully voted an additional battleship, some submarines and torpedo boats and $10 million for armor and ordnance. No mention was made of the Niles board report and any concern about the steel business was confined to Pennsylvania legislators, who worried that the naval gun factory was about to acquire a foundry facility which would conflict directly with their constituents' plant. But 1907 generally was not the year for insurgency and so Bonaparte's successor, Victor Metcalf, could anticipate a quiet period.[28]

TABLE 15

NAVY PREDICTIONS OF ARMOR COST, 1896 AND 1906

Estimator	Cost per Ton	
	Production	Full
Lieutenant Commander Rodgers	$297.54	$391.86
Ensign McVay	243.73	337.29
Rohrer Board	223.43	324.36
Secretary of the Navy	224.41	324.41
Average	247.28	344.48
Commander Rohrbacher	193.08	223.16
Commander Dieffenbach	241.76	277.73
Lieutenant Galbraith	242.33	298.77
Niles Board	244.27	295.89
Average	230.36	273.89
Combined Average	238.82	309.18
Niles Board	244.27	295.89

SOURCE: U.S. Congress, 53d Cong. 2d sess., HR Doc. 193, Cost of Armor and Armor Plant, 43.

By the end of 1907, the shifting winds of the armor question turned threatening once again as Metcalf in his annual report noted price negotiations for *Delaware* and *North Dakota* armor saw the steelmen once again bidding very high. The contracts that had been awarded in the summer for those battleships showed Carnegie and Bethlehem bidding $420 per ton for Class A and $400 for other classes (although the Pittsburgh firm stayed out of Class D bidding). Midvale this time bid the highest of all and had to be persuaded to lower its bid in order to remain competitive. The armor was subsequently divided so that Bethlehem received 3,579.34 tons, Carnegie 3,538.07 tons, and Midvale 2,258.81 tons. No mention was made of the fact that price figures were higher by $50 to $70 than prices the previous year, or that they sharply contrasted with Niles board figures. Citing the rapid construction time for the Japanese cruiser *Ibuki* (2 May–21 November 1907) as well as the *Dreadnaught* (12 months), the Navy Department was obviously more concerned with production schedules than with quibbling about prices.[29]

When Congress again took up naval matters in April 1908 it seemed obvious that either no one was reading secretarial reports or Niles board findings or, as Senator Augustus O. Bacon of Georgia noted, everyone assumed the armor problem had been solved several years before when Congress put "this matter on a business basis." Since then, said Bacon, "Congress has ceased to look after the matter at all, since we have been in the habit of passing naval appropriation bills without knowing what was in them and without the possiblity of any opportunity to dissect them or analyze them. . . ." Capitol Hill obviously knew little about what was transpiring and several members aimed to clear up the mystery.[30]

As usual, however, intent and action were not the same. "Average cost" versus "average price" deadlocked the debates. Democratic insurgents wanted to compel the secretary of the navy to buy armor on the world market, but partisanship blocked their efforts. What else could have been expected when Eugene Hale openly declared in the Senate: "I have, Mr. President, a table of the prices per ton for furnishing armor in the European countries. In Austria it is $449; in Italy $521; in Germany $450; in France $500; in England $625; and in the United States it is $416.67."

Statistics won the day. Two battleships, two destroyers, and five colliers plus $7 million for armor and armament emerged in the navy bill. "Lowest bidder," "best results and most expeditious delivery" were phrases calculated to please both insurgents and conservatives when it came to armor contracts. As usual during the Republican years, Congress sought to give maximum discretion to the secretary of navy without either tying his hands by price limitation, or giving him license to purchase abroad.[31]

Spurred by this vote of confidence, as well as the well-publicized world cruise of the "Great White Fleet," Secretary

Metcalf wholeheartedly endorsed General Board requests for more naval construction in 1909–10. The fall elections placed TR's chosen successor, former secretary of war William Howard Taft, in the presidency, so why not recommend a large ship appropriation? Navy planners looked for a $7 million reduction in costs and everyone seemed pleased, including ordnance chief Mason who observed at the end of 1908, "Armor under present contracts is being delivered in accordance with contract requirements, and it is most gratifying to the bureau that, notwithstanding the increased celerity of battleship construction, the armor makers are well ahead of the shipbuilders' schedule requirements."[32]

A "powder trust" joined the armor and shipbuilding trusts as objects of congressional ire, but that body kept on voting more ships and spending more money on naval construction. Taft tapped George von Lengerke Meyer to administer the U.S. Navy Department. Meyer came from a wealthy Boston mercantile background, and he had served as Roosevelt's ambassador to Russia as well as his postmaster general. A proven administrator and reorganizer, Meyer quickly focused upon needed changes in central departmental organization, shore installations, and the fleet. His administration provided continuity and purpose from the Roosevelt years. Meyer was an unabashed navalist, and fleet preparedness, cost effectiveness, and streamlined management (including the now redundant Board on Construction), as well as the introduction of a fourteen-inch, forty-five-caliber main battery aboard battleships numbered among Meyer's accomplishments.[33]

Meyer's superior, William Howard Taft, was certainly no Roosevelt. Taft lacked the verve and showmanship of his predecessor, and his timidity doomed Republican domestic Progressivism. Internationally, however, it was different. He encouraged Wall Street investment in the underdeveloped lands of Latin America, and then used diplomacy and naval power to effect national will in such trouble spots as Nicaraugua and Mexico. The national security team of Taft, Secretary of State Philander C. Knox, Secretary of War Henry M. Stimson, and Secretary of the Navy Meyer insured that there would be militant overtones to "dollar diplomacy."[34]

The international implications of American interest in the

Caribbean and South America became increasingly linked to the European arms race, although probably only the Navy Department sensed it. Naval rankings and detailed discussions of foreign ship development became a regular part of the department's annual report. Yet these were always juxtaposed with statistics on what percentage of American wealth was being spent on the military. Secretary Meyer was aware that politicians on Capitol Hill worried about farmers, taxpayers, industrialists, and Wall Street far more than about foreign powers.

Meyer and the bureaucrats were also concerned that congressional constraints aimed at equitable distribution of contracts often hampered construction programs. Meyer felt congressional decrees that allowed only one battleship per private yard, or forced construction at a particular navy yard or geographical facility were not cost effective. But he readily endorsed equal sharing of the armor contracts, since January 1909 agreements had almost equally divided almost 9,500 tons between Carnegie, Bethlehem, and Midvale.[35]

The armor controversy seemed to have bottomed out by the Meyer tenure, since industry and the navy both thought the equitable sharing method preserved stability. While prices for Class A armor ("which comprised 90 per cent of the total"), remained at $420.00, that of Class D rose $10.00 per ton to $415.00, Class C rose by nearly $2.00 to $460.00, Class D (hollow forgings) by $77.65 to $587.00, and Class E (bolts and nuts) was introduced at $508.00.[36]

The period after the Spanish-American War witnessed a shift from price extortion by two firms to tripartite competition in the steel industry which treatened the loss of the original armor makers due to underbidding. The naval-industrial interlock ultimately solved the problem by persuasion, leading to equitable distribution of contracts. The only threat to stability lay now beyond, not within the complex. Insurgents of the Democratic party on Capitol Hill remained unconvinced that this was all for the good of the country.

Led by Congressmen Henry T. Rainey of Illinois and Augustus O. Stanley of Kentucky (with "Pitchfork Ben" Tillman still leading the Senate charge), dissenters cried that "this Government has been for 20 years and is now fostering and maintaining a hungry, lawless monopoly in the manufacture of its armor plate and armament." Citing Andrew Carnegie's boast that his patriotic response to help Harrison and Tracy in 1890 had helped create forty-two of the forty-three millionaires, Stanley thundered in 1910: "The greatest danger to this country's Government, is not from foreign foes. It is from international combinations, and it is absurd, it is a travesty on justice to have this Government drag the Oil Trust and the Tobacco Trust into one end of the Capitol while we feed another trust out of our hands in the other end, and it is time this Government, who can make its own armor plate and who should make it, if necessary, shall say that it will not become not only the principal purchaser, but the maintainer of an illicity, illegal, and lawless combination in restraint of trade."

Congress applied the notion of nonrestraint of trade and tasked Meyer to come up with facts and figures proving fair competition in navy contracts, but continued to legislate more battleships. The narrow "minority" election victory of the Democrats under Woodrow Wilson in 1912 promised change. Lame duck administrator George Meyer's final annual report noted that 154 major firms supplied material to the Ordnance Bureau alone. While there were small concentrations of industrial buildup around the country, the naval-industrial complex of 1912 stretched in a belt from New York Harbor to the underside of the Great Lakes, with its heart in eastern Pennsylvania, centering on greater Philadelphia and environs.[37] But a drastic change from the massive big navy programs of the Roosevelt–Taft years seemed to be coming. An eastern president was about to enter the White House, but Wilson was no friend of the trusts and huge war preparations. The Democrats were back in control after fifteen years absence.

Chapter 8

Armor, Armament, and the New Freedom

American voters had a clear choice in 1912. They might continue to follow the Republican brand of Progressivism—the centralized government power of Taft and Roosevelt—or they could select Democratic "New Freedom" and Woodrow Wilson. TR and Taft had split on vital issues, but they were still the party men of big business. The country realized that it needed solutions to complex problems engendered by industrialization and mushrooming corporations. Forty-two percent of the voters thought Democratic promises to restore small business power, limit special privilege, and maintain basic fairness and decency in American life offered better possibilities. It was not a majority, but three parties were in the race.

Woodrow Wilson found that his first term in office required a great adjustment of ideals and goals. Wilsonian idealism ran counter to the special relationship which had developed between the trusts and the government. Around the turn of the century steelmen like Judge Elbert H. Gary and others had sensed the change in government attitude. They had worked out a philosophy of their own—a self-policing cooperation which business historians call "new competition." These robber barons agreed to end "cut-throat" price competition which threatened civil war between the Carnegie empire and Morgan-backed steel finishing companies like American Bridge, National Tube, and American Wire and Tube. Self-regulation would stave off federal intervention under the Sherman Anti-Trust act as well. This idea meshed nicely with the spirit of New Nationalism. The Navy Department, especially, appreciated relaxation of the tension over armor negotiations. Of course, all this seemed entirely too cozy to the Democrats and isolationist camps before 1912, when the election drew the battle lines.[1]

The reversal of business-government relations which seemed predictable with Wilson's victory eventually fell victim to international events. Industrial development also experienced profound change during the Democratic ascendancy, and the United States entered its first major war in a half-century. Even before April 1917, diplomatic crises with Japan in 1913, the Caribbean and Mexican intervention the following year, and the whole scheme of preparedness and nonneutral support of the European belligerents in World War I, influenced Wilsonian philosophy, industry's "new competition," and the navy's need for armor and armament.

International tensions provided a rationale for naval programs. In turn, these programs increased naval professionals' worry about the fact that military-industrial linkages were caught in a purely political crossfire. Complicating the problem further were the divided loyalties of a civilian naval secretary. On the one hand, he was the political spokesman for Wilsonian New Freedom, on the other, his daily responsibilities in the department were affected by the urgent needs of the U.S. Navy. Wilsonian doctrine could be implemented in principle, but at operational echelons, "armor at any price" to meet the demands of national security weighed heavily in the equation. "Detente" with the steelmen might be the aim of a Democratic secretary, but "entente" was more likely to be the goal of his naval subordinates.[2] (Detente implies a lessening of tension, especially between nations, while entente suggests an understanding or agreement, as between two nations. In this case a political secretary might desire a lessening of tensions although stopping short of any entente enjoyed between navy and steel during Republican administrations.)

The man Wilson chose to carry out responsibilities at the Navy Department was a rather unlikely character whose reputation stemmed from party loyalty. Josephus Daniels, editor of the *Raleigh News and Observer*, was provincial in background, speech, and dress. But his mind was alert, his views strong— even radical—and he made an interesting choice for the Wilson cabinet. Originally considered for the office of postmaster general, he was opposed by Walter Hines Page, but warmly supported by William Jennings Bryan, the designated secretary of state. Like the "Great Commoner," Daniels became an important member of an administration dedicated to peace, but destined to choose war. Daniels outlasted Bryan, however, and, in fact, served longer than had any secretary of the navy since Gideon Welles in the 1860s. The North Carolinian knew no more about maritime problems than most of his predecessors. Like John D. Long, Daniels was destined to have a Roosevelt— Franklin Delano—as his assistant secretary, and his own thirst for hard work and taut administration led to many interesting new directions for the navy, especially in the realm of business relations.[3]

Daniels found himself spokesman for 54,000 officers and men of ship and shore plus 10,300 Marines. The fleet now consisted of fourteen Dreadnought battleships (built or building), twenty-five predreadnought battleships, thirty-two cruisers of different classes, and numerous smaller warships and auxiliaries. As of February 1913, the fleet was concentrated in the Atlantic and stood third in strength behind British and German rivals. Serious imbalances in vessel types, deficiencies in effective command and control, and other problems were partially offset by fleet efficiency and sound strategic position. Protection of the New World seemed assured (although the U.S. Navy might have had difficulty providing for imperial contingencies in the Philippines or even Hawaii). It remained to be seen how navalism and imperialism meshed with Wilsonian isolationism and the New Freedom.[4]

The new secretary discovered opportunities and challenges in all areas. It wasn't long before the residue of correspondence from his predecessor plus communications from the president opened the issue of steel relations. H.B. Martin had written Wilson soon after the inauguration and blasted the steel companies for lining their pockets with federal money while turning out submarginal armor and other steel. The national secretary for the American Anti-Trust League noted that his organization had been hammering at this issue for years, but to no avail. Now Wilsonian Democrats had an opportunity to correct the evil.[5]

Daniels also read ex-secretary Meyer's message outlining steel market conditions and the difficulty of securing satisfactory bids to his bureau chiefs in February. The "present spasmodic demand" in the commercial world for steel, said Meyer, was taxing steelmakers who in turn seemed to be shortchanging government work in their quest for larger commercial profits. Since the government also was a customer, Meyer thought all this was rather "inconsistent" and "it is believed by the Department that preference should be given by steel manufacturers to Government business under all circumstances." The out-going secretary worried especially about "embarrassment" to the government in case of national emergency. Therefore, he wrote to all the major steelmen asking them for information "as to your facilities of manufacture under ordinary conditions, as well as the capabilities of your plant, in case of War or of great necessity.[6]

Now, as Daniels read the steelmen's response, he found the situation quite interesting. They all denied commerical preference, or that they had any bidding, delivery, or technological problems. They all refused navy desires for preference, and nearly all the steel companies felt like United States Steel Products of New York City, that there was "at the present time an extraordinary demand for steel materials of all kinds, probably the greatest in the history of the steel trade." Hence, said that firm's spokesman, "This is not a spasmodic demand, as intimated in your letter, but has existed for over a year, and the indications are that it will continue for some considerable time to come."[7]

All the corporate executives were more than willing to advise the Navy Department on how to improve naval-industrial relations. This was the aspect of the correspondence which most fascinated Josephus Daniels. Carnegie, Bethlehem, and Philadelphia Steel and Forge felt present methods were satisfactory for purchase of steel material. But others, like John A. Sutton, first vice president of Pittsburgh-based Crucible Steel, thought that government steel deliveries would always be much slower than commerical orders because of the stringent inspections, and "the most serious objection our Company has to Government orders is the ordering of steel in uncommerical quantities." J.A. Davis, second vice president of R.C. Hoffman and Company in Baltimore, and W.P. Worth of that firm agreed with Sutton. All the companies responded patriotically that their facilities and production lines would be placed at the government's disposal immediately upon the outbreak of war. But only Midvale Steel spelled out specific production statistics to help Navy Department planners.[8] (See table 16.)

TABLE 16

MIDVALE PRODUCTION IN PEACE OR WAR 1913

		Gun and Engine Forgings
Normal conditions:		(3 sets 14-inch gun forgings, and
		12 sets 5-inch gun forgings per month,
	or	(24 sets 5-inch gun forgings per month
	or	(2 sets 14-inch gun forgings, and
		6 sets 5-inch gun forgings together with
		1 set engine forgings, per month.
War conditions:		(5 sets 14-inch gun forgings, and
		18 sets 5-inch gun forgings per month,
	or	(32 sets 5-inch gun forgings per month,
	or	3 sets 14-inch gun forgings and
		9 sets 5-inch gun forgings together with
		1½ sets engine forgings per month.
In addition:		8 sets of rough castings for 5-inch gun mounts per month during peace and 12 sets per month under war conditions, and finish and assemble 3 sets and 4 sets under respective conditions.

SOURCE: Letter, President, Midvale Steel to Secretary of War, 24 February 1913, Case 9288-5-4, Box 381, Subject 9288-Steel, Entry 19, Record Group 80, General Records, Navy Department, NARS.

Daniels tucked all this information away for future reference and turned to the more pressing issue of the Martin letter. He told President Wilson on 12 April that he had been unable to discover any real collusion among armor makers in available departmental files. He frankly felt the navy had worked to secure the best material for the lowest prices. But he admitted surprise that the files showed identical bidding. In fact, as Daniels probed deeper, his pessimism increased. Eugene Grace, Bethlehem Steel president, outlined the "given" policy of industry and the navy whereby both sides worked to divide the spoils equally and "in view of that practice it has come to be understood that the naming of a lower figure by [one of the armor firms] would merely lower the price that he and each one of his competitors would receive for part of the order." This treatment of industry as a unit, the one-to-one informal, "reasonable" negotiation, the security of assured orders—all implied by Grace's discussion of the accepted arrangements of the previous administration—apparently seemed equitable to everyone but New Freedomite Josephus Daniels. Reflecting the spirit of his mentor's administration, the naval secretary bristled upon receipt of the letter from Bethlehem.[9]

By this time a disenchanted Daniels had swung to the idea of a government armor plant, or "if we are going to subsidize the Carnegie, Midvale, and Bethlehem companies, let us do so honestly, and [in a] manly fashion by statute, without hypocritical evasion of the intent of Congress to force competition." He directed his chief of ordnance to "make a preliminary study" of a government plant. He teamed up with congressional dissidents like Senator Henry F. Ashurst of Arizona, who introduced a Senate resolution in early May requiring the Navy Department to report on the whole quarter century of armor prices and contractors. Everyone was further upset when identical bids were received on armor for the battleship *Pennsylvania*. Steelmen had defied a Senate rule that contractors were supposed to sign an affadavit denying collusion in bidding. By late May, Ashurst had gone so far as to introduce legislation establishing a government armor factory.[10]

The second Ashurst measure called for the appropriation of $1.6 million for the erection of buildings and purchase of plant machinery. Furthermore, Daniels was to appoint a board to report within three months on a suitable site. Construction was supposed to begin within six months after the act went into effect. A bit later Republican representative Silas Barton of Iowa introduced a House measure to include powder with the armor investigation. Meanwhile, Secretary Daniels had his bureaucrats scurrying about for information, and he even directed Roosevelt to contact the Justice Department to find out about armor trust litigation there. Justice researchers could tell FDR nothing important, but by this time, Daniels had acquired a strong ally. His fellow southerner "Pitchfork Ben" Tillman had taken the novice secretary under his wing.[11]

The self-styled "old hand at armor plate investigations" had gone to Daniels' office on 22 May only to miss him. Returning to the hill, Tillman penned a two-page note full of "some fatherly advice," including stern warnings about too many social gatherings in the capital. "I want you not only to make a success, but a howling success, or rather a monumental one," he counseled Daniels. "There is too much hard work ahead of you for you to play with your 'belly' in the way you are doing," he noted. Moreover, the senator wanted his cabinet friend to investigate more on his own rather than relying on subordinates. He pointedly offered his Committee on Naval Affairs for help in any way, "but don't let us start it until we have had a conference and gotten some clues to work on."

Tillman pithily recalled the years of the armor battles:

> We lost the other fight for the armor plate factory after we had held up the rogues for three years. But when the Spanish-American War broke out the pressure was too great, and Mark Hanna used the party whip to drive the republicans who had supported our fight into line. We reduced the cost of armor from $600 per ton to less than $300, but immediately the naval officers and experts decided that Krupp armor was so much better than the Harveyized armor that the thieves got in their work under that plea. I feel almost certain that the then head of the Bureau of Ordnance was in collusion with the armor manufacturers or got a rake off. Whether the present head is doing the same thing I do not know, but I merely throw out the idea for you to think about, and watch.[12]

Others were in the act now also. Former Tennessee congressman John W. Gaines helped cull data from past congressional hearings, and concluded "there is not the slightest doubt in my mind but that there is an international combine, and has been for several years, in the making of armor plate." He urged creation of a government and private plant complex to be "kept going, both in war and in peace, that each may be in a going fix when war is on or threatened." R. de Tankerville, editor of *Shipping Illustrated*, wrote to reaffirm that journal's contention that earlier bureau chiefs had lied before Congress, "that the armor of our warships was studded with large surfaces left soft for the purpose of attaching fittings and making structural connections besides cutting large holes for waste pipes, scuppers, chutes etc."—all of which, claimed Tankerville, weakened American warships. Even the inventor Lewis Gathmann offered his scientific expertise, and Daniels felt obliged to ask former secretary Hilary Herbert for advice.

Tillman introduced a Senate resolution in late May asking the Navy Department for an update on armor costs, patents and processes, and the time needed to construct a government plant. The senator's office told Assistant Secretary Roosevelt that Tillman believed "if the Government has a factory equipped to build enough armor plate for one battleship, the companies will then give the Government a living price, and we will show in buying the armor plate that the Government will save as much on armor plate as we saved the other day on special treatment steel, when because we had competition, the price was 36% cheaper for Battleship No. 39 than for the *New York*."[14]

The extensive work at both ends of Pennsylvania Avenue all came together in a series of reports in the summer of 1913. In effect they were the summation of all earlier investigations since the 1890s. The reams of testimony and statistics presented a cumulative and complete picture of the armor issue. For example, Daniels' answer of 26 June in response to House resolution 176 on armor and powder noted that $77,103,483.55 had been the total United States Government expenditure for armor plate since the 1880s. Of this figure, Bethlehem had been paid $34,215,112.58 while Carnegie received $30,844,153.56

and Midvale made $12,044,217.41. Tonnage cost was difficult to compute, said the secretary, and he promised to study the matter further, introducing government plant and ordnance forging/finishing costs. He suggested that steel companies having U.S. ordnance contracts also enjoyed international markets, but "no work in connection with the finishing of these guns, wholly or in part, is done by the United States navy yards," he avowed. True, the U.S. Navy did test such guns, "the company having the contract paying all charges for same."[15]

By July Daniels and the navy bureaucrats were ready to address the larger issue raised by Tillman. When the Senate Naval Affairs Committee read Daniels' official reply, they found the U.S. Navy anxious to present the current picture, practical problems, and financial requirements. They cited the U.S.S. *Pennsylvania* as proof of the value of competition. Statistics of European as well as American armor negotiations received attention.[16] (See tables 17 and 18.)

International agitation about the "armored trust" or "cartel" had also led European governments to attack this problem. In France, for instance, a small government plant was established "to act as a guide, in order to permit the government to determine how much armor plate costs, and in this way check the bids of private manufacturers," yet also to be expansible and thus hold a "threat over the private manufacturers in case their figures do not come down to the prices shown to be reasonable by the government plant." Russia and Italy, by contrast, had either set up a plant to produce all necessary armor, or bought in America to cause a price reduction at home. Great Britain, like the United States, was still in a state of public unrest over the stranglehold of the private firms. But Daniels anticipated "it is not unlikely that England will also make its own armor in the not far distant future."[17]

The secretary suggested the history of the armor problem at home showed that only occasional threat of real competition temporarily forced prices lower. In the *Pennsylvania* case, for example, friendly shipbuilders persuaded the Navy Department to substitute thinner plates at a savings of one hundred thousand dollars, with no loss in efficiency or protection. This

TABLE 17

INTERNATIONAL ARMOR PRICES, 1912–1913

1912		
Countries	Average of All Armor	Krupp Armor
Japan*	$490.00	$490.00
Austria*	490.00	490.00
Italy	400.00–482.50	386.00–463.20
Germany*	490.00	490.00
France	443.00	448.00
England	445.00	445.00
Russia	368.00	510.00
United States	430.00	413.00

7 February 1913		
Countries	Amount in Tons	Price per Ton in $
Italy	4100	$428.00
Italy	5080	395.03
Italy	. . . . .	463.00–482.00
England	. . . . .	445.00
England	. . . . .	487.00
England	. . . . .	476.00
France	4200	558.30
France	5460	479.07
France	3400	257.81
France	3400	517.65
France	2400	525.77
France	2400	497.35
Germany	. . . . .	490.00
Japan	. . . . .	450.00–550.00
Japan	. . . . .	slightly less than above
Austria	. . . . .	548.00
Austria	. . . . .	487.00
United States	8400	420.00

1 October 1913		
Countries	Kind of Armor	Price
England	Side Armor	$503.78
England	Turret Armor	691.04
France	Curved plates: thick, cemented	978.00–1471.00
France	Curved plates: ordinary	460.81
France	Cylindrical plates, cemented	507.87
France	Cylindrical plates, special	490.22
France	Deck plating	292.17
Germany		490.00
Italy	9–11 inches thick	405.30–443.90
Italy	2–6 inches thick	353.19–366.70
Austria	Fixed armor	510.98
Austria	Turret armor	729.97
Russia	Various kinds	154.00–875.00
Japan		406.35

*Information not entirely accurate but based on best available data.

SOURCE: Memorandum, 6 January 1916, Office of Naval Intelligence, Armor 1916 folder, #1, Armor Plate 1914–17 box, Josephus Daniels papers, Library of Congress.

TABLE 18

INTERNATIONAL ARMOR PRICES, 1914

Supplier	Maximum Thickness	Cost per Ton				Date
		A-1	A-2	B	C	
Bethlehem Steel Co.	Any	$454	$518	$496	$548	1913
Midvale Steel Co.	Any	440	504		462	1913
Carnegie Steel Co.	Any	454	518	496	548	1913
Vickers Limited	Any	681	608	511	438	1906
John Brown & Co.	Any					
Carnell, Laird & Co.	Any					
Hadfield Steel Foundry Co.						
Beardmore Steel Works						
Armstrong, Whitworth & Co.						
Atlad Works	Any					
Forges Nationales de las Chaussade (G)	10 tons, wt. 2¾ inches	363		545		1909
La Compagnie des Hauts Fourneaux	Any			559		1909
Schneider & Cie.	Any		574			
Forges et Acieries de la Marine et d'Homicourt	Any					
Chatillon-Commentry et Neuves-Maisons	Any			559		1909
M.M. Marel	Any	555	678			1909
M.M. Jacob Hotzlen & Cie.						
Krupp	Any	490(?)				1913
Dillengen	light					
Witkowitz	Any	525	750			1913
Ljora Iron Works (G)	Any	325	421	207		1913
Nicopol-Marionpol	Any	463	463	287		1913
Kure Naval Station (G)	Kure	400				
Wakamatsu Iron Works (G)	Large capacity, 12 inch thickness / Small capacity 2 inch thickness					
Terni Vickers Steel Works	Any	550				1906
Ansaldo-Armstrong Co.	Any					

SOURCE: Memorandum, 6 January 1916, Office of Naval Intelligence, Armor 1916 folder, #1, Armor Plate 1914–17 box, Josephus Daniels papers, Library of Congress.

NOTE: Office of Naval Intelligence noted no other available information on this subject nor available information regarding average per capita wage paid in foreign navy yards during last years or in yards where foreign vessels were constructed.

enabled less sophisticated steel companies to bid on the thinner plate, forcing the "Big Three" to accordingly reduce their prices. None of this was particularly new to congressional audiences, yet Daniels, Tillman, and the insurgents felt new members required "re-education." Technical problems always caused the less sophisticated legislators to go along with "what the experts had to say."

Daniels and the ordnance professionals concluded "that there is nothing to interfere with the manufacture of armor plate by the Government." But, asked the secretary, was it good policy to do so? Many critics feared dire results "in time of war should the navy deprive the steelmen of their profitable business." Daniels, reflecting the professional military advice of the era, frankly doubted that the duration of a modern war would permit sufficient time to place plates on new warships. War had become too expensive for any nation to engage in it for very long, he preached. The French model permitted both government and private participation, and both George Washington and Abraham Lincoln had seen the wisdom of establishing government arms factories. "This policy is, in fact, being carried out to-day in the manufacture of powder and cartridge cases and in the manufacture of guns at the Washington Navy Yard for the Navy, and for the Army at the Watervliet Arsenal," observed Daniels. "It does not require serious consideration to reach the conclusion that no objections on the ground of public policy stand in the way of a Government plant."[18]

The real crux of the matter seemed to be economic. The chief of ordnance had computed the cost of a ten-thousand-ton per year plant (about half the requirement for a two-battleship annual program), at $8,466,000.00 or $314.00 per ton. This represented a savings of $140.00 a ton over private armor makers' prices ($454.00), but it still seemed excessive to Daniels. He suggested that doubling the annual capacity would reduce the cost to $279.00 with a net savings of $3,048,462.24. As in the past, lack of steel company cooperation kept the navy in the dark as to plant overhead, machinery, labor, etc.—all elements affecting actual cost of production. Daniels promised to keep searching for these figures, but he definitely thought some sort of government facility would introduce the desired competition.

Press coverage immediately produced private speculation that the government could produce armor for only $250 per ton. Yet, when the Navy Department opened bids for *Arizona* armor in late August 1913, all the steel companies remained committed to the $454 price tag. A surprised Daniels felt this was eloquent proof of collusion, rejected the bids, and publicly disclosed the results in order to reinvite lower bids. In turn, the business community complained loudly about the "dirty pool" tactics of the secretary. Daniels called Midvale, Carnegie, and Bethlehem representatives to Washingon and read them the riot act, despite their protests of innocence and coincidence, not collusion. When the unrepentent steelmen continued to hold out, Daniels told them to think about it overnight and come back the next day without "another coincidence."[19]

The next day's session produced no better results and the navy-steel impasse had everyone's nerves on edge. Daniels now changed his plan of attack. His desk was covered with outsiders' letters offering suggestions. One of Tillman's naval protégés, Lieutenant Commander Louis Richardson, felt that the navy should enter into armor making only in small amounts and that the steel trust kept its hold on the government merely because of a protective tariff which benefited the rich "and the fact that they can persuade the unions that if we buy our material abroad it would reduce wages." A former Midvale forge operator wrote that armor could be made for $210 a ton, but that only the Navy Department, was really to blame for the impasse. He observed, "At the time Midvale filed its initial bid with the Navy Department, I believe it was sincere in its effort to lower prices to a reasonable and competitive basis, but when the Navy Department, presumably on the advice of Admiral Mason, refused to award them more than one-third of the total contract, giving the remaining two-thirds to Carnegie and Bethlehem, at prices approximately one hundred dollars per ton more than Midvale was to receive for its metal, can you blame them for joining issue with their competitors and getting the greatest possible price?" "Call it collusion or anything you choose, for such it is, " suggested T.B.H. Stenhouse, "but there is no one to blame for this state of affairs except the Navy

Department under your predecessors."[20]

Daniels' newest scheme was to push Congress for a government plant, but to also break up the *Arizona* armor contracts into smaller amounts so as to induce bidding other than from the "Big Three." He installed an avowed government plant advocate, Captain Joseph Strauss, as naval ordnance chief, and sent Roosevelt to New York to talk with visiting English armor man Sir John Hadfield about possible ties with the British. He hinted to the press that even President Wilson was leaning toward a government armor plant. Then Daniels readvertised for *Arizona* armor.[21]

Opening the final bids on 14 October, Daniels discovered that he had three different price quotations at last. All three firms had reduced their bids, but Daniels chose to award the whole contract to Midvale, only to be told that firm could not complete the job on time. Once more the secretary had been outflanked by the steelmen and a tripartite division of contracts had to be effected although in the end the navy secured a six-hundred-thousand-dollar savings due to smaller firms like Carbon Steel being able to undercut the "Big Three" on items such as armor bolts. Daniels had won a pyrrhic victory. He secured lower prices, but the big companies had again split the main armor order, realized a handsome profit, and left the secretary of the navy grumbling to reporters, "I consider the fight only just begun."

The idea of a government plant was a major thrust in Daniels' first annual report. "Under our present system of obtaining our armor plate from private companies such improvements [in manufacture and design] become the property of all the world, and can be obtained by anybody who cares to buy them," said the secretary, citing Bethlehem experience with designing and building warships as well as an armor plant for foreign powers like Japan. Nationalism joined competition as a topic of debate. The armor issue was hot. Illinois congressman Clyde Tavenner had a $7-million plant resolution on the House calendar, and Daniels knew that even the British government was squirming with five private armor firms splitting the annual contracts equally among themselves, at ten thousand tons apiece.[22]

As the whole question of national preparedness began to trouble the nation, additional voices could be heard in favor of a government armor facility. William Allen White and even Andrew Carnegie saw positive benefits accruing from such a move. "This country is not going to continue making armor indefinitely," said the aging steel mogul, "on the contrary, I think nations generally will soon use very little of it." He thought the threat of a government plant would cause the companies to willingly open their books to department scrutiny. He suggested a typical arrangement that smelled of Republican "New Competition" philosophy—"I think you could get an agreement with the armor makers, subject to three year's notice to furnish armor at a fair percentage upon the cost." But then Carnegie also thought that "the three Teutonic nations" of Great Britain, Germany, and the United States, "united could banish war upon the seas."[23]

Much of Carnegie's thinking was sagacious. He counseled Daniels not to treat steelmen rudely since they had invested so much time and capital in the armor endeavor. He recalled using three gangs of workmen seven days a week to erect the Homestead works in 1890, sending subordinate George Lauder to get English tools and equipment, which survived the weather and an Atlantic passage, to help his government in its hour of need. He told of bonuses to English tool makers so that Carnegie could outdistance Bethlehem, yet he admitted Charles Schwab of Bethlehem was now paying great inducements to his employees for improvements in techniques and procedures in the armor field. Such vicissitudes and achievements of the "Captains of Industry" scarcely fazed Daniels, who was interested in freedom of competition and savings to the government, not liberal treatment of robber barons.

Still, a sluggish Congress could not make up its collective mind to act decisively against the trust. No less than a dozen bills had been introduced by 7 January 1914 which touched on the armor plant issue. By March, Daniels might gain some comfort from the news that the British Parliament was addressing similar questions, with M.P.s from the Midlands decrying vast private investment in expensive steel armor works spurred by government promises of long-term contracts. Winston

Churchill, among others, talked of government plants and overseas purchases to break "the armor ring." But the best that Daniels could get from Congress was an enjoinder to further study the problem and report to the next session upon the cost of erection of an armor plant.[24]

Actually, Daniels had personally shaped the composition of the new investigative body. It would include Tillman, House committee chairman Lemuel P. Padgett of Tennessee, and naval ordnance chief Admiral Strauss. However, the march of international events rapidly overtook the American armor question. When the public overcame the shock of the outbreak of the First World War in August 1914, many citizens undoubtedly agreed secretly with Tillman, who told Daniels: "It would seem to me that when the German and English fleets do meet and half of their battleships are destroyed and sunk our little navy would be very respectable. There is lots of food for thought in this war in the lessons it teaches about many things." To naval officials, the "food for thought" was probably more prosaic. Naval-industrial linkages now involved mines, torpedoes, and aviation, and Daniels spent much of the last six months of the year sorting out a variety of naval matériel problems. He utilized Hadfield's British firm in particular to cause a general reduction in American projectile prices. His success in this vein showed what might similarly be done for armor.[25]

Daniels returned to the fight for "no private gain in war preparation" by asking for two additional dreadnoughts, six destroyers, eight submarines, a gunboat, and an oiler in his 1914 annual report. He spoke of government production of all munitions so as to prevent the "philanthropy and 5 per cent" extortion of private arms makers. Reinforcing his point were the statistics—$111,875 in savings on the *Arizona* armor over that of the *Pennsylvania*, $378,261 on specially treated deck plating of the *Arizona*, and some $738,648 on the second round bidding for the latest three dreadnoughts authorized by Congress. Daniels attributed it all to the presence or threat of competition. What he failed to say was that the three dreadnought bids—on some 24,384 tons of armor— were resolved only by his return to Charles Bonaparte's stratagem of getting the high bidders to agree to lower prices and then split up the award. The government remained "at the mercy of the three manufacturers of armor plate whose policy is to make the government pay prices much beyond a fair profit."[26]

By February 1915, Secretary Daniels was anything but sanguine about the prospects for success. He wrote Padgett concerning the new appropriation:

> The Senate provisions looking toward a projectile factory and an armor plate factory, I think, are of great importance. We are now at the mercy of the manufacturers. If we insert these measures in the words of the Senate bill we do not commit the Government to any expenditure of money if we can get reasonable prices. I think the probabilities are if the items are inserted for the projectile factory and armor plate factory, the money will not be spent, certainly not until the treasury recovers from the losses due to the war in Europe, but I think they will enable us to buy these at reasonable prices; otherwise, with the war going on, I fear they will hold us up for the highest prices.[27]

Indeed, the war had introduced a new element. The steel industry experienced a recession in 1913 and 1914 from which it began to recover through the stimulus of war orders from Europe. Shrapnel and shells, barbed wire and rails, ordnance, and other matériel flowed from American shops in defiance of the government's official neutrality. Industry absorbed some of its own products for expansion of production facilities. The war spawned Charles Schwab's clandestine submarine project for the British, as well as Bethlehem's negotiations to buy up the Pennsylvania Steel Company. A merger of Midvale and Cambria was in sight; war profits and mergers were the thing.

Bethlehem loomed as America's preeminent munitions maker with its steel plant in South Bethlehem, iron ore deposits in Cuba, Union Iron Works for shipbuilding in San Francisco, and acquisition of an eastern outlet at Fore River Shipbuilding Company, Quincy, Massachusetts in 1913. If U.S. Steel earnings fell from $119 million to $82 million in the recession, Bethlehem's profits nearly doubled. Little wonder that by

November 1915, Judge Gary would opine that the demands for steel exceeded the producing capacities of American mills and furnaces. "There is nothing to indicate that there will be a decrease of the demand for some time to come," he said. All of this boded ill for Daniels' efforts to reduce naval armament prices.[28]

The Tillman committee returned its verdict on 24 February 1915. The report would be the final chapter of such investigations, and the group decided that the United States needed a government armor plant and that Congress should authorize one. Except for 110 pages of testimony, the report was generally a hard-hitting dollars and cents estimate that a plant with a yearly capacity of 10,000 tons could manufacture armor at $262.79 per ton for a $6,635,107 investment. By doubling the capacity, the price could be reduced to $230.11 for $10,331,906. Since this was a sizable reduction over private prices, it did not take much to convince the U.S. Senate to go along. House members were less sure, and in the end a conference committee struck out provisions for government facilities from the annual appropriations bill then pending.

The flood of statistics from men like Alva C. Dinkey, president of Carnegie Steel (United States Steel), Eugene Grace, president of Bethlehem, and William P. Barba, manager of Midvale, as well as their auditors and superintendents convinced readers of the Tillman report that the steel men were most cooperative and certainly not extortionists. Obviously the legislators did not understand the technical intricacies of armor making and hours of agonizing debate probably failed to sway the majority on the hill, whose minds were already made up. The steelmen certainly did not feel threatened enough to disclose corporate secrets. They had survived so many false alarms that to them the Tillman committee seemed merely another squall to wait out.[29]

Friends of private industry were still strong enough to thwart passage of armor plant provisions in the naval appropriations act of 3 March 1915. The silver-tongued spokesman for Pennsylvania steelman, Senator Bois Penrose, pooh-poohed the proposed plant with the observation, "We simply have the ladle dipped into the bucket and the money of the taxpayer poured

out like water in a lavish and improvident way." Two battleships, six destroyers, two submarines, $18,957,998 for
private armor and ordnance contracts, and no armor plant were
the result.[30]

The prolonged and bloody warfare in Europe began to create
pressures even on this side of the Atlantic. European demands
drove steel prices ever upward; naval preparedness proponents
heckled the Navy Department about combat readiness; and
Daniels struck back at Republican criticism by admitting to
Henry Cabot Lodge, "Instead of being satisfied with the Navy
as it is to-day, I am strongly in favor of steadily increasing it in
every actual unit experience teaches is necessary, as well as
increasing the personnel." But the navy could not secure
preference from an industrial sector bloated with ship and
matériel orders. "First come, first served," Daniels was told by
businessmen. He should have seen the crunch coming a year
before, they claimed.[31]

Daniels resorted to navy yard construction insofar as Congress would allow, but he found normal steel prices 25 percent
higher than before. His 1915 annual report fairly brimmed with
frustration and anger at private manufacturers' taking advantage of the war market to raise prices or deny their services to
the American government. Surprisingly, he now espoused what
naval professionals had been advocating for years—a set, five-
year, well-defined building program which would permit order-
ly and sustained growth, as well as firm goals for industry. He
apparently sensed no inherent irony in his opening recommendation for massive fleet buildup, and his closing avowal that
what was necessary was "an international agreement to end
competition in big naval programs."[32]

Election year 1916 opened with Admiral Strauss estimating
113,200 tons of armor would be needed from 1917 to 1921 to
fulfill Daniels' five-year program. "Preparedness" questions
were in the air, and Senator Tillman returned to the armor
battle with a vengeance. "The greedy capitalists, who have the
Government by the throat, are not going to release their grip if
they can possibly hold it," he told Daniels, "and the inordinate
profits they have been making heretofore are not going to be
relinquished without much squealing. We must be prepared at

all points when the debate begins; and we are evidently going to have much talk before the bill becomes law, if it becomes a law at all." Tillman still hoped to get an armor plant provision through Congress.[33]

The senator was no fool. Tillman did not think the country could "afford to have several millions of dollars tied up in an Armor Factory unable to make anything else; and we ought to go to the limit of diversifying the products to be turned out." He was also concerned that industry not try to corner the supply of raw materials once an armor plant was fact. Daniels agreed but saw no problems in securing pig iron, nickel, ferro-chromium, ferrosilicon, spiegeleisen, ferro-manganese, limestone, flospar, A.M.S. metal or coal. But the secretary was less sanguine about product diversification. "The plan esti-mated upon was for the production of heavy face hardened armor, and can not very well be utilized for any other purposes without large additional outlay of money," he told Tillman. He added, however, that co-located plants could turn out projectiles or other heavy materials.

Both men solicited the help of President Wilson. But the chief executive was caught between election year fears about heavy spending and winning the votes of the common man yet retaining the hard-won confidence of the business community. Wilson promised support at the strategic moment. Now Till-man had momentum in his favor. Committee hearings in 1916 surfaced the usual steel industry arguments and desires to return to Republican era policies, but willingness to sit down and negotiate with Secretary Daniels. This time, however, the end of the titanic struggle was in sight. The secretary turned a deaf ear to industry price figures varying from $395.00 to $402.50 per ton, and guarantees of a five-year, forty-thousand-ton price-stabilized program. He simply refused to admit that immunity to market fluctuations, stable prices and materials, insurance, taxes, profits, research waste, and other indicators were valid considerations which might drive prices up in actual production circumstances.[34]

The disconcerted steelmen struck back with a threat to raise the price of armor two hundred dollars per ton should Congress vote for an armor plant. Fearing the loss of $20 million in investment, men like Grace, Dinkey, and Barba apparently thought this ploy would bludgeon a docile Congress back into its usual submissive position. The effort backfired for the industrialists, who were overconfident, perhaps, or merely blinded by past success and fat wartime profits. A tide of public opinion erupted in favor of the government facility and the *Manufacturers Record* declared on 7 February that the steelmen's announcement was "one of the most unfortunate statements ever issued in this country by any great business organization dealing with the Government." Tillman reacted by promising immediate introduction of a bill authorizing government seizure of all munitions plants in event of war or even threat thereof. Newspaper editors across the country urged construction of a government plant as proof that the United States Government would not be robbed, extorted, or exploited by robber barons.[35]

Armor was but the tip of the iceberg in 1916. The question of socialism versus private enterprise in munitions production bothered official Washington. Administration backers pointed to government experience in running its own plants for ordnance, powder, and torpedoes. U.S. Army ordnance facilities proved capable of underbidding Midvale and Bethlehem on fourteen-inch guns by $18,000 per item, thus getting the naval contract. The navy had undercut the powder trust by making that material at $.38 when the market price was $.53—with a savings of $1,169,000 in just three years. Similarly, government torpedo production had been increased from seventy-five to four hundred torpedoes a year at nearly $1,100 less per item than prices demanded from private sources. These statistics pointed to similar benefits in armor.[36]

The fight in both houses of Congress was bitter. On 21 March, the U.S. Senate voted for an armor plant by 58 to 23, with 14 abstentions, including Progressive Republican Robert M. LaFollette of Wisconsin. The House was more stubborn, as always, and late minute indications from Bethlehem that it might lower prices, a barrage of newspaper propaganda on behalf of industry, and the lukewarm pressure from the White House nearly doomed the bill. It wasn't until June that the House followed the Senate, by 263 to 135, and it took until 18

August to iron out differences between the two versions of the naval appropriations legislation. Daniels thought the victory already won and queried the steel moguls if they would like to sell their plants to the government.

Final passage of the most militaristic appropriation bill in the country's history contained the key provision:

> The Secretary of the Navy is hereby authorized and directed to provide, either by erection of a factory or by the purchase of a factory or both, for the manufacture of armor for the vessels of the Navy; said factory or factories to have an annual capacity of not less than 20,000 tons of armor; to be located at a place or places approved by the General Board of the Navy, with especial reference to considerations of safety in time of war; and the sum of $11,000,000 is hereby appropriated, out of any money in the Treasury not otherwise appropriated, to be immediately available, for the purposes of this paragraph. And if the United States owns no suitable site or sites, authority is hereby given to acquire by purchase, condemnation, or gift such site or sites as may be necessary. The expenditures for drafting, technical, expert and clerical assistance necessary shall be paid from the appropriation herein made. The Secretary of the Navy shall keep an accurate and itemized account of the cost per ton of the product of such factory or factories and report the same to Congress in his annual report.[37]

Later, Henry Cabot Lodge wrote his old friend Theodore Roosevelt that the Republicans had forced Wilson and Daniels into line on the big preparedness program, but the secretary himself claimed a great Democratic victory, observing, "This act of Congress is by far the most important law that was ever passed in regard to the United States Navy and its effect on the future history of the United States will be far reaching and probably beyond anything that anyone can visualize today." If for no other reason than quantity, the legislation escalated the naval-industrial linkages with provisions for ten battleships, six battle cruisers, nine fleet and fifty-eight coastal submarines, two gunboats, a repair ship, a transport, a hospital ship, two destroyer tenders and a submarine tender, two ammunition ships, and $47,110,000 for armor and armanent. Besides the armor plant provision, there was a clause for establishment of a Federal naval reserve, improvements in organizational and personnel matters, and the principle of a legally established, set naval construction program spread over three years. When combined with other legislation of the year, such as a revised shipping bill and a revenue bill, the package helped reelect Wilson in November on a platform of reasonable preparedness, but conscious nonintervention in the European war.[38]

Actually, the year was quite profitable even for the steel industry, notwithstanding the defeat on an armor plant. Bethlehem earnings, for example, exceeded $61 million. Even without foreign munitions orders, that company was devoting less than one-third of its effort directly to guns, ships, and projectiles. The industry as a whole witnessed mergers (Bethlehem/Pennsylvania Steel, and Midvale/Cambria), new plant openings, and reactivation of all facilities. Around board rooms, a generally euphoric atmosphere was threatened only by worries that demands might outdistance supply.[39]

Ironically, the nation which voted for the president who promised to keep it out of war soon found itself in the thick of the fighting. With similar irony, while major powers like the United States worried about dreadnoughts and armor prices, the unsung submarine was the instrument which plunged the Wilson administration into a really world-wide conflict. America had been preparing for several years—the first of its roles as arsenal of democracy in the twentieth century. But the declaration of war in April 1917 changed many things, not the least of which were business-government relations. From 1917 to 1919 the military-industrial complex, which had been evolving since the eighties and nineties, came of age as ranks of "dollar-a-year" men from industry and business joined the soldiers and sailors marching to "make the world safe for democracy." Modern, industrialized, bureaucratized mobilization of men and matériel exploded across the whole country, and the war preparedness effort included not only manpower for the army and armored ships for the navy, but also a War Industries Board, and figures like Bernard Baruch, William Goethals,

Peyton March, and Walter S. Gifford.[40]

Key men behind the scenes, like Secretary of the Navy Daniels, had to deal with the munitions and new institutional arrangements forged in the preparedness campaigns of 1915 and 1916. Even provision for a government armor factory failed to solve all the steel procurement problems for Daniels. Fortunately, competition did exist for special treatment steel protective deck plates, projectiles, torpedoes, and gun forgings. Carbon Steel had underbid Carnegie on *California* deck plates while only British munitions policies prevented Hadifield Ltd. from providing foreign competition on projectiles. Supply and demand continued to be the most acute problem as America entered the war.

Private shipbuilders were unable or unwilling to undertake new orders with an assurance of completion even at prices which normally would have caused the Navy Department great distress. The department could not get fixed price bidding for the battle cruisers in December 1916, four private firms submitting bids based on cost plus profit. Daniels told Congressman Padgett that this was totally unacceptable, that the navy had to expand its own construction facilities, and that Midvale, Carnegie, and Bethlehem were continuing to extort high prices for gun shells.[41] (See tables 19–22.)

The secretary's battles with industry evoked varied responses from the public. One Midvale stockholder, Thomas B. Stenhouse, urged him to "stick to your guns—you are dead right," claiming it was absurd that "the American manufacturers cannot produce an article equal to the European shell . . . because they either don't want to or are asleep." Yet C.F. Roberts, a Detroit manufacturer, protested the shabby treatment accorded industry by the government. Daniels could only reply that he preferred American products, but they had to be useful. Accommodation between industry and government was obviously necessary, and at the request of Bernard Baruch, Daniels attempted to ameliorate the navy's needs through Elbert H. Gary, president of the American Iron and Steel Institute.[42]

Gary's response was mixed. His citation of base prices for plates, structural shapes, and bars, f.o.b. Pittsburgh, was in excess of what Daniels thought equitable and fair "to the nation in the crisis which faces it." Yet Gary had assembled some of the most important figures in the field—James A. Ferrell, Charles A. Schwab, Alva C. Dinkey, James A. Burden, E.A.S. Clarke, John A. Topping, and Willis L. King—to comprise a committee on steel and steel products. This group improved the

TABLE 19

MUNITIONS PRICES—PROJECTILES

Size	Date	Price per Item	Supplier
14-inch	November 1912	$490.00	
	January 1914	315.00*	
	October 1914	415.00	
	July 1915	410.00	
	October 1916	492.00	
	15 November 1916†	535.00–545.00	
	(later modification)	535.00	Midvale Steel
	(later modification)	530.00	Crucible Steel
	3 January 1917†	356.00	Hadfield Ltd.
		500.00	Washington Steel and Ordnance
		550.00	Midvale Steel
		543.50	Crucible Steel
	(later modification)	750.00	Crucible Steel
	(later modification)	750.00	Bethlehem Steel
16-inch	3 January 1917‡	513.00	Hadfield Ltd.
		750.00	Washington Steel and Ordnance
		900.00	Midvale Steel
		768.50	Crucible Steel
		775.00	Bethlehem Steel
	(later modification)	750.00	Crucible Steel
	(later modification)	750.00	Bethlehem Steel

*Low prices due to possible Hadfield bid.
†No contracts awarded. Figures represent bids.
‡Only 10 16-inch projectiles were manufactured—by Midvale for $843. Figures represent bids.

SOURCE: Memoranda, Chief of Ordnance to Secretary of the Navy, 15 January and 13 February 1917, both in Ordnance, 1917 Folder, Ordnance Bureau Box, Subject File, Naval Affairs, Josephus Daniels papers, Library of Congress.

lines of communication between Washington and private industry and was another important ingredient in the growth of the military-industrial complex.

The March 1917 naval appropriations bill provided three more battleships, another battle cruiser, three scout cruisers, fifteen destroyers, a destroyer tender, a submarine tender, eighteen coastal submarines, and $44,180,000 to arm and armor the vessels. Meanwhile, an offer of free land at Charleston, West Virginia had been a determining factor in the selection of the armor plant site. Daniels had directed the General Board in November 1916 to establish a special group to select the site and an extensive search had examined the cost of assembling material for plate manufacture, labor, freight rates, etc. Rear Admiral Frank F. Fletcher, Commander F.H. Clarke, and Civil Engineer R.E. Bakenhus worked hard before submitting a preliminary report on 7 April.

TABLE 20

MUNITIONS PRICES—POWDER

Cost of Manufacture at Indian Head, Maryland—U.S. Government Plant

	1912, per lb.	1913, per lb.	1914, per lb.	1915, per lb.	1916, per lb.
Direct	$.30511	$.29929	$.27261	$.24912	$.321061
Overhead and interest (3% on plant)	.08025	.08025	.08403	.072243	.096052
Total:	$.40746	$.40164	$.38072	$.341256	$.440782

Purchased from E.I. Dupont de Nemours

$.60	$.60 and $.53	$.53	$.53	$.50

SOURCE: Memoranda, Chief of Ordnance to Secretary of the Navy, 15 January and 13 February 1917, both in Ordnance, 1917 Folder, Ordnance Bureau Box, Subject File, Naval Affairs, Josephus Daniels papers, Library of Congress.

Just as the private steel firms had predicted, the subject became more complex than the Navy Department had originally anticipated. A final, definitive report on the best location seemed impossible pending expert advice on process, raw materials, sources of supply, transportation, and marketing systems throughout the country, not to speak of labor and

TABLE 21

MUNITIONS PRICES—GUNS

U.S. Naval Gun Factory: one 1-inch, 45 caliber gun = $77,058.00.		
Computation Table with Breech Mechanism		
Caliber	Naval Gun Factory	Lowest Private Bid
16-inch, 45 caliber	. . . . .	$167,295.00
16-inch, 50 caliber	$89,560.00	116,000.00
14-inch, 45 caliber	56,900.00	74,770.00
12-inch, 50 caliber	56,700.00	72,800.00
12-inch, 45 caliber	54,400.00	66,912.00
6-inch, 50 caliber	11,233.00	12,283.00
5-inch, 51 caliber	5,840.00	9,500.00
4-inch, 50 caliber	. . . . .	5,772.46

NOTE: Bids made in 1916 were made upon material for gun forgings that had advanced in price nearly 60 percent since forgings for the guns made at the naval gun factory were obtained. Comparisons hence were difficult, cost of guns to the gun factory did not include any charge for plant or overhead. Sixteen-inch gun construction necessitated new lathes and machinery at Midvale and Bethlehem for which their estimate was practically naval gun factory cost plus machinery add-on.

SOURCE: Memoranda, Chief of Ordnance to Secretary of the Navy, 15 January and 13 February 1917, both in Ordnance, 1917 Folder, Ordnance Bureau Box, Subject File, Naval Affairs, Josephus Daniels papers, Library of Congress.

TABLE 22

MUNITIONS PRICES—TORPEDOES AND MINES

	Torpedoes		
	Torpedo Station	Naval Gun Factory	E.W. Bliss Company
Mark-VII	$5,119.34	$7,860.91 on first order 5,618.62 on second order	$6,125.91
Mark-IX	4,332.30		7,627.86

Mines	
Norfolk Navy Yard	Vickers Ltd.
$321.96	$498.95

SOURCE: Memoranda, Chief of Ordnance to Secretary of Navy, 15 January and 13 February 1917, both in Ordnance, 1917 Folder, Ordnance Bureau Box, Subject File, Naval Affairs, Josephus Daniels papers, Library of Congress.

power supply, now that the report was not merely gathering data for some congressional committee but was the data base for actual construction of the whole plant complex. Schwab and the others had been right, and Daniels and his naval professionals really lacked the expertise to be in the armor plant construction business—especially now that America had entered the actual fighting.[43]

When the Armor Plant Board's final report reached Daniels' desk in mid-May, it was impressive and detailed. Yet, since speed was of the utmost importance, the details seemed sadly out of touch with the realities of the new war effort. Daniels had also already accepted the Charleston location despite board preference for Pittsburgh among twenty-nine competitors. Advertisement for machinery, concern for overtime pay, union versus nonunion construction, and legal battles about water rights all plagued the project. But the contractor, American Bridge Company, plunged on, and both Daniels and ordnance chief Rear Admiral Ralph Earle waxed enthusiastic about what the former termed "a concrete declaration of a new national policy in the making of weapons of war."[44]

The "Giant Naval Plant and Projectile Factory" at Charleston eventually provided employment for 2,363 men including 18 officers, 3 seamen, and a marine contingent of 34 officers and men. Upon the settlement of various contracts on a cost-plus basis, a large amount of navy-owned machinery became available for installation at the facility. The armor plant, or "South Unit" alone covered one hundred and fifty acres and was designed as five buildings to house armor plate and major gun forging operations (the latter added from "Increase of the Navy funds" in August 1918). A second, or "North Unit" was completed and in full operation producing six-inch gun forgings and sixteen-inch armor-piercing projectiles.

Earle's successor, Charles B. McVay, bragged to Daniels in 1920 that during the previous year, the plant had been especially successful in producing torpedo air flasks and armor plate bolts, as well as 5,959 tons of ingots, 291 tons of steel castings, 465 tons of iron castings, 20 tons of brass castings, while at the same time forging 4,644 tons of ingots, annealing 4,282 tons of forgings, and heat treating 2,582 tons of the same. The war weary secretary by this time was probably happier when Captain George R. Marvell, the plant commandant, recommended abolishment of the ten dollar per day position of labor superintendent after the armistice. "This is the first piece of good news I have had in a long time," said Daniels, "everybody is writing in asking for new positions and higher pay and it is a delight to get this news on this dreary, rainy day, and that somebody has really recommended that we abolish a place."[45]

Daniels finally visited the plant in September 1919 "to see the cornfields of his last visit transformed into massive steel and concrete structures, to hear the hum of wonderful machinery, and to gaze upon the largest modern steel plant in the entire world." The secretary praised the progress of construction "and . . . the product so far obtained," as well as the "harmony, the teamwork, and the splendid comradeship" of the naval station. Yet, in the end, Daniels was denied the privilege of witnessing the first armor plate ingot cast on Wednesday, 2 February 1921. Daniels was by then a lame duck administrator, and he could only read with interest how the sixty-ton ingot excited those dignitaries present at the festivities.[46]

The government armor plant never produced sizable quantities of armor plate. When the United States entered World War I, a priority was given to ship construction, not building plants. The need for projectiles and smaller caliber guns rather than battleship armor took priority even at Charleston. Armor secured from private sources during the war drew $425 per ton in 1917 from Carnegie Steel, and a return to identical bidding in 1919 netted Carnegie, Midvale, and Bethlehem $520 per ton as well as $525 the following year. Wartime necessity supplanted Progressive idealism, and the postwar environment focused attention on international, not domestic crusades.

What Daniels may have sought all along was simply a yardstick, a government measuring device against which to judge private price and quality. The steelmen failed to understand such motives, and the secretary failed to look beyond the *bete noire* of robber baron profits and closed markets. When the smoke of war had cleared, the situation had gone nearly full cycle. The advent of Warren G. Harding and the Republicans in

1921 left the Navy Department with its armor plant but with no emphasis on its use. The steel firms thus not only retained their high prices and possibly excess profits, but also regained their solid political position in Washington and its concomitant return to the pleasant triangular arrangements of the New Nationalism and New Competition.

Meanwhile, an elaborate and costly plant rusted from neglect. Skilled workmen and their families who had been wrenched from other jobs to staff the West Virginia facility drifted away in the 1920s. A token guard watched over a disintegrating plant. Even the Democrats' return with the New Deal in the 1930s signaled no rebirth of earlier enthusiasm. President Franklin D. Roosevelt ignored all pleas to reopen the Charleston armor plant. He had never fully understood Daniels' motives when he served as his assistant, and probably had no interest in the project when he gained the White House. Final victory belonged not to Herbert, Tillman, Daniels, or the Democrats, but rather to Carnegie, Linderman, Harra, and Schwab—even, perhaps, to the line of Republicans from Tracy and Bonaparte to Henry Cabot Lodge. The nation had a naval-industrial complex, but it didn't know it. Americans had other things on their minds as the country returned to normalcy.

Postscript

Some Reflections
on the Steelmen and the Navy

It may have been inevitable. Marriage between two strong American institutions—national government and the business community—was meant to be. The technological revolution and the unification of the country, followed by rise to world power, guaranteed that various essential ingredients would have to congeal in pursuit of national goals and policies. The Civil War was a start—a wedding of sorts. But the postwar absence of necessity delayed real consummation of the sacrament. The oldest armed service, the United States Army, took nearly a half-century to seal the knot. With the United States Navy, however, it was different.

For one thing, the tools of the trade were vastly different, as was the place of the navy in the philosophy of national policy and goals. If a century of carefully orchestrated isolationism was accepted national policy, the navy was the arbiter of that policy. It formed the first line of national defense and enforced the Monroe Doctrine. Its mission was to insure American people and property against threat both at home and abroad. To accomplish such a mission required the largest and most sophisticated man-made engines of war, complicated weapons systems which packaged men, ships, and ordnance even in the days of "hearts of oak." By the time iron and steel supplanted the New England forests as the source of matériel, it was inevitable that the United States Navy, like its counterparts across the world, would lead the effort to establish ties with other national institutions, in particular business and industry, in shaping and securing common goals.

Methods and means became all important. While the military establishment might need these other institutions, the reverse was not necessarily true, or so it seemed. Naturally, national defense was fundamental to securing the rights of life, liberty, and the pursuits of property and happiness, and the subtle ties between defense and industry escaped many Americans too busy exploring and populating a continent, forging political, economic, and cultural institutions—or simply paying the bills. An unfamiliar government in Washington, an unseen gunboat on the ocean, or a faceless cavalry troop in the West would provide for the common defense. If an impertinent Briton or Gaul crossed through the ocean barriers, then American manhood would Cincinnatus like spring forth to repeat the mythical exploits of Lexington and Bunker Hill.

However, the government and its armed services needed tools to fulfill their mission, and the U.S. Navy, in particular, turned to a burgeoning industrial sector when it began modernization in the late nineteenth century. The navy apparently needed industry far more than entrepreneurs like Joseph Wharton and Andrew Carnegie thought they needed the navy. Of course, the government was a customer. But so were railroads, bridge builders, and construction firms. There was an assured market there, without the risk that changes in federal budget or in technology would overtake investment and programs. To most businessmen of the age, the United States Government was a most intransigent customer.

Naval officials persevered. Whether Carnegie's motives were pure and patriotic or not in 1890, the navy and the government did offer revenue subsidies and opportunities for expansion. The Pittsburgh steelmen were no fools. Carnegie, who could consistently underbid rivals in the industry, smelled profit in steel armor profits. True, uncertainty always remained, in the form of congressional inconsistency, government inspectors, production costs, etc. But why not use U.S. funds to build another sector of one's industrial empire? Products from armor and ordnance could be sold to other government represent- atives than those in Washington. Besides, Carnegie and Beth- lehem officials quickly discovered that naval contracts helped offset those troublesome depressions and other growing pains of robber barons at work.

The early era of naval-industrial association was mutually beneficial. The U.S. Navy received first-rate facilities and products and put a modernized fleet in the water. The U.S. government gained a vital tool for joining the imperialist scramble of the era while winning world power status and protecting its national interests. The steelmen secured new tools, new techniques, and new processes which could be transferred from naval armaments to domestic market uses. For a time, the honeymoon in the marriage seemed destined never to end!

The era was also one of severe competition and cutthroat practices in the steel industry. Wide open negotiations, idea sharing, political accommodations—all were double-edged weapons for both government and big business. It helped to have the party of big business in power, although in reality, modern naval-industrial ties began under a Democrat, Grover Cleveland, not the Republicans, and continued virtually unin- terrupted during the periodic inroads made by the Democrats from 1893 to 1897 and 1913 to 1921. It was also useful that Alfred Thayer Mahan and Stephen B. Luce provided an ideological rationale. Seapower and imperialism necessitated battlefleets, which in turn generated the need for heavier armor and armament, leading to heavy industrial involvement, which then returned full cycle when domestic firms needed a strong national defense to assure their capitalist prosperity. While the 1880s witnessed a tenuous reaching out by both naval and steel officials in the interest of patriotism and profit, the advantages to both became readily apparent by the 1890s.

Even then there were rough edges and strains to the rela- tionship. These men were products of an age of individualism —not cooperation. Nickel steel was to be used in any profitable manner, no matter that the U.S. government had provided the mills, greased the patent process, insured favorable tariff provisions, and winked at naval officials' "double-dipping" on corporate payrolls while in uniform. Social Darwinism, Horatio Alger, and Mahanite seapower were all cut from the same cloth. If civilians like Whitney, Tracy, Herbert, and Long entered office determined to maintain civilian supremacy, they all became militarized by their duties, obligations, missions, and policy making. The push and shove of strong willed naval officials and captains of industry was part of the climate of the age. What they wrought was all of the circumvention of rules and regulations, accommodated principles, and power ploys which became main threads of the later military-industrial complex.

At the time, however, these men only dimly perceived the potential of modern military-industrial interdependence, and none of them saw any threat of the hydra-headed monster destined to haunt a later generation of Americans. Not surprisingly, they were both the founders of the complex and the first to become disenchanted with their brainchild. Naval officials came to see private profit as incompatible with national interest. The resulting guidelines and checks instituted by the government soon led the steelmen into distrust and discontent over curtailment of their right to wealth.

Excess profits became the rallying cry for the opposition, and by 1900, the Sherman Anti-Trust Act sought to regulate the freewheeling spirit which had built great industrial empires. The government and the people began to view private entrepreneurship with misgivings, and the ground swell of Populism reflected disenchantment in America's ranks. The Horatio Alger myth seemed to lead only to combines, high prices, class structure, and labor exploitation. Hilary Herbert became the first naval secretary to lead what would become a twenty-year Democratic crusade for lower armor prices and the maintenance of private competition, since navy desires for teamwork with industry had created a Frankenstein in Bethlehem and Carnegie armor mills, and company officials seemed to be "mind-reading" what the Navy Department would pay for their products. Herbert's investigations and talk of a government production facility were one aspect of general confusion as to what course America wanted its economic activity to take.

Cabinet officials like Herbert and Long wanted more armor for their naval construction programs, but discontents from western farms to small towns in the New South often forced the administration to change its tack. Opposition to "armor and shipbuilding trusts" formed on Capitol Hill under the banner of "Pitchfork Ben" Tillman. The administrations of Harrison, Cleveland, and McKinley may have matched overseas expansionism with domestic neglect of the Sherman Act (in fact the Supreme Court all but emasculated the law in its 1895 ruling concerning the American Sugar Refining Company), but the advent of a new century and a new administration— Rooseveltian Progressivism—suggested a new direction.

The steelmen read the signs of the times, and reacted accordingly. Industrial warfare was tiresome and unproductive. The merger of the House of Morgan and Carnegie Steel at the turn of the century meant not only bigness, but frank avowal of a new internal doctrine designed to bring stability and order. The philosophy of New Competition was enunciated by Judge Elbert H. Gary and embraced by a second generation of steelmen coming in the wake of Wharton, Carnegie, and the original robber barons. Men like Schwab, J. Leonard Berlogle, Charles J. Harrah, and George W. Perkins readily accepted the stability of price and growth.

All of this accounts for the relatively stable armor-ordnance picture from 1900 to 1912. Even here there were inconsistencies. Moderate price advances were in line with the New Competition. Hence, moderate armor price raises could be anticipated, and the Navy Department under Roosevelt went along with this until the voices of protest became too strident on Capitol Hill. Half-hearted moves by Secretaries Moody, Morton, Bonaparte, and Newberry reflected the tightrope approach taken by the navy. The government encouraged reintroduction of competition (Midvale's entry into the marketplace), yet acquiescence to industry demands meshed with the stability and cooperation which the Republican administration and Republican corporations wanted desperately. Cabinet officials, congressmen, and industrialists of the GOP welded a close-knit team to build the new navy. They carried it victoriously through its first war, and moved it into the halcyon dreadnought days when consistency in naval construction programs was the rallying cry for bureau chiefs and secretaries, to the benefit of uninterrupted profits for the industrialists.

The military-industrial accommodation on steel worked smoothly until 1912. The return of the Democrats to the White House threatened to undo all of this. In the battle between New Freedom and New Competition, initial victory belonged to Populist-Progressive Wilsonian Democrats. Two Democratic southern politicians, Josephus Daniels and Benjamin Tillman, won authority to place a government armor and projectile factory beside other successful government ventures manufacturing guns and smokeless powder. Yet they failed in the end, largely because of events beyond their control.

World War I forged an even stronger alliance between government and business. Cutting across more than just naval programs, the exigencies of industrial mobilization led to cooperation between Wilson and the captains of industry. Adequate production supplanted adequate price controls as the main concern of government watchdog committees like the War Industries Board. President Wilson turned increasingly to his dream for "making the world safe for Democracy" and an international league of nations to avoid the debacle of 1914. As many have observed, Wilsonian New Freedom simply turned its back on what it symbolized to voters in 1912.[1]

The coup de grace was administered in 1920. The return of the Republicans was one thing, but on 1 March 1920 the Supreme Court found in favor of the United States Steel Corporation in an antitrust suit which had been pending since the Taft administration. No monopolistic control had been exerted over the industry, asserted the judges. Big steel had triumphed. In the wake of private victory were strewn the good intentions of Populists, New Freedom progressives, and supporters of a government armor factory. The navy and the nation returned to the notion that what was good for U.S. Steel was good for the country.

World War I changed much. For years congressional insurgents had complained about high armor prices and the need for a government yardstick. That yardstick, the armor factory, had been possible only with the advent of the war. But when the United States actually entered the fighting, its naval arm found that it had been preparing for the wrong conflict. There was to be no vindication of the Mahanite battlefleet. Jutland was fought to a draw between German and British navies in 1916. America faced battle in the North Atlantic with U-boats, and this required smaller, faster, unarmored antisubmarine craft. The government armor plant represented obsolete requirements, a fact rendered even clearer as aerial bombardment provided new dimensions to warfare in the postwar period.[2]

Still, the military-industrial linkage had been forged. It had all begun with steel, armor, and ordnance in the rush to create a new navy in the eighties and nineties. Navy needs spawned new methods, matériel, products, and relationships. New breeds of naval professional, cabinet secretary, and steel mogul alike were forged upon the anvil of armor. Theodore Roosevelt cut his teeth worrying about the question as assistant secretary on the eve of the war with Spain. Charles Schwab served as manager of the Homestead works in the bloody strike of 1890, and he used his armor-making expertise later as head of the Bethlehem empire. For twenty years, Senator Benjamin Tillman carved out a reputation in the United States Senate on the question of naval armor prices and government facilities for manufacture and production.

Questions of nickel steel, structural shapes, and federal money for plant growth all faded into history in the end. Possibly the most irritating problem, that of armor prices, became quite academic by the end of World War I. Even the commandant of the naval armor plant at Charleston, Captain George Marvell, seemed to waver when he wrote Secretary Daniels on 9 February 1921:

> There can be no doubt that looking back through the years since the agitation started, that the prevailing undercurrent, and I might say surface-current, in the Senate and the House has been that the armor makers have overcharged the Government for armor. The various Boards that have been appointed to investigate the cost of armor plate have one and all run up against a stonewall, because the armor plate manufacturers have refused to give to any

officers connected with the government a true statement,
or in fact, any statement at all as to what their armor cost
them. Personally, I feel that they could not have told us,
because their methods of manufacture were so intimately
connected with the manufacture of commercial articles,
that it was almost impossible to separate them.[3]

From that statement we may guess the answer to the
question, was it all worth it? It is doubtful that many naval
officials five years before would have seen Marvell's point. The
government had gained a yardstick of sorts, a greater appreciation of the hardships, imponderables, and difficult statistical
computations with which it had hounded private industry for
years. If experience is the best teacher, then Marvell's
statement reflects a gaining of knowledge, hence a tempering of
a hard-line viewpoint. If anything, the events from 1913 to 1921
represented an overall tempering of viewpoints. Wilsonian
idealism and the notion of the reintroduction of competition in
order to balance the public welfare with business gain receded
from the lofty campaign platitudes of 1912 and 1913. Wartime
growth of independent entrepreneurs eclipsed the near
monopoly enjoyed by U.S. Steel and reinforced steel executive
commitment to the tenets of New Competition. Wilson had
feared for the result of the Great War and its solidification of
the power of big business, but his administration had tempered
its hard line on armor.

The United States Navy had been in at the beginning, it had
been an important part of the forging of America's industrial
might. Somewhat unsung by later historians, the story of the
navy and the steel industry cut across economics, politics, and
the culture of the time. Experimentation, renegotiation, and
amelioration pervaded the marriage of steel and the navy. From
need came the seeds of a complex. If naval armor no longer
forms the tip of the military-industrial iceberg today, it nonetheless provided its beginning.

Appendix

TABLE 1

APPROPRIATIONS FOR THE NEW NAVY, 22 FEBRUARY 1883–JULY 1921

Year, Congress, Session	Naval Appropriation Acts	Miscellaneous Acts	Total
1883 (42–2)	$16,037,512.23	$882,776.57	$16,920,288.50
1884 (48–1)	8,931,856.12	1,757,293.14	10,689,149.26
1885 (48–2)	21,460,929.54	1,145,386.43	22,606,315.97
1886 (49–1)	16,489,556.72	922,143.49	17,411,700.21
1887 (49–2)	25,786,847.79	37,257.79	25,824,105.58
1888 (50–1)	19,913,281.05	1,034,551.56	20,977,832.61
1889 (50–2)	21,692,510.27	1,963,027.17	23,655,537.44
1890 (51–1)	23,136,035.53	2,318,815.22	25,454,850.75
1891 (51–2)	31,541,645.78	1,234,394.86	32,776,040.64
1892 (52–1)	23,543,266.65	450,972.19	23,944,238.84
1893 (52–2)	22,504,061.38	121,553.68	22,625,615.06
1894 (53–2)	25,366,826.72	325,073.75	25,691,900.47
1895 (53–3)	29,416,077.31	170,578.78	29,586,656.09
1896 (54–1)	30,862,660.95	596,161.18	31,458,822.13
1897 (54–2)	34,128,234.19	705,216.85	34,833,451.04
1897 (55–1)		557,561.02	557,561.02
1898 (55–2)	56,098,783.68	88,458,157.09	144,556,940.77
1899 (55–3)	48,099,969.58	9,197,600.20	57,297,569.78
1900 (56–1)	61,140,916.67	5,808,369.95	66,949,286.62
1901 (56–2)	78,101,791.00	4,918,299.23	83,020,090.23
1902 (57–1)	78,858,761.07	6,488,584.22	85,347,345.29
1903 (57–2)	81,876,791.43	3,116,906.56	84,993,697.99
1904 (58–2)	97,505,140.94	6,347,029.97	103,852,170.91
1905 (58–3)	102,836,679.94	15,623,217.62	118,459,897.56
1906 (59–1)	102,371,670.27	3,443,672.23	105,815,342.50
1907 (59–2)	99,971,449.79	921,982.19	100,893,431.98
1908 (60–1)	122,666,133.27	7,347,020.33	130,013,153.60
1909 (60–2)	136,935,199.05	3,107,456.80	140,042,655.85
1910 (61–2)	131,510,246.01	1,706,447.18	133,216,693.19
1911 (61–3)	126,478,338.24	1,340,984.17	127,819,322.41
1912 (62–2)	128,908,196.96	830,217.99	129,738,414.95
1913 (62–3)	141,050,643.53	1,499,720.94	142,550,364.47
1913 (63–1)		193,802.80	193,802.80
1914 (63–2)	145,503,963.48	2,750,368.93	148,254,332.41
1915 (63–3)	149,763,563.45	1,270,344.58	151,033,908.03
1916 (64–1)	312,888,060.25	5,324,147.52	318,212,207.77
1917 (64–2)	520,553,908.27	203,573.00	520,757,481.27
1917 (65–1)		524,286,603.58	524,286,603.58
1918 (65–2)		653,225,023.06	653,225,023.06
1918 (65–2–3)	1,895,610,070.53	402,557,410.27	2,298,167,480.80
1919 (66–1–2)	613,691,744.88	22,692,149.68	636,383,894.56
1920 (66–2–3) ...... ⎫ 1921 (67–1) .... ⎭	433,211,780.00	341,991,227.17	775,203,007.17
Total	6,016,475,104.52	2,128,873,080.94	8,145,348,185.46

NOTE: Table does not include 3 March 1875 act authorizing expenditures each year of $75,000 from ordnance material sales nor appropriations for clerical and contingent expenses of the Navy Department. Further, all reappropriations warranted by the Treasury Department have been treated the same as new appropriations. Total expenditures for the new navy 1884–1921 inclusive: $7,486,204,201.65.

SOURCE: Elwin A. Silsby, compiler, *Navy Yearbook 1920–1921* (Washington, 1922), p. 805.

TABLE 2

CONTRACT PRICES FOR CLASS A ARMOR (SIDE BELT) 1887–1920

Year	Bethlehem	Carnegie	Midvale
1887	$510		
	545		
1890		$510	
		500	
		525	
		575	
1893	520	575	
	575		
1896	515	565	
	565	515	
1898	400	400	
1899	410	400	
1900	420	420	
1903	420	420	398
1904		420	
1905	420	420	398
1906	346	346	346
1907	420	420	420
1909	420	420	420
1911	420	420	420
1912	420	420	420
1913	454	454	454
			440
1914	425		425
1916	420	425	
1917		425	
1919	520	520	520
1920	525	525	525

SOURCE: Memorandum, Chief of Ordance to Secretary of the Navy, Data on Armor, 24 August 1920, Folder Armor Plate 1920, Box Armor Plate 1921–35, Subject File, Naval Affairs, Josephus Daniels Papers, Library of Congress.

TABLE 3

ARMOR CONTRACTS: BETHLEHEM STEEL COMPANY

Vessels	Authorization Act	Date of Contract	Amount, Tons	Cost per Ton including Royalties
Amphitrite	3 Mar. 1887	1 June 1887	237.17	$604.85
Puritan	3 Mar. 1887	1 June 1887	1,126.46	604.85
Texas (old)	3 Mar. 1887	1 June 1887	1,064.77	604.85
Maine (old)	3 Mar. 1887	1 June 1887	1,221.00	634.85
Monterey	3 Mar. 1887	1 June 1887	174.26	694.85
Oregon	30 June 1890	1 Mar. 1893	899.74	646.41
Massachusetts (old)	30 June 1890	1 June 1887 } 1 Mar. 1893	2,191.25	{ 604.85 646.41
Brooklyn	19 July 1892	1 Mar. 1893	40.73	646.41
Iowa (old)	19 July 1892	1 Mar. 1893	791.63	646.41
Kearsarge	2 Mar. 1895	1 June 1896	2,830.00	547.96
Alabama	10 June 1896	9 June 1898	2,559.00	411.20
Illinois	10 June 1896	3 June 1898	1,406.00	411.20
Maine (new)	4 May 1898	28 Nov. 1900	2,419.00	{ 411.20 453.00
Ohio	4 May 1898	28 Nov. 1900	1,213.00	{ 411.20 453.00
Florida (old)	4 May 1898	4 Oct. 1899	541.44	411.20
Cheyenne (Wyoming)	4 May 1898	4 Oct. 1899	541.44	411.20
Virginia	3 Mar. 1899	28 Nov. 1900	1,948.00	{ 411.20 453.00
Nebraska	3 Mar. 1899	28 Nov. 1900	3,332.00	{ 411.20 453.00
Georgia	3 Mar. 1899	28 Nov. 1900	3,332.00	{ 411.20 453.00
Pennsylvania (old)	3 Mar. 1899	28 Nov. 1900	1,908.00	{ 411.20 453.00
West Virginia	3 Mar. 1899	28 Nov. 1900	954.00	{ 411.20 453.00
Colorado	7 June 1900	28 Nov. 1900	1,908.00	{ 411.20 453.00
Maryland	7 June 1900	28 Nov. 1900	954.00	{ 411.20 453.00
St. Louis	7 June 1900	28 Nov. 1900	365.00	{ 411.20 453.00
Milwaukee	7 June 1900	28 Nov. 1900	731.00	{ 411.20 453.00
Louisiana	1 July 1902	28 Feb. 1903	3,542.00	{ 411.20 453.00
Washington	1 July 1902	28 Feb. 1903	2,190.00	{ 411.20 453.00

TABLE 3 (continued)

Vessels	Authorization Act	Date of Contract	Amount, Tons	Cost per Ton including Royalties
Kansas	3 Mar. 1903	31 Dec. 1903	1,772.00	411.20 / 453.00
Minnesota	3 Mar. 1903	31 Dec. 1903	3,543.00	411.20 / 453.00
New Hampshire	27 Apr. 1904	1 Apr. 1905	3,038.00	411.20 / 453.00
North Carolina	27 Apr. 1904	1 Apr. 1905	1,021.00	411.20 / 453.00
South Carolina	3 Mar. 1905	10 Aug. 1906	1,794.00	345.89
Delaware	29 June 1907	15 Aug. 1907	2,198.00	417.65
North Dakota	2 Mar. 1907	15 Aug. 1907	1,382.00	416.54
Florida	13 May 1908	20 Jan. 1909	1,983.00	422.36
Utah	13 May 1908	20 Jan. 1909	1,154.00	421.99
Arkansas	3 Mar. 1909	27 Sep. 1909	3,946.00	424.25
Wyoming	3 Mar. 1909	27 Sep. 1909	648.00	440.69
Texas	24 June 1910	17 Feb. 1911	2,257.00	432.00
New York	24 June 1910	13 June 1911	2,212.00	430.64
Oklahoma	4 Mar. 1911	15 Jan. 1912	1,899.00	420.00 / 480.00
Nevada	4 Mar. 1911	15 Jan. 1912	3,124.00	460.00 / 508.00
Pennsylvania	22 Aug. 1912	1 Mar. 1913	2,666.00	454.00 / 496.00 / 518.00
Idaho	30 June 1914	6 Nov. 1914 }	16,256.00	425.00 / 486.00 / 466.00 / 376.00
New Mexico	30 June 1914	6 Nov. 1914 }		
California	3 Mar. 1915	11 Apr. 1916 }	60.00	395.00
Tennessee	3 Mar. 1915	11 Apr. 1916 }		
Iowa	29 Aug. 1916 } 1 July 1918 }	29 Oct. 1919 }	21,010.00	520.00 / 581.00 / 555.00
Massachusetts	1 July 1918	29 Oct. 1919 }		
Colorado	29 Aug. 1916	28 Dec. 1916 }	16,021.20	420.00 / 485.00 / 466.00 / 395.00 / 785.00
Washington	29 Aug. 1916	28 Dec. 1916 }		
Lexington	29 Aug. 1916	27 Apr. 1917 }	8,841.00	525.00 / 586.00 / 560.00
Saratoga	29 Aug. 1916	19 May 1920 }		

SOURCE: Elwin A. Silsby, compiler, *Navy Yearbook, 1920–1921* (Washington, 1922), pp. 916–17.

TABLE 4

ARMOR CONTRACTS: CARNEGIE STEEL COMPANY

Vessels	Authorization Act	Date of Contract	Amount, Tons	Cost per Ton including Royalties
Amphitrite	3 Mar. 1887	20 Nov. 1890	427.00	$574.00
Monadnock	3 Mar. 1887	20 Nov. 1890	675.00	574.00
Terror	3 Mar. 1887	20 Nov. 1890	629.00	574.00
Monterey	3 Mar. 1887	20 Nov. 1890	532.00	574.00
New York (old)	7 Sept. 1888	20 Nov. 1890	517.00	574.00
Olympia	7 Sept. 1888	20 Nov. 1890	227.44	599.04
Cincinnati	7 Sept. 1888	20 Nov. 1890	47.00	599.04
Raleigh	7 Sept. 1888	20 Nov. 1890	47.00	599.04
Montgomery	7 Sept. 1888	20 Nov. 1890	22.00	599.04
Detroit	7 Sept. 1888	20 Nov. 1890	22.00	599.04
Marblehead	7 Sept. 1888	20 Nov. 1890	20.00	599.04
Machias	2 Mar. 1889	20 Nov. 1890	20.85	599.04
Castine	2 Mar. 1889	20 Nov. 1890	21.00	599.04
Columbia	30 June 1889	20 Nov. 1890	76.44	599.04
Katahdin	30 June 1889	20 Nov. 1890	775.00	574.00
Oregon	30 June 1889	20 Nov. 1890	1,867.00	574.00
Massachusetts	30 June 1889	20 Nov. 1890 ⎱ 28 Feb. 1893 ⎰	582.00	{ 574.00 671.00
Indiana	30 June 1889	1 Mar. 1893 ⎱ 20 Nov. 1890 ⎰ 28 Feb. 1893 ⎰	2,316.00	{ 605.00 646.00
Minneapolis	2 Mar. 1891	28 Feb. 1893	75.68	657.93
Iowa	19 July 1892	28 Feb. 1893	1,812.00	671.00
Brooklyn	19 July 1892	28 Feb. 1893	661.00	671.00
Nashville	3 Mar. 1893	11 Feb. 1895	37.00	298.15
Helena	3 Mar. 1893	11 Feb. 1895	29.00	304.64
Wilmington	3 Mar. 1893	11 Feb. 1895	29.00	307.61
Kentucky	2 Mar. 1895	1 June 1896	2,830.00	552.50
Illinois	10 June 1896	9 June 1898	1,153.00	411.00
Wisconsin	10 June 1896	9 June 1898	2,559.00	411.20
Ohio	4 May 1898	26 Nov. 1900	1,214.00	{ 411.20 453.00
Missouri	4 May 1898	26 Nov. 1900	2,409.00	{ 411.20 453.00
Arkansas (old)	4 May 1898	30 Aug. 1899	538.00	411.20
Nevada (old)	4 May 1898	30 Aug. 1899	538.00	411.20
Virginia	4 May 1898	26 Nov. 1900	1,384.00	{ 411.20 453.00
West Virginia	4 May 1898	26 Nov. 1900	954.00	{ 411.20 453.00
California	4 May 1898	26 Nov. 1900	1,908.00	{ 411.20 453.00
New Jersey	7 June 1900	26 Nov. 1900	3,332.00	{ 411.20 453.00
Rhode Island	7 June 1900	26 Nov. 1900	3,332.00	{ 411.20 453.00
Maryland	7 June 1900	26 Nov. 1900	954.00	{ 411.20 453.00

TABLE 4 (continued)

Vessels	Authorization Act	Date of Contract	Amount, Tons	Cost per Ton including Royalties
South Dakota	7 June 1900	26 Nov. 1900	1,908.00	411.20 / 453.00
St. Louis	7 June 1900	26 Nov. 1900	365.00	411.20 / 453.00
Charleston	7 June 1900	26 Nov. 1900	731.00	411.20 / 453.00
Connecticut	1 July 1902	28 Feb. 1903	3,542.00	411.20 / 453.00
Tennessee	1 July 1902	28 Feb. 1903	2,190.00	411.20 / 453.00
Vermont	3 Mar. 1903	9 Jan. 1904	3,543.00	411.20 / 453.00
Kansas	3 Mar. 1903	9 Jan. 1904	1,772.00	411.20 / 453.00
Montana	27 Apr. 1904	3 Apr. 1905	1,921.00	411.20 / 453.00
South Carolina	3 Mar. 1905	13 Aug. 1906	1,865.00	345.95
Delaware	29 June 1906	22 July 1907	2,491.00	416.35
North Dakota	2 Mar. 1907	22 July 1907	1,047.00	418.36
Florida	13 May 1908	6 Jan. 1909	977.00	422.20
Utah	13 May 1908	6 Jan. 1909	2,176.00	423.07
Arkansas	3 Mar. 1909	13 Sept. 1909	1,098.00	420.00
Wyoming	3 Mar. 1909	13 Sept. 1909	3,506.00	420.68
Texas	24 June 1910	10 Feb. 1911	2,207.00	431.44
New York	24 June 1910	10 Feb. 1911	2,323.00	426.69
Nevada	4 Mar. 1911	15 Jan. 1912	4,540.00	420.00
Oklahoma	4 Mar. 1911	15 Jan. 1912	591.00	480.00 / 460.00 / 508.00
Pennsylvania	22 Aug. 1912	1 Mar. 1913	2,683.00	454.00 / 496.00 / 518.00
Tennessee / California	3 Mar. 1915	7 Apr. 1916	15,901.20	486.00 / 460.00 / 425.00
Maryland / West Virginia	29 Aug. 1916	2 Jan. 1917	15,901.20	486.00 / 460.00 / 425.00
Indiana / Montana	20 Aug. 1916 / 4 Mar. 1917	27 Oct. 1919	17,910.00	520.00 / 581.00 / 555.00
Constellation	20 Aug. 1916 / 4 Mar. 1917	11 Apr. 1917	11,788.00	525.00 / 586.00 / 560.00
Ranger	20 Aug. 1916 / 4 Mar. 1917	18 May 1920		

SOURCE: Elwin A. Silsby, compiler. *Navy Yearbook, 1920–1921* (Washington, 1922), pp. 917–18.

TABLE 5

ARMOR CONTRACTS: OTHER COMPANIES

Midvale Steel Company

Vessels	Authorization Act	Contract Date	Amount, Tons	Cost per Ton including Royalties
Mississippi	3 Mar. 1903	15 Dec. 1903	3,090.00	$385.00 / 398.00
Idaho	3 Mar. 1903	15 Dec. 1903	3,090.00	385.00 / 398.00
New Hampshire	27 Apr. 1904	5 Apr. 1905	504.00	385.00 / 398.00
North Carolina	27 Apr. 1904	5 Apr. 1905	269.00	385.00 / 398.00
Montana	27 Apr. 1904	5 Apr. 1905	269.00	385.00 / 398.00
Michigan	3 Mar. 1905	6 Aug. 1906	3,660.00	345.92
North Dakota	2 Mar. 1907	29 Aug. 1907	2,259.00	406.56
Florida	13 May 1908	14 Jan. 1909	1,748.00	420.73
Utah	13 May 1908	14 Jan. 1909	1,380.00	418.31
Arkansas	3 Mar. 1909	10 Sept. 1909	1,445.00	422.19
Wyoming	3 Mar. 1909	10 Sept. 1909	2,341.00	421.91
Texas	24 June 1910	20 Feb. 1911	2,274.00	426.71
New York	24 June 1910	2 June 1911	2,202.00	435.05
Oklahoma	4 Mar. 1911	15 Jan. 1912	5,189.00	420.00 / 480.00 / 460.00 / 508.00
Pennsylvania	22 Aug. 1912	1 Mar. 1913	2,723.00	454.00 / 518.00 / 496.00
Arizona	4 Mar. 1913	17 Nov. 1913 / 20 May 1914	252.00	440.00 / 504.00 / 471.00

TABLE 5 (continued)

Vessels	Authorization Act	Date of Contract	Amount, Tons	Cost per Ton including Royalties
Midvale Steel Company (continued)				
Mississippi	30 June 1914	7 Nov. 1914	8,128.00	425.00 486.00 466.00 376.00
Tennessee ⎫ California ⎭	3 Mar. 1915	12 Apr. 1916	60.00	376.00
Maryland	29 Aug. 1916	2 Jan. 1917	58.00	385.00
South Dakota	29 Aug. 1916 ⎱ 4 Mar. 1917 ⎰	28 Oct. 1919 ⎱		520.00 581.00 555.00
			21,010.00	
North Carolina	29 Aug. 1916 1 July 1918	28 Oct. 1919 28 Oct. 1919 ⎰		
Constitution ⎫ Saratoga ⎭	1 July 1918	18 Apr. 1917 ⎱ 4 June 1920 ⎰	8,841.00	525.00 586.00 560.00
Pittsburgh Screw & Bolt Company				
Maryland	29 Aug. 1916	8 Mar. 1917	2.00	$2,240.00
West Virginia	29 Aug. 1916	8 Mar. 1917	60.00	548.80 2,240.00
Constellation	29 Aug. 1916	12 Apr. 1917	30.00	548.80 2,240.00
Ranger	29 Aug. 1916	12 Apr. 1917	30.00	548.80 2,240.00
Constitution	4 Mar. 1917	12 Apr. 1917	1.30	2,240.00
Carbon Steel Company				
Arizona	4 Mar. 1913	10 Oct. 1913	61.00	$448.00

SOURCE: Elwin A. Silsby, compiler. *Navy Yearbook 1920–1921* (Washington, 1922), pp. 918–19.

TABLE 6

ARMOR CONTRACTS FOR INCREASE OF NAVY, 1887–1915

Contract	Tons	Cost	Average Price per Ton
Bethlehem Steel Company			
18: 1 June 1887	6,891.00	$4,168,000.00	$604.85
48: 1 Mar. 1893	3,882.00	2,510,000.00	646.41
71: 1 June 1896	2,800.00	1,534,272.00	547.96
100: 9 June 1898	3,965.00	1,586,000.00	400.00
132: 4 Oct. 1899	1,142.00	456,800.00	400.00
141:28 Nov. 1900	18,588.00	7,684,700.00	413.42
165:28 Feb. 1903	5,798.00	2,386,440.00	411.60
189:31 Dec. 1903	5,372.00	2,239,640.00	416.91
202: 1 Apr. 1905	4,959.00	2,038,780.00	411.13
246:10 Aug. 1906	1,824.00	630,813.00	345.84
282:15 Aug. 1907	3,579.00	1,493,240.00	417.22
319:20 Jan. 1909	3,137.00	1,324,502.00	422.22
347:27 Sept. 1909	4,594.00	1,959,643.00	426.57
387:17 Feb. 1911	2,257.00	977,221.00	432.97
398:13 June 1911	2,212.00	952,573.00	430.64
421:15 Jan. 1912	5,022.00	2,160,384.00	430.18
447: 1 Mar. 1913	2,669.00	1,242,901.00	465.68
483: 6 Nov. 1914	16,256.00	6,975,320.00	429.09
: 3 Mar. 1915	60.00	23,700.00	395.00
	95,007.00	$42,344,937.00	$445.70
Carnegie Steel Company			
28:20 Nov. 1890	6,054.00	$3,475,000.00	$574.00
47:28 Feb. 1893	3,120.00	2,094,000.00	671.15
70: 1 June 1896	3,073.00	1,697,808.00	552.50
99: 3 June 1898	3,712.00	1,484,800.00	400.00
131:30 Aug. 1899	1,134.00	453,600.00	400.00
140:26 Nov. 1900	18,588.00	7,684,700.00	413.42
164:28 Feb. 1903	5,666.00	2,333,640.00	411.87
186: 9 Jan. 1904	5,258.00	2,194,040.00	417.26
203: 3 Apr. 1905	1,921.00	772,660.00	402.22
248:13 Aug. 1906	1,865.00	645,206.00	345.95
284:22 Jul. 1907	3,538.00	1,475,140.00	416.94
320: 6 Jan. 1909	3,153.00	1,333,095.00	422.80
344:13 Sept. 1909	4,604.00	1,936,065.00	420.52
386:10 Feb. 1911	2,207.00	952,180.00	471.44
392:25 May 1911	2,323.00	991,200.00	423.69
420:15 Jan. 1912	5,123.00	2,194,572.00	427.63

TABLE 6 (continuted)

Contract	Tons	Cost	Average Price per Ton
	Carnegie Steel Company (continued)		
448:28 Feb. 1913	2,684.00	1,236,671.00	460.76
3 Mar. 1915	15,901.20	6,829,100.00	429.47
	89,933.20	39,783,497.00	$442.36
	Midvale Steel Company		
182:15 Dec. 1903	6,180.00	$2,453,422.00	$396.39
204: 5 Apr. 1905	1,041.00	411,972.00	395.74
247: 6 Aug. 1906	3,690.00	1,276,363.00	345.89
285:29 Aug. 1907	2,259.00	941,020.00	416.56
321:14 Jan. 1909	3,128.00	1,312,706.00	419.66
343:10 Sept. 1909	3,786.00	1,597,756.00	422.02
388:20 Feb. 1911	2,274.00	970,349.00	426.71
395: 2 June 1911	2,202.00	957,985.00	435.05
419:15 Jan. 1912	5,189.00	2,218,656.00	427.57
446: 1 Mar. 1913	2,723.00	1,262,645.00	463.70
465:17 Nov. 1913	7,739.00	3,462,760.00	447.44
485: 7 Nov. 1914	8,128.00	3,487,664.00	429.09
: 3 Mar. 1915	60.00	22,560.00	376.00
	48,399.00	20,375,858.00	420.99
	Carbon Steel Company		
464:10 Oct. 1913	61.00	$27,328.00	$448.00
	Totals–Aggregate		
Bethlehem	95,007.00	$42,344,937.00	$445.70
Carnegie	89,933.20	39,783,497.00	442.36
Midvale	48,399.00	20,375,858.00	420.99
Carbon Steel	61.00	27,328.00	448.00
	233,400.20	$102,531,620.00	$439.29

NOTE: The average price per ton is an average of the prices of the various classes of armor, not of any one class.

SOURCE: Secretary of the Navy to Hon. Clyde H. Tavenner, 26 January and 11 December 1915, Folder 1914–15, Box Armor Plate, 1914–17, Josephus Daniels papers, Library of Congress.

TABLE 7

Foreign Prices for Armor Plate

Year		Japan	Austria	Italy	Germany	France	Great Britain	United States	Russia
1906	a.	$400.00	$449.00	$521.00	$450.00	$569.00	$626.00	$345.92	
	b.	400.00	557.00	550.00	450.00	572.00	681.00	346.00	
1907	a.	400.00	449.00	521.00	450.00	569.00	626.00	416.97	
	b.	400.00	557.00	550.00	450.00	572.00	681.00	420.00 class-A	
1908	a.	400.00	449.00	521.00	450.00	569.00	626.00	421.57	
	b.	400.00	557.00	550.00	450.00	572.00	681.00	420.00 class-A	
1909	a.	400.00	449.00	521.00	450.00	569.00	626.00	423.00	
	b.	400.00	557.00	550.00	450.00	572.00	681.00	420.00 class-A	
1911	a.	400.00	449.00	521.00	450.00	569.00	525.00	430.00	
	b.	400.00	557.00	550.00	450.00	572.00	525.00	426.00 class-A	
1913	a.	490.00	729.00	444.00		598.00	693.00	518.00	510.00
	b.	490.00	511.00*	405.00*	490.00	460.00*	503.00*	454.00	368.00*
1915	a.	490.00	729.00	444.00		598.00	691.00	496.00	510.00
	b.	490.00	511.00	405.00	490.00	460.00	503.00	425.00	368.00
1917–18	a.	490.00	729.00	444.00		598.00	691.00	496.00	510.00
	b.	490.00	511.00	405.00	490.00	460.00	503.00	425.00	368.00
1919	a.	490.00	729.00	444.00		598.00	691.00	496.00	510.00
	b.	490.00	511.00	405.00	490.00	460.00	503.00	425.00	368.00
1920–21	a.	490.00	729.00	444.00		598.00	691.00		510.00
	b.	490.00	511.00	405.00	490.00	460.00	503.00		368.00

*Doubtful, from unofficial sources.

SOURCE: Various compilers, *Navy Yearbook*, 1906-21, pp. 562, 600, 641, 674, 761, 842, 541, 827, 804, 919.

Notes

Introduction

1. Examples of the "traditionalist" approach are: Frank M. Bennett, *Steam Navy of the United States: A History of the Growth of the Steam Vessel of War in the U.S. Navy, and of the Naval Engineer Corps* . . . ; Harold and Margaret Sprout, *The Rise of American Naval Power, 1776–1918;* George T. Davis, *A Navy Second to None;* and even Samuel P. Huntington, *The Soldier and the State.* "Revisionist" interpretation begins with Robert Seager II, "Ten Years before Mahan: The Unofficial Case for the New Navy, 1880–1890," *Mississippi Valley Historical Review* 40 (December 1953):491–512; and includes John D. Alden, *The American Steel Navy;* as well as Lance C. Buhl, "Mariners and Machines: Resistance to Technological Change in the American Navy, 1865–1869," *Journal of American History* 61 (December 1974):703–27.

2. See Merritt Roe Smith, *Harpers Ferry and the New Technology;* and Gaddis Smith, *Britain's Clandestine Submarines, 1914–1915.* New trends among business historians include Joseph Frazier Wall, *Andrew Carnegie;* Robert Hessen, *Steel Titan: The Life of Charles M. Schwab;* and Melvin I. Urofsky, *Big Steel and the Wilson Administration;* although some newer steel accounts still neglect the military

link; for example, Peter Temin, *Iron and Steel in Nineteenth Century America: An Economic Inquiry;* William T. Hogan, S.J., *An Economic History of the Iron and Steel Industry in the United States;* and Duncan Burn, *The Economic History of Steelmaking 1867–1939: A Study in Competition.*

3.   D.D. Porter to C.S. Boutelle, 3 January 1890 Case 6172, Selected Letters Received, Secretary of the Navy, 1890, RG 80, General Records of Navy Department, NARS.

4.   Dean Allard, "The Influence of the United States Navy Upon the American Steel Industry, 1880–1900," M.A. thesis, Georgetown University, 1959; and Walter I. Brandt, "Steel and the New Navy, 1882–1893," Ph.D. dissertation, University of Wisconsin, 1920.

Chapter 1

1.   The general background for the post-Civil War era in light of modern scholarship can best be followed in John A. Garraty, *The New Commonwealth, 1877–1890;* Robert Wiebe, *The Search for Order, 1877–1920;* Foster Rhea Dulles, *Prelude to World Power: American Diplomatic History, 1860–1900;* John A.S. Grenville and George B. Young, *Politics, Strategy, and American Diplomacy: Studies in Foreign Policy, 1873–1917;* Milton Plesur, *America's Outward Thrust, Approaches to Foreign Affairs 1865–1890;* Rembert W. Patrick, *The Reconstruction of the Nation;* and bibliographic/interpretive essays such as those by Walter T.K. Nugent, J. Carroll Moody, and Daniel M. Smith on politics, economics, and diplomacy during this period in William H. Cartwright and Richard L. Watson, eds. *The Reinterpretation of American History and Culture.*

2.   Concerns of business and military professionals in this period may be gleaned from Samuel P. Huntington, *The Soldier and the State,* 222–270; Walter Millis, *Arms and Men,* chapter 3; Thomas C. Cochran, *Business in American Life: A History,* part 3; Edward W. Sloan, *Benjamin Franklin Isherwood, Naval Engineer: The Years as Engineer in Chief, 1861–1869,* 65.

3. On U.S. naval buildup and modernization during the Civil War, see John Niven, *Gideon Welles, Lincoln's Secretary of the Navy*, 506–7.

4. *Annual Report, Secretary of the Navy, 1877,* 33–34; *1874,* 199; Walter I. Brandt, "Steel and the New Navy, 1882–1893," Ph.D. dissertation, University of Wisconsin, 1920, chapter 1; John D. Long, "The Birth of the New Navy," *Outlook,* September 1902, 490–91.

5. The essential ambivalence of professionals in this period and consequent difficulty for understanding by later analysts was appropriately discerned by Millis, *Arms and Men,* 133–34, 145–46; and Peter Karsten, *The Naval Aristocracy,* chapter 6.

6. Studies of foreign navies in this period can best be traced in Arthur Marder, *The Anatomy of British Sea Power,* part 1; Theodore Ropp, "The Development of a Modern Navy, French Naval Policy, 1871–1904," Ph.D. dissertation Harvard University, 1937; and Jonathan Steinberg, *Yesterday's Deterrent: Tirpitz and the Birth of the German Battle Fleet.* For a useful overview, see Clark G. Reynolds, *Command of the Sea,* chapter 13.

7. On Porter's contribution, compare Lance C. Buhl, "Mariners and Machines: Resistance to Technological Change in the American Navy, 1865–1869," *Journal of American History,* 61 no. 3 (December 1974): 703–27; and Kenneth P. Hagen, "Admiral David Dixon Porter, Strategist for a Navy in Transition," *Proceedings of the United States Naval Institute* (USNIP) 94 (July 1968): 140–43.

8. Karsten, *Naval Aristocracy,* 65–69, 95, 292, 327–29, 355–61, 380.

9. Elting E. Morison, *Men, Machines, and Modern Times,* chapters 2 and 6 especially.

10. Virtually no recent American scholarship adequately integrates the numerous and confusing aspects of technology and national defense. The closest approach is Brandt, "Steel and the New Navy," chapters 1–3; Emanuel Raymond Lewis, *Seacoast Fortifications of the United States: An Introductory History,* 66–89; H. Garbett, *Naval Gunnery,* chapters 2–4; and Peter Padfield, *Guns at Sea,* chapters 24–28.

11. Garbett, *Naval Gunnery,* vii–viii; Rogers Birnie, *Gun Making in the United States,* chapters 1–4.

12. U.S. Navy Department, *Annual Report, 1882,* Chief of Ordnance report, 243; U.S. Congress, 38th, 2d session, Sen. Rept. 121, *Report of the Joint Committee on the Conduct of the War on Heavy Ordnance (CCW),* 1–7, 12–13, 90–91, 124–26, 169–71; and U.S. Congress, 49th,

1st session, Sen. Rept. 90, *Report of the Select Committee on Ordnance and Warships*, xxiii.

13.   Such a philosophy may be found in such period reports as Report of Chief of Naval Ordnance, *Annual Report, SN, 1882*, 220; Report of Whitely Heavy Ordnance Board, *Annual Report, Secretary of War, 1872*, 326–484 inter alia; U.S. Cong., 44th, 2d session, Sen. Ex. Doc. 27, *Report of Chief Engineer J.W. King, USN on European Ships of War*, 29, 156, 157; and U.S. Cong., 48th, 2d session, Ex. Doc. 13, *Report of the Gun Foundry Board*, 16 February 1884, 15 ff.

14.   William H. Jaques, *Modern Armor For National Defense*, 3.

15.   U.S. Cong., 44th, 2d sess., Sen. Ex. Doc. 27, *Report of Chief Engineer J.W. King*, 31, 61; Frank Bennett, *Steam Navy of the United States*, 1: 280.

16.   U.S. Cong., 49th, 1st sess., Sen. Rpt. 90, *Report of the Senate Committee on Ordnance and Warships*, 24–28, 48, 210.

17.   These "promisory contracts" were not authorized by Congress and each one contained the proviso that no money should be paid until appropriated by that body. See U.S. Cong., 45th, 2d sess., House Rept. 112, *Investigation of the Navy Department*, 1878, 4; *Annual Report, SN, 1883*, 6; and *Army and Navy Journal*, 27 September 1879, 141, 11 October 1879, 182–83, 29 November 1879, 324.

18.   For detailed accounts of the development of the steel industry, see Peter Temin, *Iron and Steel in Nineteenth Century America* and William T. Hogan, *Economic History of the Iron and Steel Industry in the United States*. Useful synopses with relevance to the U.S. Navy appear in Dean Allard, "The Influence of the United States Navy upon the American Steel Industry," 6–14; Edward C. Kirkland, *Industry Comes of Age*, 165–66; and John W. Oliver, *History of American Technology*, 315–29.

19.   U.S. Cong., 46th, 2nd sess., *Congressional Record*, 10, pt. 3: 2410 ff, 2441; and 3d sess., 11, pt. 3: 2205.

20.   Original records of the board including report, journal, and correspondence are in entry 199, Report of Naval Advisory Board, RG 45, National Archives and Records Service (NARS), while the published version of the report appears in *Annual Report, SN, 1881*, 27–81.

21.   Ibid., 29–30, 37–38; Allard, "Influence of the Navy," 16.

22.   See minority members' views in published Advisory Board, *Annual Report, SN, 1881*, 39–46, as well as notes of meeting of House and Senate Naval Affairs Committees with the Rodgers board, printed

in U.S. Cong., 47th, 1st sess., House Rept. 653, *Construction of Vessels for the Navy*, 200–205. On Pusey and Jones development see 376 ff. of published advisory board report and J.G.B. Hutchins, *The American Maritime Industries and Public Policy*, 456–57.

23. Advisory Board, *Annual Report, SN, 1881*, 7.

24. Ibid., 33, 36.

25. Report of the Naval Advisory Board on Mild Steel printed in *Annual Report, SN, 1885*, 29, 34, 111, 118, 376 ff.

26. For full text of bill as introduced see *Army and Navy Journal*, 4 March 1882; committee changes are reflected in U.S. Cong., 47th, 1st sess., House Rept. 1433, 696; the floor debate is found in U.S. Cong., 47th, 1st sess., *Congressional Record*, 13, pt. 6, 23 June–25 July 1882, and pt. 7, 25 July–8 August 1882: 5452–6969 inter alia; and the final law is contained in U.S. *Statutes at Large*, 22: 291.

27. See "Discussion: The Use of Iron and Steel in the Construction of Vessels of War," USNI-Boston Branch, 28 February 1882, *USNIP*, 13 (1882): 267–84.

28. Rodgers–E. Simpson, "A Proposed Armament For the Navy," Ibid., 7 (1882): 81.

Chapter 2

1. Secretary of the Navy, *Annual Report, 1882*, 40; Chandler's personal papers in the Library of Congress portray the politician more than the administrator. The latter emerges in Leonard Swann, *John Roach, Maritime Entrepreneur*, 170–71.

2. Roach–Chandler, 5 June 1882, vol. 53, Chandler papers, LC.

3. Swann, *John Roach*, 171; John D. Long, *The New American Navy*, 1; 29–30; and compare William Brinker, "Robert W. Shufeldt and the Changing Navy," Ph.D. dissertation, 1973, 182, with Kenneth J. Hagen, *American Gunboat Diplomacy and the Old Navy, 1877–1889*.

4. *Army and Navy Journal* 20 (1882–1883), 11 November 1882; U.S. Cong., 47th, 2d sess., House Ex. Doc. 32, *Report of Naval Advisory Board*, 1–2. Original journals, correspondence, and report may be

found with entry 172, Record Group 80, National Archives and Records Service (NARS).

5. U.S. Cong., 47th, 2d sess., House, *Congressional Record*, 14, pt. 2, 1548–68 inter alia; pt. 4, 3101–16.

6. *Navy Yearbook, 1914*, 11 ff; SN, *Annual Report, 1883*, 54–56.

7. See correspondence in Naval Advisory Board records, Box 1, RG 80, NARS.

8. Swann, *John Roach*, 176–77.

9. R. Gatewood, compiler, Report of Naval Advisory Board on Mild Steel, pt. 1, 13–29, NAB Records, NARS; also Dean Allard, "Influence of U.S. Navy Upon American Steel Industry, 1880–1900," M.A. thesis, 1959, 26–28; SN, *Annual Report, 1883*, 54–56.

10. Gause–Chandler, 19 July 1883, v. 63, Chandler papers, LC.

11. Swann, *John Roach*, 181–82; Shufeldt–Chandler correspondence, 28 July, 4 August, Roach–Chandler, 6, 13 August, all 1883, all vol. 63, Chandler papers, LC; and Long, *The New American Navy*, 1: 32–33.

12. SN, *Annual Report, 1884*, esp. 6, 232. The report included various Shufeldt board communications from 1882 through 1883.

13. Ibid.

14. Ibid., 9, 410, 415, 416.

15. Ibid., 415; *1885*, vii.

16. Walter I. Brandt, "Steel and the New Navy, 1882–1893," Ph.D. dissertation, 1920, 43–44.

17. Anderson, Du Puy and Co.–Simpson, 22 May 1883, appendix G in U.S. Cong., 48th, 1st sess., House Ex. Doc. 97, *Report of Gun Foundry Board (GFB Report)*, 57. See also report of proceedings 72–89, Simpson–Chandler 19 May 1883 with reports of GFB, Record Group 45, NARS, and for foreign tour reports, see, W.H. Jaques–Chandler 5, 11, 18 August and 1, 7 September, all 1883, vol. 63, Chandler papers, LC.

18. Krupp–Simpson correspondence 30 July–17 September 1883, 63–67, and Board proceedings, 73–89 in *GFB Report*.

19. Allard, "Influence," 50–51.

20. *GFB Report*, 46–47.

21. Ibid., 48.

22. Ibid., appendices H, J, N, 57–59, 61–63.

23. Allard, "Influence," 54–55.

24. Edward Simpson, "The Navy and Its Prospects of Rehabilita-

tion," *U.S. Naval Institute Proceedings*, 12, no. 1, (1886): 20–22.

25.   See U.S. Cong., 48th, 1st and 2d sess., *Congressional Record*, 15, pts. 1–6: 1425–26, 1453–56, 1459, 1481.

26.   Ibid., pt. 2: 1382.

27.   Ibid.

28.   Ibid., pt. 2: 1424, also 1430, 1462, 2759–64, 2806, 2927; pt. 6: 6159–64.

29.   Swann, *John Roach*, 189–208 inter alia; correspondence on the *Dolphin* may be followed in vols. 69–71 in Chandler papers, LC.

30.   SN, *Annual Report, 1884*, 3, 4; also Church–Chandler, 6 December 1884, and H.C. Lodge–Chandler, 10 December 1884, both vol. 71 as well as W.H. Beeler–Chandler 26 December 1884, vol. 72, all Chandler papers, LC.

31.   SN, *Annual Report, 1884*, 9, 10–11, 30–31.

32.   See Supplementary Gun Foundry Board Report, Ibid., 3, 345–82; also Hale–Chandler, n.d. [December 1884], vol. 72, Chandler papers, LC.

33.   *Navy Yearbook, 1918*, 29–38; post election debates appear in *Congressional Record*, 16, pt. 1: especially 39–40, 67, 305–13, 327–28, 359–62, 395–410, 610–12, 685–86; pt. 2: 1019–20, 1041–42; pt. 3: 1910–20, 1967–74, 2036–3041, 2228–31.

34.   Simpson–Chandler, 10 August 1885, vol. 73, Chandler papers, LC.

35.   W.H. Jaques, "The Establishment of Steel Gun Factories in the United States," 10, no. 4 (1884): 532–868; and Edward W. Very, "The Development of Armor for Naval Use," 9, no. 3 (1883): 349–583, both in *U.S. Naval Institute Proceedings*.

36.   Very–Chandler, 13 May, 3 October, both 1884, vols. 68–70; Simpson–Chandler, 19 July 1884, vol. 69, all Chandler papers, LC.

37.   Allard, "Influence of the Navy," 33.

Chapter 3

1.   On Whitney, see Mark D. Hirsch, *William C. Whitney, Modern Warwick*, especially 277–88; and Leonard Swann, *John Roach*,

240 / GRAY STEEL AND BLUE WATER NAVY

Maritime Entrepreneur, chapter 9.

2. In addition to Hirsch and Swann, see Secretary of the Navy (SN), *Annual Report, 1885*, 217–22, 290–365; U.S. Cong., 49th, 1st sess., Sen. Ex. Doc. 153, *Information Relative to Chicago, Boston, Atlanta, Dolphin*, especially 1, 36, 158, 161.

3. Walter R. Herrick, Jr., *The American Naval Revolution*, 35–36; B. Franklin Cooling, *Benjamin Franklin Tracy*, 74–76, 103, 123.

4. *New York Herald*, 9 May 1889; SN, *Annual Report, 1886*, 5; Hirsch, *Whitney*, 297, 323.

5. See U.S. Cong., 49th, 1st sess., House Rept. 1450, Commission on Ordnance and Gunnery, *Report of the Commission*, 1886 (Randall Report); U.S. Cong., 49th, 1st sess., Sen. Rept. 90, Select Committee on Ordnance and Warships, *Report*, 1886 (Hawley); U.S. Cong. 49th, 1st sess., House Doc. 49, *Report of the Board on Fortifications or Other Defenses*, 1886 (Endicott Board Report).

6. Randall Report, ii, iv, vi, 10 as well as Samuel J. Randall–Whitney, 9 April 1887, vol. 43, Whitney papers, Library of Congress (LC); Hawley Report, xiv–xxx inter alia; U.S. Cong. 48th, 2d sess., House Doc. 70, *Estimates for Building a Government Gun Factory*, 1885 (Gun Factory Report), 300; Endicott Board Report, 5–10, 13–15, 23, 26–29, 260–65. Indicative of this board's sweeping study were separate committee studies of armor and ordnance, torpedoes and torpedo boats, warships (armament, armor, draught), navigable draught of American forts and harbors, capacity of country to furnish armor and guns, floating batteries (coast defense vessels), and gun carriages.

7. GFB Report, 376–77; *Bulletin of Iron and Steel Association*, 19 (1885): 5: 36, 45, 349; and Edward Simpson, "The Navy and Its Prospects of Rehabilitation," *Proceedings of the United States Naval Institute*, 12, no. 1 (1886): 25.

8. SN, *Annual Report, 1885*, vii–ix, xxvii–xli, 252–66, 273–90.

9. In addition to Simpson, "The Navy and Its Prospects of Rehabilitation," 1–39; see William Bainbridge Hoff, "A View of Our Naval Policy and a Discussion of Its Factors," 121–33; F.M. Barber, "A Practical Method of Arriving at the Number, Size, Type, Rig, and Cost of the Vessels of Which the U.S. Navy Should Consist in Time of Peace," 418–22, all volume 12 of the *Naval Institute Proceedings (USNIP)*; and W.H. Jaques, "Memorandum to the Secretary," n.d. [December 1885?] volume 29, Whitney papers, LC.

10.   On foreign plan negotiations see Chadwick–Whitney, 20 September and Jaques–Whitney, 21 September, both 1885, vol. 24; Chadwick–Whitney, 24, 26, and 29 September, 3 October 1885, vol. 25; and Scott–Whitney, 2 July 1886, vol. 35, all Whitney papers, LC; also SN, *Annual Report, 1885*, xvii–xviii.

11.   Debates on increasing the naval establishment in 1886 may be followed in U.S. Cong., 49th, 1st sess., *Congressional Record*, 17, pt. 7: 7476–503; pt. 8: 7742–43, 7855–58.

12.   Knight, *Navy Yearbook, 1913*, 49–51.

13.   On Wharton see W. Ross Yates, "Joseph Wharton's Nickel Business," *Pennsylvania Magazine of History and Biography* 101, no. 3 (July 1977): 287–321; also Wharton–Randall, 12 June 1886, vol. 34, and Francis Wharton–Whitney, 21 July enclosing letters from his father, 17 July, and J. Wharton–H. Schneider, 25 June 1886, vol. 35, all Whitney papers, LC.

14.   Dean Allard, "The Influence of the United States Navy upon the American Steel Industry," 73–74.

15.   Wharton–Randall, 12 June, vol. 34, Wharton–Whitney, 29 July, vol. 36, and Schneider–Wharton ?June, vol. 35, all 1886, all Whitney papers, LC.

16.   Draft, "To Manufacturers of American Steel," 16 August 1886 and Draft Circular, "New Cruisers and Gun Boats of the United States Navy, 16 August 1886, both vol. 36; and Additional Notice, October 1886, vol. 38, all Whitney papers, LC.

17.   Wharton–Whitney, 7 September; Remey–Whitney, 11 September, both 1886, both vol. 37, Whitney papers, LC; SN, *Annual Report, 1886*, 9.

18.   Wharton–Whitney, 18, 22 September 1886, vol. 37, Whitney papers, LC.

19.   Chadwick–Whitney, 28 September, 1 December, vol. 37, 38 respectively, G.A. Oates–Whitney, 15 December, vol. 39, G.W. Bennett–Whitney, 26 October and John Ericsson–Whitney, 4 November, vol. 38, all 1886, all Whitney papers, LC.

20.   Barber–Chandler, 6, 11 November, 1886, vol. 75, Chandler papers, LC.

21.   Church–Whitney, 8 December 1886, vol. 38, Whitney papers, LC.

22.   Hirsch, *Whitney*, 325–26.

23.   SN, *Annual Report, 1886*, 8–9, 11–12.

24. Hirsch, *Whitney*, 301; also Walter I. Brandt, "Steel and the New Navy," 68–71.

25. Whitney–President, Midvale Steel, 5 December 1886, vol. 38, Whitney papers, LC.

26. Carnegie–Whitney, 8 December 1886, vol. 39, Whitney papers, LC.

27. Carnegie–Whitney, 27 December 1886, vol. 39; 28 February, 9 March 1887, vol. 41; see also Whitney–Herbert, 25 January, vol. 40 and February [1887] vol. 41; Wharton–Whitney, 21 January, vol. 40, 1 February, vol. 41, 14, 16 March, vol. 42, all 1887; and Whitney–Wharton, 5 December 1886, Letterbook 4, vol. 40, all Whitney papers LC.

28. Allard, "Influence," 79–80; also Barber–Whitney, 18 March 1887, vol. 42, and 6 August 1886, vol. 46, both Whitney papers, LC.

29. Jaques–Chandler, 16 November 1883, vol. 64, Chandler papers; Jaques–Whitney, 21 September 1885, vol. 34; Wharton–Whitney, 8 September 1886, Whitney papers, LC; also Allard, "Influence," 80–81.

30. SN, *Annual Report, 1887*, 460, 466–72, 474; Wharton–Whitney, 23 March and R.W. Davenport–Whitney, 4, 22 March 1887, vol. 42; Powell Stackhouse–Whitney, 23 March 1887, vol. 41, all Whitney papers, LC. For copies of armor contract, Folder 2, Misc. Data, Subject File BR-Armor, Subject Files 1774–1910 (1860–1910), Naval Records Collection of Office of Naval Records and Library, RG 45, NARS.

31. Hirsch, *Whitney*, 328–29; SN, *Annual Report, 1887*, 235–36, 257–63.

32. See *Congressional Record* 18: 1214–17, 1429–31, 1710–14, 1805–14, 1856–57.

33. SN, *Annual Report, 1887*, iii–viii, xxvii, xxviii–xxxix.

34. Hirsch, *Whitney*, 335; Cramp–Whitney, 22 March 1888, vol. 55, Whitney papers, LC.

35. Clippings attached to E. Summer–Whitney, 2 April, vol. 52; on search for superintendent, W. Vollmer–Whitney, 19 April, vol. 52; on construction problems, W. Malson–Whitney, 28 April, vol. 52; Commandant, NY Navy Yard–SN, 10 May, vol. 53; Commandant Norfolk Navy Yard–SN, 21 June, vol. 53, all Whitney papers, LC.

36. Wharton–Whitney, 18 October, 16 November, vol. 56; 6 December, vol. 57; R.H. Sayre–Whitney, 9 September, vol. 55, all

1886, all Whitney papers, LC.

37.   Pulsifer, *Navy Yearbook, 1908*, 81–82.

38.   *Congressional Record*, 19: 5150–59, 5675–78, 5709–36, 6118–32; 20: 2492–95.

39.   SN, *Annual Report, 1888*, iii–ix. *Philadelphia Press*, 3 February, *Philadelphia Public Ledger* 14, 15 February, all 1888.

40.   Pulsifer, *Navy Yearbook, 1908*, 99–100.

41.' Frank Bennett, *Steam Navy of the United States*, 805–6.

42.   SN, *Annual Report, 1887*, 368; *1888*, 297; *1889*, 15, 526–27; *1890*, 7; *1892*, 3.

43.   Ibid., *1890*, 249; *1891*, 223; Stephen L. Goodale, *Chronology of Iron and Steel*, 212; W.H. Jaques, "The Establishment of Steel Gun Factories in the United States," *USNIP* 10, no. 1 (1884): 158.

44.   "American Steel For The New Cruisers," *USNIP* 13, no. 3 (1887): 496–97; Allard, "Influence," 86–89; W. Paul Strassman, *Risk and Technological Innovation: American Manufacturing Methods during the Nineteenth Century*, 64.

45.   Allard, "Influence," 84–85; on symposia presentations see for example, Edward B. Dorsey, "Steel For Heavy Guns," [delivered 5 January 1887] 13, no. 1: 2–125; William J. McAlpine, "The Most Suitable Metal for Naval Guns" [delivered 8 March 1887] 13, no. 2 (1887); 141–46; Alfred Cowles, "Aluminum Bronze For Heavy Guns," [delivered 27 October 1887] 13, no. 4 (1887): 601–79 and 14, no. 1 (1888): 235–47; Stephen B. Luce, "Annual Address," 14, no. 1 (1888): 1–8; E.I. Zablinski, "The Naval Uses of the Pneumatic Torpedo Gun," [delivered 8 December 1887] 14, no. 1 (1888): 10–55; William Metcalf, "Steel: Its Properties; Its Uses in Structures and Heavy Guns," 14, no. 2 (1888): 445–53; Albert Gleaves review of Eaton, "Notes on Steel Inspection of Structural and Boiler Material," 14, no. 4: 641–53, all *USNIP*.

Chapter 4

1.   On the state of the Union at the time, see Harry J. Sievers, *Benjamin Harrison, Hoosier President;* and H. Wayne Morgan, *From*

Hayes to McKinley.

2.   On Tracy's accomplishments, see Benjamin Franklin Cooling, *Benjamin Franklin Tracy; Father of the Modern American Fighting Navy;* and W. R. Herrick, *The American Naval Revolution.* For development of military-industrial linkage, see Cooling, "The Formative Years of the Naval-Industrial Complex: Their Meaning for Studies of Institutions Today." *Naval War College Review* 17 (March-April 1975): 53–62.

3.   Cooling, *Tracy,* 60.

4.   Tracy–McCann, 16 July 1889, Appendix A, U.S. Cong., 51st, 1st sess., Sen. Ex. Doc. 43, *Letter from Secretary of the Navy,* 29 January 1890; *New York Times,* 31 July 1889.

5.   Secretary of the Navy, *Annual Report, 1889,* 1: 5, 49–50.

6.   Cooling, *Tracy,* 76–78; Tracy–Hale, 27 September 1889, Box 24, Tracy papers, LC.

7.   Luce–Tracy, 18 March 1892, Box 9, S.B. Luce papers, Naval Historical Foundation, LC; U.S. Cong., 50th, 2d sess., *Congressional Record,* 1889, 20, pt. 3: 2426.

8.   Folger–Tracy, 19 January 1890, Box 4, and Chandler–Tracy, 9, 10 January 1890, Box 4 Tracy papers, LC.; U.S. Cong., 51st, 1st sess., *Congressional Record,* 21: 3163–70.

9.   "Report of the Policy Board," *Proceedings of the U.S. Naval Institute* 16 (1890): 201–73, esp. 206–7.

10.   U.S. Cong., 51st, 1st sess., House Rept. 1178 to accompany HR 8909, Appropriation for the Naval Service, 1 April 1890, 26; *Congressional Record,* 21: 3161–71, 3221, 3256–71 (all House), and 5173–82, 5236–38, 5276–97 (Senate).

11.   *Congressional Record,* 21: 3169–70. Apparently Henry Cabot Lodge coined the phrase "sea-going coastline battleships" as a political maneuver, see especially 3395, 5297; Walter Millis, *Arms and Men,* 190; SN, *Annual Report, 1890,* 37.

12.   Bisphan–Tracy, 15 May 1889, Box 2, Tracy papers, LC; Tracy testimony, 6 February 1896, U.S. Cong., 54th, 2d sess., Sen. Rept. 1453, *Prices of Armor For Vessels of the Navy,* 11 February 1897, 22.

13.   Ibid., 122–24; Tracy–Ritchie, 7 March 1892, Letterbook 43, Box 26 and G.A. Evans (Bethlehem Steel Rails)–Tracy, 15 October 1889, Box 3, both Tracy papers, LC; Dean Allard, "Influence of the United States Navy upon the American Steel Industry," 90–91.

14.   Sen. Rept. 1453, *Prices of Armor,* 124; Barber–SN, 16 November 1889, Box 4, Tracy papers, LC.

15. SN *Annual Report, 1892,* 14; Vice President Bethlehem Iron–SN and J.W. Philip–Tracy, both 23 December 1889; Barber–Tracy, 19 January 1890, all Box 4, Tracy papers, LC; and Robert Lindemann–Tracy, 25 January 1890 in SN, *Annual Report, 1890,* and *1891,* 17–18, and 19 respectively.

16. Sen. Rept. 1453, *Prices of Armor,* 143, also 131–32.

17. Various undated letters, Carnegie–W.L. Abbott, October 1889–April 1890, vol. 240, Andrew Carnegie papers, LC.

18. See for example, F. Ray–Abbott, 6, 30 May; J.S. Morgan–Carnegie, 7, 20 June; Abel Ray–Carnegie, 16, 23, 26 June; W.H. Emory–Carnegie, n.d. and 26 June, all 1890, all vol. 11, Carnegie papers, LC; also Naval Attache (London)–Chief, Bureau/Navigation, 16–18, 21 June 1890, London Attache Letterbook, 1890, RG 38, Office of Naval Intelligence, National Archives and Records Services (NARS).

19. Carnegie–Tracy, 5, 19 July; Abbott–Tracy, 17 July, all 1890, all Box 6, Tracy papers, LC; Emory–Carnegie, 30 June 2, 3 July; Ray–Carnegie 3 July; J.F. Hull–Carnegie, 4, 6 July; J. Scott–Carnegie, 6 July; Carnegie–Carnegie, Phipps and Company, 7 July, all 1890, all vol. 11, Carnegie papers, LC.

20. Carnegie–Tracy, 23 July; miscellaneous telegrams, Carnegie–home office, all 1890, all Box 11, Carnegie papers, LC.

21. Sen. Rept. 1453, *Prices of Armor,* 143–45.

22. SN, *Annual Report, 1890,* 20–21; L.A. Kimberly, "Report of the Board on the Competitive Trial of Armor Plate," *USNIP* 16 (1890): 620–45.

23. Carnegie–Tracy, 10 September 1890; Ritchie–Carnegie, Phipps copy, 28 June 1890, Box 6, Tracy papers; Abbott–Carnegie, 23 June 1890, vol. 11, Carnegie papers, all LC.

24. Tracy–McKinley, 15 March 1890, Box 25; Ritchie–Tracy, 30 March 1891, Box 8, Tracy papers; Folger–Luce, 24 February 1890, Box 9, S.B. Luce papers, NHC, all LC; *Congressional Record,* 21, pt. 2: 10452, 10460–63.

25. *New York Times,* 6 October 1890; miscellaneous letters regarding conference, cases 9984, 9985, 9499 in Letters Received, 1890, Office, Secretary/Navy, RG 80 NARS.

26. SN, *Annual Report, 1892,* 19; Copy of contract in folder, Contract for Steel Armor, 1890, BR, Armor and Armament Subject File, RG 45, Naval Records Collection NARS; Carnegie–Tracy, 27

November 1890, Box 7, Tracy papers, LC; Carnegie–Tracy, 1 December 1890, Case 10388, Letters Sent, 1890, OSN, RG 80, NARS.

27. Tracy–Cameron, 4 November 1890, Box 24, Tracy papers, LC; Richard K. Morris, *John P. Holland*, 62.

28. SN, *Annual Report, 1890*, 38, 40, 41.

29. Morgan, *From Hayes to McKinley*, 354–56; Cooling, *Tracy*, 102–3.

30. Hale–Tracy, 30 December 1890; Boutelle–Luce, 19 December 1890, both Box 7, Luce papers, LC.

31. Assistant SN–Commandant, New York Navy Yard, 24 December 1891, Letterbook, SN, 1892, RG 80, NARS; also ASN–SN, 12 July 1892, Box 9, Tracy papers, LC.

32. Cooling, *Tracy*, 241–43.

33. Carnegie–Tracy, 9 May 1891, Box 9, Tracy papers, LC; Carnegie–J.G. Blaine, 10 May 1891, Letterbook 17, Carnegie papers, LC.

34. Tracy–W.H. Emory, 27 October 1891, Box 2, William Emory papers (NHF), LC; Folger–Dewey, 31 July 1891 and Case 3712, Records of Proceedings of U.S. Navy Board on Armor, RG 80, NARS.

35. Stephen Gwynne, ed., *Letters and Friendships of Sir Cecil Spring-Rice*, 2: 118; see Cooling, *Tracy*, chapter 6 for a fuller account of chauvinism.

36. *Navy Yearbook, 1908*, 141–58.

37. Joseph Frazier Wall, *Andrew Carnegie*, chapter 16; Cooling, *Tracy*, 130–31.

38. SN–Bethlehem, 10 October 1892, Box 25, Tracy papers, LC.

39. *Philadelphia North American*, 15 October 1892; Tracy–National Advisory Board of Amalgamated Association of Iron and Steelworkers, 5 November 1892, Box 25, Tracy papers, LC.

40. *New York Herald*, 22, 29, 31 August, 13 September 1892. The issue probably arose from an April 1892 request from Bethlehem for an additional $150 per ton for inclined armor which management claimed was harder to fabricate. The technical problem was by no means solved when the *Herald* broke the story. See Bethlehem Iron Company requests, case 3691, Selected Letters Received, 1892, Records OSN, RG 80, NARS.

41. SN, *Annual Report, 1892*, 5.

42. Sampson–ASN, 21 February 1893, case 919, Letters Received and Sent, 1892/93, OSN RG 80, NARS.

43. *Navy Yearbook, 1908*, 161, 176; Morris, *John P. Holland*, 64–65.

44. U.S. Congress, 52nd, 2d sess., House Rept. 2489, *Appropriations for the Naval Service*, 13 February 1893, 6.

Chapter 5

1. Modern historians like Walter La Feber and W.R. Herrick mistakenly believe that both Tracy and Herbert were won over to the battleship concept from reading Alfred Thayer Mahan's work. See Hugh Bernard Hammett, "Hilary Abner Herbert; A Southerner Returns to the Union," and the published version, especially chapters 6, 7, and 8.

2. *St. Louis Republic*, 1 June 1893; Hammett, *Herbert*, 150; Hilary Herbert, "The Lesson of the Naval Review," *North American Review*, 156 (June 1893): 641–47.

3. Ltr. Hunsicker–Secretary of the Navy, 17 May 1893, case 2869; Chief, Bureau of Construction and Repair–SN, 2 May 1893, case 2681, both General Correspondence, Navy Department, RG 80, NARS.

4. Secretary of the Navy, *Annual Report, 1893*, 16.

5. Ibid., 22–32, 35, 39, 40; R.B. Dashiell, "Report on the Test of a 14-inch Nickel Steel Harveyed Armor Plate," *Proceedings of the United States Naval Institute (USNIP)* 19, no. 1 (1893): 117–20; "Armor Question Puzzles," *USNIP* 19, no. 3 (1893): 312–19; Russell W. Davenport, "Gun Forgings and Armor Plate in the United States," *USNIP* 19, no. 4: 485–86, and "Trail of Schneider's Nickel Steel Armor for Russia," *USNIP* 19, no. 4: 491–92, in which he declared the tests "more severe than demanded in any other country."

6. *Navy Yearbook, 1908*, 196; Congressional debate may be followed in U.S. Cong., 53d, 2d sess., *Congressional Record*, 26, pt. 5: 4506–8, 4621–39, and pt. 7: 4779–86.

7. *New York Times*, 3 September 1893; Hammett, *Herbert*, 163–68; SN, *Annual Report 1894*, 9–10.

8. Statement of ex-Secretary Benjamin F. Tracy before Senate Naval Affairs Committee, U.S. Congress, 54th, 2d sess., Sen. Rept.

1453, *Prices of Armor For Vessels of the Navy*, 137 ff.

9. On armor scandals see: U.S. Cong., 51st, 2nd sess., Sen. Ex. Doc. 74, *Communication from SN relative to defective castings of Standard Steel Casting Company, 1893*, 18–45; U.S. Cong., 51st, 2nd sess., Sen. Ex. Doc. 75, *Communication from Sec. Navy relative to counterfeit stamping of steel plates by Linden Iron Works*, 1893; and U.S. Cong., 53rd, 2d sess., House Ex. Doc. 160, *Communication from SN relative to report of alleged violation of contract by Carnegie, Phipps, and Company,* 1894.

10. Ibid., 19 ff.; Hammett, *Herbert*, 174–76; *New York Times*, 3, 5, 24 March 1894.

11. Cleveland–Herbert, 10 January 1894 in Allan R. Nevins, editor, *Letters of Grover Cleveland*, 343–44, quoted in Hammett, *Herbert*, 175.

12. Herbert–Frick, 18 January; Herbert–Smith, 12 January, both 1894, both in vol. 27, (Sept. 1893–Jan. 1897), Confidential Letters Sent, SN, Naval Records Collection, Office of Naval Records and Library, RG 45, NARS.

13. U.S. Cong., 53d, 2d sess., House Rept. 1468, *Report on Armor Plate Investigation*, 1894, 17; Sampson Report–SN, 4 June 1894, General Correspondence files, Navy Department, RG 80; also Burton J. Hendrick, *The Life of Andrew Carnegie*, 2: 401–5; U.S. Cong., 53d, 2d sess., *Congressional Record*, 26, pt. 8: 8637–49 and 54th, 2d sess., 29, pt. 3: 2558–62.

14. Dean Allard, "Influence of the United States Navy upon the American Steel Industry, 1880–1900," 109–11.

15. See William Manchester, *The Arms of Krupp*, 221.

16. SN, *Annual Report, 1894*, 22, 248; *1895*, 206–7; C.A. Stone–Millard Hunsicker, 17 September 1894, vol. 27, Carnegie papers, LC.

17. Knight, *Navy Yearbook, 1913*, 227–28; and a brief treatment may be found in Hammett, *Herbert*, 176–80.

18. Herrick, *American Naval Revolution*, 174–75; SN, *Annual Report, 1895*, xiv, lvii, 207; SN–President, Carnegie Steel, 13 January 1895, Confidential Letters Sent, SN, v. 27, 1895, RG 45 and President Bath Iron Works–SN, 25 November 1896 in Armor Plate Investigation files, Records of the Hydographic Office, RG 37, both NARS; also U.S. Cong., 53d, 3d sess., Sen. Ex. Doc. 1453, *Report of SN Relative to Cost of Armor Plate for Vessels of US Navy*, 1895, 2.

19.   U.S. Cong., 54th, 1st sess., *Congressional Record*, 28, pt. 7: 6022–23, 6045–58, 6082–85, 6185–95, 6225–26, 6357.

20.   Knight, *Navy Yearbook, 1913*, 252.

21.   Herbert–Linderman, 13 June, 18 July; Herbert–Leischman, 13, 25 June, all 1896, all General Correspondence, RG 80; also SN–President, Carnegie Steel, Bethlehem Iron, 13 June, and SN–Secretary of Treasury, 12 December, all 1896, all Confidential Letters Sent, SN, RG 45, all NARS; and Sen. Ex. Doc. 56, *Cost of Armor*, xvi–xx.

22.   U.S. Cong., 54th, 2d sess., House Doc. 151, *Report of SN on Cost and Price of Armor*, 1897, 20; Sen. Ex. Doc. 56, *Cost of Armor*, 268–69; SN–Naval Attaches, Paris and London, 18 June 1896, Confidential Letters Sent, SN, RG 45, NARS.

23.   See for example, Naval Attache, Paris–SN, 11 September 1896; McVay–C.H. Laucheimer, USMC, OJAG, 27 July 1896, both Armor Plate Investigation 1896, RG 37, as well as SN–President, Bethlehem Iron, 12 December 1896, and Telegram SN–Carnegie Steel and vice versa, 18, 19 January 1897, all Confidential Letters Sent, SN, RG 45, all NARS.

24.   Allard, "Influence," 117–19; House Doc. 151, *Report of SN on Cost and Price of Armor*, 8–10; Sen. Rept. 1453, *Prices of Armor*, xvi–xx.

25.   Ibid., xxiii, 274–75.

26.   Ibid., iii–xiii, inter alia.

27.   Allard, "Influence," 120; Knight, *Navy Yearbook, 1913*, 274–75.

28.   SN, *Annual Report, 1896*, 5–15; see also Herrick, *American Naval Revolution*, 190.

29.   SN, *Annual Report, 1896*, 26–29.

30.   Ibid., 5, 9, 56, 57; Herrick, *American Naval Revolution*, 159–60, 183–88.

Chapter 6

1.   Carleton Hunt–Long, 4 March 1897 in Gardner Weld Allen, ed. *Papers of John Davis Long 1897–1904*, 3–5; John R. Alden, *American*

Steel Navy, 354; Walter K. Herrick, *The American Naval Revolution*, 194.

2. U.S. Congress, 55th, 1st sess., *Congressional Record*, 30, 1897, pt. 1: 22, 91.

3. Roosevelt–Lodge, 3 August 1897, in *Selections from Correspondence of Roosevelt and Lodge*, 1: 268; Robert Hessen, *Steel Titan; The Life of Charles Schwab*, 93–95.

4. U.S. Congress, 55th, 2d sess., House Doc. 95, *Report of the Armor Board (RAB)* 4; Secretary of the Navy, *Annual Report, 1897*, 288; Lodge–Roosevelt, 5 August 1897, *Selections*, 1: 270; and *Congressional Record*, 3, 1897, pt. 2: 1171, 1222, 1593.

5. *RAB*, 4; SN, *Annual Report, 1897*, Report, Chief of Ordnance, 290.

6. *RAB*, 4,5; see also, Records of Armor Factory Board, 1897, Box 3, RG 74, Bureau of Ordnance, National Archives and Records Service (NARS).

7. Memoranda, Interview of Assistant Secretary, 20,29 September; Outlining Directions for Negotiations with John Fritz, 22 September; Agreement with John Fritz, 11 October; and Memorandum of Conference with Acting Secretary of Navy, 4 September, all 1897, all Ibid.

8. *RAB*, 11–20; Memorandum, Subdivision of Work by Committee, 28 September 1897, Records of Armor Factory Board, RG 70, NARS.

9. *RAB*, 20–21.

10. Roosevelt–Lodge, 5 November 1897, *Selections*, 294; SN, *Annual Report, 1897*, 41–42.

11. Dean Allard, "The Influence of the United States Navy upon the American Steel Industry, 1880–1900," 122–123; SN, *Annual Report, 1897*, 12–18, 34–36.

12. *Congressional Record*, 31, pt. 4: 3458–79.

13. Ibid., pt 4: 3225, 4238; pt 8: 268–70.

14. Knight, compiler, *Navy Yearbook, 1913*, 300–302; *Congressional Record*, 31, pt 4: 3232, 4242.

15. Hessen, *Steel Titan*, 95; Allard, "Influence," 123; Harold and Margaret Sprout, *Rise of American Naval Power*, 230–45.

16. SN, *Annual Report, 1898*, pt. 1, 31; see also Daniel Costello, "Planning For War: A History of the General Board of the Navy,

1900–1914," 16–17; also SN–Hon. William Greene, Data on Ammunition expended at battle of Santiago, 27 May 1910, Box 9, Gunnery at Santiago, File BG–Guns and Gunnery, Subject File 1774–1910, RG 45, Naval Records Collection and Library, NARS.

17. *Congressional Record*, 32, pt. 3: 2158–66, 2188–96, 2244–57; William Manchester, *The Arms of Krupp*, 220–21.

18. See Kirkpatrick's speech especially on 23 February in *Congressional Record*, 32, pt. 3: 2225.

19. On Senate debate, see Ibid., 2620–38, 2752–55, 2844–51, 2811–16.

20. Ibid., 2862, 2866; Knight, *Navy Yearbook, 1913*, 326–28.

21. The steelmen's side of the story is ably recounted by Hessen, *Steel Titan*, 97–102.

22. Ibid., 98.

23. SN, *Annual Report 1899*, 8, 59–64; Mahan–Long, 31 January, 5 February, both 1900, in Allen, *Papers of John Davis Long*, 306–8.

24. *Congressional Record*, 33, pt. 5: 4226, 4228, 4230–72, 4312–47, 4482–4501, 4525–26. All deficiency and regular appropriations totaled $53,400,000 in 1899.

25. Cramp–Long, 3 March 1900, Allen, *Papers of John Davis Long*, 313–15.

26. *Congressional Record*, 33, pt. 5: 4254, 4258, 4327–47, 4482–4501.

27. Ibid., pt. 6: 54–55, with full Senate debate 5401–95.

28. Knight, *Navy Yearbook, 1913*, 355; *Congressional Record*, 34, pt. 2, 1353–55.

29. Quoted in Hessen, *Steel Titan*, 102; also see SN, *Annual Report, 1900*, 15.

30. Long–Dewey, 30 March 1900, quoted in Costello, "General Board," 26.

31. *Congressional Record*, 34, pt. 2: 1353, 1413–30 inter alia.

32. SN, *Annual Report, 1900*, 15, 31; Costello is also good on this point.

33. On submarine see Allison W. Saville, "The Military-Industrial Complex for American Submarine Technology, 1888–1941," in B.F. Cooling, ed., *War, Business, and American Society*, chapter 7.

34. See Wendell Garrett, "John Davis Long, Secretary of the Navy, 1897–1902: A Study in Changing Political Alignments," *The New England Quarterly*, 31: 291–311; also Roosevelt–Long, 2 October

1903, Allen, *Papers of John Davis Long*, 432–33.

35. *Congressional Record*, 35, pt. 6: 5374.

36. Allard, "Influence," 126–27.

Chapter 7

1. Peter Karsten, "The Nature of 'Influence': Roosevelt, Mahan, and the Concept of Sea Power," *American Quarterly*, 23 (October 1971): 585–600.

2. John B. Hattendorf, "Technology and Strategy," *Naval War College Review* 24 (November 1971): 34–35; Gordon C. O'Gara, *Theodore Roosevelt and the Rise of the Modern Navy*, chapters 1 and 4.

3. This area is substantially covered by Albert C. Stillson, "The Development and Maintenance of the American Naval Establishment: 1901–1909," Ph.D. dissertation, Columbia University, 1959 and "Military Policy without Political Guidance: Theodore Roosevelt's Navy," *Military Affairs* 25 (Spring 1961): 18–31; Daniel Costello, "Planning for War: A History of the General Board of the Navy, 1900–1914," Ph.D. dissertation, Fletcher School, 1968, chapters 3, 7; and Vincent Davis, *The Admiral's Lobby*, chapters 1–4.

4. Davis, *Admiral's Lobby*, 49–53, for example, emphasizes the military ramifications of aviation for the spread of political-military-industrial relationships away from maritime constituencies into the hinterland. This certainly took place later, but arose only from a well-founded base of contracts and subcontracts in the period 1880–1917, not only in seacoast districts but inland where small naval stores and shipbuilding projects (including steel making) were popular.

5. J.J. Woodward, "The Necessity of a Definite Program of Naval Construction," lecture, Naval War College, 25 September 1902, RG 7, Intelligence and Technical Archives, 1894–1945, Naval War College Files, Naval Historical Collection, NWC, Newport, Rhode Island; Stillson, "Military Policy Without Political Guidance," 31.

6. John D. Alden, *American Steel Navy*, 357; Robert Sobel, editor, *Biographical Directory of the United States Executive Branch*, 28–29,

239–40, 246, 250, 254.

7. Elting E. Morison, editor, *The Letters of Theodore Roosevelt*, vol. 4, *The Square Deal 1903–1905*, 847–48; also "Brief Account of the General Board 26 October 1903," Box 3, Personal Files of Henry V.L. Meyer, RG 80, General Records of the Navy Department, NARS.

8. U.S. Cong., 64th, 1st sess., Hearing Before Committee on Naval Affairs, United States Senate on S. 1417; *A Bill to Erect a Factory for the Manufacture of Armor*, 1916, 6.

9. Speech, "The Navy," volume B, William Moody papers, Library of Congress.

10. Secretary of the Navy, *Annual Report, 1902*, 5; also Table 2, fn.; Stillson, "Development and Maintenance," 29, 280.

11. Quoted in Robert Hessen, *Steel Titan; The Life of Charles Schwab*, 167; see also Henry M. Moyt–Moody, 29 July 1903, vol. 8; John G. Johnson–Moody, 23 October 1903, vol. 9; John Keane–Moody, 6 January 1903; L.M. McComas–Moody, 8 January 1903, both vol. 5; S.M. Weld–Moody, 9 June 1903, vol. 7; all in Moody papers, LC.; also, W.S. Sims–SN, 26 August 1903, file BO–Subject File 1774–1910 (1871–1910) RG 45, NARS.

12. U.S. Cong., 58th, 2d sess., *Congressional Record*, 38, pt. 3: 2064–74.

13. Ibid., 2078, 2153–55, 2211–21, 2232.

14. Ibid., 2910–11. For internal navy deliberations see, President General Board–SN, 17 October 1903, 26 January 1904; Chairman Conference Committee–SN, 26 January 1904; Board on Construction–SN, 27 November 1903, all RG 7, NWC files, Naval War College Archives, Newport.

15. Knight, compiler, *Navy Yearbook, 1913*, 480–81; *Congressional Record*, 38, pt. 3: 2382, 2441–47; also O'Neil–H.A. Herbert, 11 March 1904, Box 13, R.M. O'Neil papers, LC.

16. Speech, 16 February 1904, vol. 16, Moody papers, LC; General Board–SN, "Recommendations on Number and Types of Ships to be Authorized by Congress at the Sessions of 1904–1905," 28 October 1904, 1–2, 6–7, RG 7, NWC files, Naval War College Archives, Newport.

17. SN, *Annual Report, 1904*, 1–7, 13–16, 568–69; *Congressional Record*, 39, pt. 3: 2563, 2576, 2744, 2945–47, 2950–52.

18. Ibid., pt. 4: 3505, 3508, 3877, 3883, 3942, 3982.

19. Knight, *Navy Yearbook, 1913,* 510–11; Sobel, editor, *Biographical Directory,* 28.

20. SN, *Annual Report, 1905,* 17, 19–20, 22–24, 491–92; Bonaparte–Roosevelt and reverse, 2, 3 August 1905, Boxes 126, 174; miscellaneous newspaper clippings, all Scrapbook 7, Box 258, all Bonaparte papers, LC. See also H.C. Lodge–Roosevelt, 29 September 1905 in *Selections from the Correspondence of Theodore Roosevelt and Henry Cabot Lodge, 1884–1918,* 2: 203–4.

21. U.S. Cong., 59th, 1st sess., House Doc. 889, *Cost of Armor Plate and Armor Plant,* 13 June 1906, 1–2.

22. *Congressional Record,* 40, pt. 7: 6991–94; pt. 8: 7895; Knight, compiler, *Navy Yearbook, 1913,* 546–47.

23. SN, *Annual Report, 1906,* 21–22; Midvale actually bid $346 for Class A, $345 for Class B, $344 for Class C, and $343 for Class D.

24. Ibid., 22; Roosevelt–Bonaparte, 14 July 1906, Box 126 Bonaparte papers, LC; U.S. Cong., 59th, 2d sess., House Doc. 193, *Cost of Armor and Armor Plant,* 14.

25. See representative clippings, *Baltimore News, Baltimore American, Philadelphia Record, Milwaukee Free Press, Washington Post, Brooklyn Times, New Orleans Picayune, New York Evening Post, Norfolk Landmark,* all volumes 8 and 9, Box 259, Bonaparte papers, LC.

26. House Doc. 193, *Cost of Armor and Armor Plant,* inter alia.

27. SN, *Annual Report, 1906,* 513–15; Acting SN–Chief Bureau of Ordnance, Subject Bethlehem Steel Company and Midvale Steel Co. Bids on 8–12″, 2–8″, and 10–6″ guns, 4 August 1908, Case 26548-1, RG 80, General Records, Navy Department, NARS.

28. *Congressional Record,* 41, pt. 3: 2603–5, 2911–13; pt. 4: 3047–68, 3437.

29. SN, *Annual Report, 1907,* 12, 464.

30. *Congressional Record,* 62, pt. 5: 4685–86, 4830–33.

31. Ibid., pt. 6, 5104–13, 5287; Knight, *Navy Yearbook, 1913,* 619–20.

32. SN, *Annual Report, 1908,* 5–7, 37–38, 428.

33. "Resume of the Useful, Interesting, and Important Achievements of the Navy Department since March 4, 1909," Personal Files of George Von L. Meyer, RG 80, General Files, Navy Department, NARS.

34. For treatment of U.S. Navy and diplomacy in this period, see, Seward W. Livermore, "The American Navy as a Factor in World Politics, 1903–1913," *The American Historical Review* 63 (July 1958),

863–79; Ronald Spector, "Roosevelt, the Navy, and the Venezuela Controversy: 1902–1903," *The American Neptune* 32, 257–263; and Richard D. Challener, *Admirals, Generals, and American Foreign Policy 1898–1914*, chapter 4.

35. SN, *Annual Report, 1909*, 7–20, 402–3.

36. Ibid., *1910*, 39–41, 345–46. Knight, compiler, *Navy Yearbook, 1913*, 703–4, 735–37.

37. Ibid., *1912*, 17–19, 26–33, 210–21, 236–38; *Congressional Record*, 66, pt. 4: 3093–4000; 68, pt. 7: 7023–41; pt. 8: 7851–53; pt. 9: 8646–51; pt. 11: 11266–68; U.S. Cong., 62nd, 2d sess., House Doc. 782, *Increase of the Navy*, 31 May 1912; and "The Necessity For Battleships Each Year," January 29, 1912, Box 5, Personal Files of George Von L. Meyer, RG 80, NARS.

Chapter 8

1. See Melvin I. Urofsky, *Big Steel and the Wilson Administration*, Prologue, where he notes that other business spokesmen of this philosophy include George W. Perkins of the financial House of Morgan, Cyrus H. McCormick of International Harvester, and John D. Rockefeller, Jr. of Standard Oil in addition to Judge Gary of United States Steel.

2. A concise treatment of Wilsonian diplomacy and the military can be found in Richard Challener, *Admirals, Generals and American Foreign Policy*, chapter 5.

3. Concerning Daniels and the Navy department, see Joseph L. Morrison, *Josephus Daniels; The Small-d Democrat*, chapters 3 and 4, and E. David Cronon, *The Cabinet Diaries of Josephus Daniels 1913–1921*, Preface.

4. Edward H. Brooks, "The National Defense Policy of the Wilson Administration, 1913–1917," Ph.D. diss., Stanford University, 1950, 30–35.

5. H.B Martin–Wilson, 7 April 1913, Wilson–Daniels, 9 April 1913 as cited in Urofsky, "Josephus Daniels and The Armor Trust," *North*

Carolina Historical Review 45 (July 1968): 237.

6.   Secretary of the Navy (SN)–Lackawanna Steel Co., 17 February 1913, Case 9288/5, Box 381, Subject 9288–Steel, Entry 19, RG 80, General Records of Navy Department, NARS.

7.   President, United States Steel Products Co.–SN, 27 February 1913, Ibid. For other responses see similar letters from heads of Carnegie Steel, Midvale, Bethlehem, Crucible, Worth Brothers, Philadelphia Steel and Forge, Jones and Laughlin, Lackawanna, Pennsylvania Steel, Pollock, Carbon, R.C. Hoffman, conveniently summarized in Memorandum. Aid material–SN, 7 April 1913, all Ibid.

8.   General Manager, Midvale–SN, 24 February 1913, Case 9288–5–4, Ibid.

9.   Grace–Daniels, 19 April 1913, H.M. Deamer (Midvale)–Daniels, 16 May 1913, all Armor Plate 1913 Folder 1, Box, Appropriations–Armor Plate 1913, Josephus Daniels papers, LC; and Urofsky, "Daniels and The Armor Trust," 241–42.

10.   *Washington Post*, 22 May 1913 quoted in U.S. Cong., 63d, 1st sess., *Congressional Record*, 50, pt. 2: 1689, see also 1612–14, 1686–89; SN–CBUORD, 10 April 1913, Case 4174/157, in General Correspondence SN, RG 80, NARS.

11.   *Congressional Record*, 50, pt. 2: 1760–64, 1937, pt. 3: 2053, 2150–51; pt. 6: 5535–37.

12.   Tillman–Daniels, 22 May 1913, Armor Plate 1913 Folder 1, Box Appropriations, Armor Plate 1913, Daniels papers, LC.

13.   Gaines–Howard N. Banks and McH. Howe, 22 May, Tankerville–Daniels, 24 May, Gathmann–Daniels, 2 June and Daniels–Herbert, 27 May, all 1913, all Ibid.

14.   Memo, OASN–SN, 28 May 1913, Ibid.

15.   U.S. Cong., 63rd, 1st sess., Sen. Doc. 129, *Letter from Secretary of the Navy to the Chairman of the Committee on Naval Affairs with Reference to the Cost of Armor Plate and Its Manufacture*, 1913, Appendix A, hereinafter cited, *Cost of Armor Plate*.

16.   Soliciter–SN, 23 June 1914, Armor Plate 1914–1915 Folder, Box Armor Plate 1914–1917, Daniels papers, LC.

17.   *Cost of Armor Plate*, 2–3, also "Suggested Form of the Report to Congress on Armor Plate Question," Appendices B, C, and D, all drafts in Armor Plate 1913 Folder 3, Box Appropriations–Armor Plate, Daniels papers, LC.

18.   *Cost of Armor Plate*, 4–8.

19. As described in Urofsky, "Daniels and the Armor Trust," 244.

20. T.D.H. Stenhouse–Daniels, 24 September and Richardson–Daniels, 10 September, President and General Manager of Baldwin Steel–Daniels, 1 October all 1913, all Armor Plate 1913 Folder 2, Box Appropriations–Armor Plate 1913, Daniels papers, LC.

21. Urofsky, *Big Steel*, 127.

22. SN, *Annual Report, 1913*, 10–13; Tavenner–Daniels, 15, 26 November 1913, Folder 3, Draft, Daniels–"My Dear Mr. Congressman," 29 September 1913, Folder 2, all Armor Plate 1913, all Daniels papers, LC; Urofsky, "Daniels and the Armor Trust," 244–46.

23. Carnegie–Daniels 9 December 1913 and Director ONI–SN, 5 December 1913, both Folder 3, Armor Plate 1913, Box Appropriations–Armor; Confidential Memo, Savings in Cost of Armor-Piercing Projectiles, 9 December, General Folder, Ordnance Bureau Box, Naval Subject Files 1913–1914, all Daniels papers, LC.

24. *London Times* account, 4 March 1914, Folder 1914–1915, Armor Plate, Box 1914–1917; "HAB"–SN, 7 January 1914, General Folder, Ordnance Bureau Box, both Naval Subject Files, 1913–1914, Ibid.; also *Congressional Record*, 51, pt. 7: 6851–53, 7018–25, 7264, 7281–86; pt. 8: 7395–99, 8247–67; pt. 9: 9309–19; pt. 10: 9365–77, 9634–36, Appendix 551–59, 643–44.

25. Tillman–Daniels, 4 June, 22 August, 21 September, 8 November; Daniels–Tillman, 28, 29 May, 1 October, all 1914, all Folder 1914, Box, Senate Naval Affairs Committee, Special Correspondents File. Projectiles, ship construction, torpedoes, and powder matters may be followed in various boxes of Naval Subject Files; all Daniels papers, LC.

26. SN, *Annual Report, 1914*, 8–9, 14–15, 22–23; and Daniels–Padgett, 29 January 1915, Folder 1915–1916, Box, House Committee on Naval Affairs, Ibid.

27. BUORD Memo, "Improvement and Savings Accomplished in Ordnance during the Past Two Years," 4 February 1915, Ordnance Bureau 1915–1916 Folder, Box Ordnance Bureau, Naval Subject Files; Daniels–Padgett, 27 February 1915, Folder 1915–1916, Box House Committee on Naval Affairs, both Daniels papers, LC.

28. Robert Hessen, *Steel Titan: The Life of Charles Schwab*, 227–29; Gaddis Smith, *Britain's Clandestine Submarines 1914–1915*, especially chapter 2.

29. U.S. Cong., 63d, 2d sess., House Doc. 1620, *Report of the*

Committee to Investigate the Cost of an Armor Plant for the United States 1915; and Urofsky, "Daniels and the Armor Trust," 248–49.

30. Silsby, *Navy Yearbook 1920–1921,* 420–22; U.S. Cong., 63d, 3d sess., *Congressional Record,* 52, pt. 3: 2689–95; pt. 6: 5237–51, esp. 5241; and Appendix 417–41.

31. Daniels–Lodge, n.d., Folder 1915, Box, Senate Naval Affairs Committee, Special Correspondents File; Memo, President, General Board–SN, 30 July, Folder, George Dewey, Box Dewey–Edison; Daniels–S.A. Williams, 19 October, Daniels–Tavenner, 19 August, Daniels–Ferguson, 26 November, all Folder 1914–1915, Armor Plate 1914–1917 Box; Daniels–Barringer, 4 December, Folder, Ordnance Bureau 1915–1916, Ordnance Bureau Box, all 1915, all Naval Subject Files, all Ibid.

32. SN, *Annual Report, 1915,* 1–8, 56–70.

33. CBUORD–SN, 6 January, Folder Armor 1916 no. 1, Box Armor Plate, 1914–1917; Tillman–Daniels, 11 January and reverse 12 January, Folder 1916, Box Senate Naval Affairs Committee, Special Correspondents File, all documents 1916, all Daniels papers, LC.

34. See U.S. Cong., 64th, 1st sess., *Hearings... S. 1417, a Bill to Erect a Factory for the Manufacture of Armor,* 1916, with Grace's statement, 5–63, 151–52, 169–72; Barba, 65–77; Dinkey, 77–133; Strauss, 133–48; and Daniels, 149–69; Presidential support is discussed in Urofsky, "Daniels and the Armor Trust," 250–51.

35. See *Manufacturers Record* (Baltimore), 7, 17 February 1916; Urofsky, "Daniels and the Armor Trust," 255–56.

36. Unidentified paper, "Mr. President," c. 21 March 1915, Armor Plate Folder no. 1, Box Armor Plate 1914–1917, Daniels papers, LC.

37. Silsby, compiler, *Navy Yearbook, 1920–1921,* 430–31, 490–94; Daniels–C.A. Swanson, 11, 17, 18 March 1916, Folder Armor Plate 1916 no. 1, Box Armor Plate 1914–1917; various statistical memoranda 18 May, 17 June, 1916, Appropriations Folder, Box Armor Plate Appropriations 1913–; and Daniels–C.G. Van Dyke, 2 June 1916, Folder 1916–1917, Box House Committee on Naval Affairs, all Daniels papers, LC; *Congressional Record,* pts. 9–15 inter alia.

38. Lodge–Roosevelt, 10 July 1916 in *Selections from the Correspondence of Theodore Roosevelt and Henry Cabot Lodge 1884–1914,* 2: 491–92; Arthur S. Link, *Woodrow Wilson and the Progressive Era 1910–1917,* especially chapter 7, and SN, *Annual Report, 1916.*

39. Hessen, *Steel Titan,* 228–34.

40.   For discussion of this expansion, see Robert D. Cuff, *The War Industries Board.*

41.   Daniels–Padgett, 8, 22 January, Folder 1916–1917, Box House Committee on Naval Affairs; Miscellaneous undated position papers in Armor 1917 Folder 2, Box Armor Plate 1914–1917; Memo BUORD–SN, 10, 15, 16 January and Daniels–W.A. Oldfield, 16 March, Folder 1917, Ordnance, Box–Ordnance, all documents 1917, all Daniels papers, LC.

42.   Stenhouse–Daniels, 22 January, Roberts–Daniels, 25 January, Daniels–Hersch, 26 January, all 1917, all Ordnance Folder 1917, Box Ordnance Bureau; Daniels–J.C. McGuire, 1 February 1917, Folder 1916–1917, Box Civilian Naval Consulting Board, Daniels–Baruch, 27 March and Gary–Daniels, 29 March with reverse 30 March; J.A. Farrell–Daniels 5 April, all Folder Armor 1917 no. 1, Box Armor Plate 1914–1917, Daniels papers, LC.

43.   Silsby, *Navy Yearbook 1920–1921*, 521; Daniels–R.H. Engle, 12 April 1917, Folder Armor Plate 1917 no. 2, Box Armor Plate 1914–1917, Ibid.

44.   SN, *Annual Report, 1917*, 55–56; Report of Armor Plant Board, 17 May 1917, Folder Armor 1917 no. 2 and Daniels–Senator Ollie H. James, 20 June 1917. Armor Folder 1917 no. 3, both Box Armor Plate 1914–1917; Memo CBUORD–SN, 2 June 1917, Folder Armor 1917, Box Ordnance Bureau, Subject File Naval Affairs, Daniels papers, LC.

45.   Daniels–Marvell, 23 October 1919; Memo CBUORD–SN, 23 August 1920 in Folders Armor 1918–1919, and 1920 [1921–1935] respectively, Box Armor Plate, Ibid.

46.   Charleston Chamber of Commerce, "The Automobile Owner," 25 August 1920; Daniels–Marvell, 1 September 1920, 29 January 1921, and a description of the whole project was ably covered in Roger M. Freeman, "The Armor-Plate and Gun Forging Plant of the U.S. Navy Department at South Charleston, W. Va.," American Society of Engineers, 1920; and Inspector of Ordnance in Charge–SN, 4 February 1921; CBUORD–SN, "Data on Armor," 24 August 1920, all in Ibid.

Postscript

1. Melvin I. Urofsky, *Big Steel and the Wilson Administration*, Preface and Epilogue.

2. An early expostulation of this irony may be found in Guysbert B. Vroom and William Oliver Stevens, "The Fate of the Dreadnaught," *United States Naval Institute Proceedings* 47 (February 1921): 191–200.

3. Marvell–Daniels, 9 February 1921, Folder Armor Plate 1921, Box–Armor Plate 1921–35, Subject File Naval Affairs, Daniels papers, LC.

Bibliography

UNPUBLISHED SOURCES

Manuscript Division—Library of Congress

Charles J. Bonaparte papers
Andrew Carnegie papers
William E. Chandler papers
Josephus Daniels papers
William H. Hunt papers
John D. Long papers
George v. L. Meyer papers
William L. Moody papers
Paul H. Morton papers
Naval Historical Foundation collection
   George Washington Chambers papers
   Albert Gleaves papers
   Charles O'Neil papers
   Montgomery Sicard papers
Benjamin F. Tracy papers
William C. Whitney papers

National Archives and Records Service (NARS)

Record Group 19—Bureau of Ships
Record Group 38—Office, Chief of Naval Operations
Record Group 45—Naval Records Collection, Office of Naval Records and Library
Record Group 74—Bureau of Ordnance
Record Group 80—General Records of the Navy
Record Group 125—Judge Advocate

Naval War College Archives, Newport, R.I.

Record Group 1—Early Records 1884 ca. 1910
Record Group 7—Intelligence and Technological Archives 1894–1945
Record Group 14—Lectures 1884–1950

PUBLIC DOCUMENTS

U.S. Commissioner of Patents. *Annual Report of US Patent Office, 1847, 1861, 1862.* Washington: 1847, 1861, 1862.

U.S. Congress. *Congressional Record,* vols. 10–55.

U.S. Congress. *US Statutes at Large,* vols. 17, 20, 21, 22. Boston: Little Brown, 1873; and Washington: Government Printing Office, 1879–83.

U.S. Congress. House of Representatives. *Appropriation for Naval Service, 1 April 1890.* 51st Cong., 1st sess. HR 1178 to accompany HR 8909. Washington: Government Printing Office, 1890.

————. *Appropriations for the Naval Service. 13 February 1913.* 52d Cong., 2d sess., HR 2489. Washington: Government Printing Office, 1893.

————. *Hearings before Subcommittee of Appropriations Committee in Charge of Deficiency Appropriations for 1908 and Prior Years on Urgent Deficiency in Appropriation for Armament and Armor for Naval Vessels.* Washington: Government Printing Office, 1908.

————. *Armor Plate and Armor Plant, Board on Cost of, Report.* 6 December 1906. 59th Cong., 2d sess., House Document 193.

————. *Armor Plant for United States, Hearings Pursuant to Provision of Naval Appropriation Act, Fiscal Year 1915,* Approved 30 June 1914. 26 February 1915. 63d Cong., 3d sess., House Document 1620.

————. *Estimates for Building a Government Gun Factory.* 48th Cong., 2d sess. 1885, House Document 70.

————. *Improvements in Naval Engineering in Great Britain.* 47th Cong., 2d sess., 1883, House Document 48.

————. *Information Regarding the Amounts of Armor Purchased by the Navy from Bethlehem Iron Co. and Carnegie Steel Co.* 55th Cong., 1st sess., 1897, House Document 147.

————. *Letter from the Secretary of the Navy regarding the Carnegie Armor Frauds.* 53d Cong., 2d sess., 1894, House Document 160.

————. *Letter from the Secretary of the Navy Transmitting to the Inquiry of the House, a Letter from the Chief of Ordnance in Relation to Contracts for Armor Plate.* 18 February 1905. 58th Cong., 3rd sess., House Document 351.

————. *Letter from the Secretary of the Navy with Enclosures in Response to a Resolution of the House Calling for Information as to Expenditure of the Naval Advisory Board Also as to Any Changes in the Plans for Hulls, Boilers, and Machinery &c. in the Ships Chicago, Boston, Atlanta, and Dolphin.* 12 February 1885. 48th Cong., 2d sess., House Document 220.

————. *Letter from Secretary of War Relative to the Future of Permanent Works with an Estimate for $500,000 to Convert Smooth-Bore Guns into Rifles, and for an Experimental and Proving Ground for Heavy Ordnance.* 18 December 1874. 43 Cong., 2d sess., House Document 38.

————. *Letter from Secretary of the Navy Replying to Resolution Asking for Information concerning Contract and Payment Thereon under Increase of Navy* [torpedo-boats, and armor and armament] *and Advising* [that] *As Soon As Information Can Be Collated It Will Be Forwarded.* 8 May 1912. 62d Cong., 2d sess. House Document 745.

————. *Letter from Secretary of the Navy Pursuant to Resolution, Information Relative to Bids and Contracts Made with Various Persons and Corporations* [for torpedo-boats and for armor and armament]. 31 May 1912. 62d 2d sess. House Document 782.

————. *Report of the Naval Advisory Board,* 1882. 47th Cong., 2d sess. House Document 32.

————. *Report of the Armor Factory Board.* 54th Cong., 2d sess., 1897, House Document 95.

————. *Report of the Board of Ordnance and Fortifications.* 52d Cong., 1st sess., 1892, House Document 12.

————. *Report of the Board on Fortifications or Other Defenses.* 49th Cong. 1st sess., 1886, House Document 49.

————. *Report of the Gun Foundry Board.* 16 February 1884. 48th Cong., 2d sess., House Document 13.

————. *Report of the Gun Trial Board.* 43d Cong., 2d sess., 1875, House Document 126.

————. *Report of the Secretary of the Navy on the Cost and Price of Armor.* 54th Cong., 2d sess., 1897, House Document 151.

————. *Response of the Secretary of the Navy to Request for Information as to Cost of Armor Plate and Armor Plant.* 14 June 1906. 59th Cong., 1st sess., House Document 889.

————. Commission on Ordnance and Gunnery. *Report of the Commission on Ordnance and Gunnery.* Report Number 1450. 49th Cong., 1st sess., 1886.

————. Committee on Naval Affairs. *Report, Amending by Substitute H.R. 363, Calling for Information Relating to Contracts Entered into by Navy Department under Provisions "Increase of Navy, Torpedo Boats" and "Increase of Navy, Armor and Armament" in Act Making Appropriations for Naval Service. Fiscal Year, 1912.* 16 January 1912. 62d Cong., 2d sess., House Report 234.

————. *Report Favoring H.R. 528, Calling for Information Relative to Cost of Armor-Plate and Armor Plant.* 5 June 1906. 59th Cong., 1st sess., House Report 4778.

————. *Heavy Ordnance.* 48th Cong., 2d sess., 1885, House Report 2546.

————. *Investigation of the Navy Department,* 45th Cong., 2d sess., 1878, House Report 112.

————. *Report of Board of Assistants for Navy.* 45th Cong., 2d sess., 1878, House Report 662.

————. *Report on the Increase of the Naval Establishment.* 49th Cong., 1st sess., 1886, House Report 993.

————. *Report on the Navy Appropriations Bill.* 53d Cong., 2d sess.,

1893, House Report 2489.

————. *Violation of Armor Contracts.* 53d Cong., 2d sess., 1894, House Report 1460.

U.S. Congress, Senate. *Hearings on S. 1417, a Bill to Erect a Factory for the Manufacture of Armor,* 1916. 64th Cong., 1st sess., Washington: Government Printing Office, 1916.

————. *The Counterfeit Stamping of Material at Linden Steel Works.* 51st Cong., 2d sess., 1891, Senate Document 75.

————. *Defects in the Castings of the Standard Steel Casting Co.* 51st Cong., 2d sess., 1891, Senate Document 74.

————. *Extract from Report to Navy Department on Location of Water-Line Armor Belt upon Battleships.* 7 April 1908. 60th Cong., 1st sess., Senate Document 422.

————. *Information Regarding the Armor Question.* 56th Cong., 1st sess., 1899, Senate Document 10.

————. *Letter from Acting Assistant Secretary of the Treasury Transmitting a Letter from Secretary of the Navy, Asking for Appropriation for Steel Cruisers.* 30 June 1886. 49th Cong., 1st sess., Senate Document 195.

————. *Letter from Secretary of the Navy Communicating Report of Board Appointed 6 July 1867 to Examine the Claims of Certain Contractors for the Construction of Vessels of War and Steam Machinery under an Act of Congress.* 2 March 1867. 40th Cong., 2d sess., Senate Document 3.

————. *Letter from Secretary of the Navy to Chairman of the Committee on Naval Affairs with Reference to the Cost of Armor Plate and Its Manufacture.* 63d Cong., 1st sess., 1913, Senate Document 129.

————. *Letter from Secretary of the Navy, Transmitting Certain Data and Information Collated and Arranged by the Chief of the Bureau of Ordnance Relating to the Armor Question.* 6 December 1899. 58th Cong., 1st sess., Senate Document 10.

————. *Letter from Secretary of the Navy Transmitting in Compliance with Senate Resolution 13 February 1883, Report of the Naval Advisory Board, Organized under Act of 5 August 1882.* 47th Cong., 2d sess., Senate Document 74.

————. *Letter of Secretary of the Navy, Transmitting Information in Relation to Construction of the Monitor.* 25 July 1868. 40th Cong., 2d sess., Senate Document 86.

————. *Letter from Secretary of the Navy, Transmitting, in Response to*

Senate Resolution of 5 March 1886, Information Relative to the Chicago, Boston, Atlanta, and Dolphin. 49th Cong., 1st sess., Senate Document 153.

—————. *Letter from Secretary of the Navy Relative to the Purchase Abroad of Designs for Naval Vessels.* 50th Cong., 1st sess., 1883, Senate Document 241.

—————. *The Prices of American Armor in the United States and Abroad.* 53d Cong., 3d sess., 1895, Senate Document 56.

—————. *Report of the Board on Heavy Ordnance and Projectiles* [Getty Board] 47th Cong., 1st sess., 1882, Senate Document 178.

—————. *Report of Chief Engineer J.W. King USN on European Ships of War.* 44th Cong., 2d sess., 1877. Senate Document 27.

—————. *Steel Material Used in Construction of Naval Vessels.* 55th Cong., 1st sess., 1897, Senate Document 57.

U.S. Senate. Committee on Naval Affairs. *Hearings before . . . 19 January and 2 February 1893, and Bids for Constructing a Government Armor Factory.* 55th Cong., 2d sess., 1893, Senate Document 127.

—————. *Prices of Armor for Vessels of the Navy.* 54th Cong., 2d sess., 1897, Senate Report 1453.

—————. *Report to Accompany S. 1181, Claims of Heirs of John Roach.* 54th Cong., 1st sess., 1896, Senate Report 754.

—————. Joint Committee on the Conduct of the War. *Report of . . . on Heavy Ordnance.* 38th Cong., 2d sess., 1865, Senate Report 121.

—————. *Report of Joint Committee on Heavy Ordnance.* 40th Cong., 2d sess., 1869, Senate Report 266.

—————. Select Committee on Heavy Ordnance and Projectiles. *Report of . . . .* 47th Cong., 2d sess., 1883, Senate Report 969.

—————. Select Committee on Ordnance and War Ships. *Report of . . . .* 49th Cong. 1st sess., 1886, Senate Report 90.

U.S. Department of the Navy. *Annual Report of the Navy Department, 1864, 1870–1920.* Washington: Government Printing Office and Predecessors, 1864, 1871–1921.

—————. Bureau of Ordnance. *Advertisement and Circulars Concerning Armor for Naval Vessels, 1906, 1907, 1908, 1909, 1910, 1913.* Washington: Government Printing Office, 1906–1913.

U.S. War Department. *Annual Report of Chief of Ordnance, 1865, 1880.* Washington: Government Printing Office and predecessors, 1865, 1880.

BOOKS

Alden, John D. *The American Steel Navy.* Annapolis: Naval Institute Press, 1972.

Allen, Gardner Weld, editor. *Papers of John Davis Long 1897–1904.* 2 vols. Boston: Massachusetts Historical Society, 1939.

American Iron and Steel Association, compilers. *History of the Manufacture of Armor Plate for the United States Navy.* Philadelphia: American Iron and Steel Association, 1899.

Bennett, Frank M. *The Steam Navy of the United States.* Pittsburgh: Warren, 1896.

Bernado, C. Joseph, and Eugene H. Bacon. *American Military Policy: Its Development Since 1775.* Harrisburg: Military Service Publishing Co., 1955.

Birnie, Rodgers. *Gun Making in the United States.* Washington: Government Printing Office, 1907.

————. *The Manufacture of Coiled Wrought-Iron Tubes, for the Conversion of 10-inch Rodman Smooth-bore Guns into 8-inch Rifles.* Ordance Memoranda 25. Washington: Government Printing Office, 1884.

Boynton, Charles B. *The History of the Navy during the Rebellion.* 2 vols. New York: D. Appleton, 1870.

Burn, Duncan. *The Economic History of Steelmaking 1867–1939; A Study in Competition.* Cambridge: Cambridge University Press, 1961.

Carrison, Daniel J. *The Navy From Wood to Steel.* New York: Watts, 1965.

Cartwright, William H., and Richard L. Watson, editors. *The Reinterpretation of American History and Culture.* Washington: National Council for the Social Studies, 1973.

Challener, Richard G. *Admirals, Generals, and American Foreign Policy 1898–1914.* Princeton: Princeton University Press, 1973.

Cochran, Thomas C. *Business in American Life; A History.* New York: McGraw Hill, 1972.

Cooling, Benjamin Franklin. *Benjamin Franklin Tracy: Father of the Modern American Fighting Navy.* Hamden, Ct.: The Shoe String Press, 1973.

————. *War, Business and American Society.* Port Washington, N.Y.: Kennikat, 1977.

Cronon, E. David., editor. *The Cabinet Diaries of Josephus Daniels*

1913–1921. Lincoln: University of Nebraska Press, 1963.

Cuff, Robert D. *The War Industries Board; Business–Government Relations during World War I*. Baltimore: Johns Hopkins University Press, 1973.

Davis, George T. *A Navy Second to None*. New York: Harcourt, Brace, 1940.

Davis, Vincent. *The Admiral's Lobby*. Chapel Hill: University of North Carolina Press, 1967.

Dulles, Foster Rhea. *Prelude to World Power; American Diplomatic History, 1860–1900*. New York: Harper and Row, 1954.

Freeman, Roger M. *The Armor-Plate and Gun-Forging Plant of the U.S. Navy Department at South Charleston, W. Va*. New York: The American Society of Mechanical Engineers, 1920.

Garbett, H. *Naval Gunnery*. London: 1897. Reprint. S.R. Publishers Ltd., 1971.

Garraty, John A. *The New Commonwealth, 1877–1890*. New York: Harper and Row, 1968.

Goodale, Stephen L. *Chronology of Iron and Steel*. Pittsburgh: Pittsburgh Iron and Steel Co., 1920.

Grenville, John A.S., and George B. Young. *Politics, Strategy, and American Diplomacy; Studies in Foreign Policy 1873–1917*. New Haven: Yale University Press, 1966.

Gwynne, Stephen, editor. *The Letters and Friendships of Sir Cecil Spring-Rice; A Record*. 2 vols. Boston and New York: Houghton-Mifflin, 1929.

Hagen, Kenneth J. *American Gunboat Diplomacy and the Old Navy, 1877–1889*. Westport, Ct.: Greenwood, 1973.

Hammett, Hugh B. *Hilary Abner Herbert; A Southerner Returns to the Union*. Philadelphia: American Philosophical Society, 1976.

Hammond, Paul Y. *Organizing for Defense; The American Military Establishment in the Twentieth Century*. Princeton: Princeton University Press, 1961.

Hendrick, Burton J. *The Life of Andrew Carnegie*. 2 vols. New York: Doran, 1932.

Herrick, Walter R., Jr. *The American Naval Revolution*. Baton Rouge: Louisiana State University Press, 1966.

Hessen, Robert. *Steel Titan; The Life of Charles M. Schwab*. New York: Oxford University Press, 1975.

Hirsch, Mark D. *William C. Whitney, Modern Warwick.* New York: Dodd, Mead, 1948.

Hogan, William T., S.J. *Economic History of the Iron and Steel Industry in the United States.* Lexington, Mass.: D.C. Heath, 1971.

Holley, Alexander L. *A Treatise on Ordnance and Armor.* New York: D. Van Nostrand, 1865.

Hunt, Thomas H. *The Life of William H. Hunt.* Brattleboro, Vt.: E.L. Hildrith, 1922.

Huntington, Samuel P. *The Soldier and the State.* Cambridge, Mass.: Harvard University Press, 1965.

Hutchins, John G.B. *The American Maritime Industries and Public Policy, 1789–1914; An Economic History.* Reprint. New York: Russell and Russell, 1968.

Jaques, William H. *Modern Armor for National Defense.* New York: Putnams, 1885.

Karsten, Peter. *The Naval Aristocracy; The Golden Age of Annapolis and Emergence of Modern American Navalism.* New York: Free Press, 1972.

Kirkland, Edward C. *Industry Comes of Age; Business, Labor and Public Policy, 1860–1897.* New York: Holt, Rinehart and Winston, 1961.

Knight, J.B., compiler. *Navy Yearbook; Compilation of Annual Naval Appropriation Laws from 1883 to 1913.* 63d Cong., 2d sess., Senate Document 247. Washington: Government Printing Office, 1913.

Knox, Dudley. *A History of the United States Navy.* New York: Putnams, 1948.

Lewis, Emanuel Raymond. *Seacoast Fortifications of the United States: An Introductory History.* Washington: Smithsonian Institution Press, 1970.

Link, Arthur S. *Woodrow Wilson and the Progressive Era, 1910–1917.* New York: Harper, 1954.

Lodge, Henry Cabot, and Charles F. Redmond, editors. *Selections from the Correspondence of Theodore Roosevelt and Henry Cabot Lodge, 1884–1918.* Reprint. New York: Da Capo, 1971.

Long, John D. *The New American Navy.* 2 vols. New York: Outlook, 1903.

Mahan, Alfred Thayer. *From Sail to Steam; Recollections on Naval Life.* 2 vols. New York: Harper, 1908.

Manchester, William. *The Arms of Krupp 1587–1968.* Boston: Little,

Brown, 1968.

Marder, Arthur. *The Anatomy of British Sea Power; A History of British Naval Policy in the Pre-Dreadnought Era, 1880–1905.* New York: Knopf, 1940.

Miller, Francis T., editor. *Photographic History of the Civil War.* 10 vols. New York: Review of Reviews, 1911.

Millis, Walter A. *Arms and Men: A Study of American Military History.* New York: Putnams, 1956.

Mitchell, Donald. *History of the Modern American Navy.* New York: Knopf, 1946.

Morgan, H. Wayne. *From Hayes to McKinley, National Party Politics 1877–1896.* Syracuse: Syracuse University Press, 1969.

Morison, Elting E. *Men, Machines, and Modern Times.* Cambridge, Mass.: MIT Press, 1966.

————, editor. *The Letters of Theodore Roosevelt.* Cambridge, Mass.: Harvard University Press, 1952.

Morris, Richard K. *John P. Holland, 1814–1914; Inventor of the Modern Submarine.* Annapolis: U.S. Naval Institute, 1966.

Morrison, Joseph L. *Josephus Daniels; The Small-d Democrat.* Chapel Hill: University of North Carolina Press, 1966.

Niven, John. *Gideon Welles, Lincoln's Secretary of the Navy.* New York: Oxford University Press, 1973.

Officers of the Ordnance Department, U.S. Army. *Reports of Experiments on the Strength and other Properties of Metals For Cannon.* Philadelphia: Henry Carey Baird, 1856.

O'Gara, Gordon C. *Theodore Roosevelt and the Rise of the Modern Navy.* New York: Greenwood, 1943.

Oliver, John W. *History of American Technology.* New York: Ronald Press, 1956.

Padfield, Peter. *Guns at Sea.* New York: St. Martins, 1974.

Patrick, Rembert W. *The Reconstruction of the Nation.* New York: Oxford University Press, 1967.

Paullin, Charles O. *Paullin's History of Naval Administration, 1775–1911: A Collection of Articles from the U.S. Naval Institute Proceedings.* Annapolis: Naval Institute Press, 1968.

Peck, Taylor. *Round Shot to Rockets; A History of the Washington Navy Yard and Naval Gun Factory.* Annapolis: U.S. Naval Institute, 1949.

Plesur, Milton. *America's Outward Thrust, Approaches to Foreign Af-*

fairs 1865–1890. DeKalb, Ill.: Northern Illinois University Press, 1971.

Potter, E.B., and C.W. Nimitz, editors. *Sea Power: A Naval History*. Englewood Cliffs, N.J.: Prentice Hall, 1960.

Reynolds, Clark G. *Command of the Sea; The History and Strategy of Maritime Empires*. New York: Morrow, 1974.

Richardson, Leon Burr. *William E. Chandler, Republican*. New York: Dodd Mead, 1940.

Rodman, T.J. *Reports of Experiments on the Properties of Metals for Cannon, and the Qualities of Cannon Powder; with an Account of the Fabrication and Trial of a 15-inch Gun*. Boston: Charles H. Crosby, 1861.

Sievers, Harry J. *Benjamin Harrison, Hoosier President*. Indianapolis: Bobbs-Merrill, 1968.

Silsby, Elwin A., compiler. *Navy Yearbook 1920–1921*. U.S. Cong., 66th, 3d sess., Senate Document 428. Washington: Government Printing Office, 1922.

Simkins, Francis B. *Pitchfork Ben Tillman*. Baton Rouge: Louisiana State University Press, 1944.

Simpson, Edward. *Report on a Naval Mission to Europe*. 2 vols. Washington: Government Printing Office, 1873.

Sloan, Edward W. *Benjamin Franklin Isherwood, Naval Engineer; The Years as Engineer in Chief, 1861–1864*. Annapolis: U.S. Naval Institute, 1965.

Smith, Gaddis. *Britain's Clandestine Submarines 1914–1915*. New Haven: Yale University Press, 1964. Reprint. Hamden, Ct.: The Shoe String Press, 1973.

Smith, Merritt R. *Harpers Ferry and the New Technology*. Ithaca: Cornell University Press, 1976.

Sobel, Robert. *The Age of Giant Corporations: A Microeconomic History of American Business 1914–1970*. Westport, Ct.: Greenwood, 1972.

————, editor. *Biographical Directory of the United States Executive Branch*. Westport, Ct.: Greenwood, 1971.

Spears, John R. *The History of Our Navy from Its Origin to the Present Day*. New York: Scribners, 1897–98.

————. *A Short History of the American Navy*. New York: Scribners, 1907.

Sprout, Harold and Margaret. *The Rise of American Naval Power*

1776–1918. Princeton: Princeton University Press, 1946.

Steinberg, Jonathan. *Yesterday's Deterrent; Tirpitz and the Birth of the German Battle Fleet*. New York: Macmillan, 1965.

Strassman, W. Paul. *Risk and Technological Innovation: American Manufacturing Methods during the Nineteenth Century*. Ithaca: Cornell University Press, 1959.

Swann, Leonard. *John Roach, Maritime Entrepreneur*. Annapolis: U.S. Naval Institute, 1965.

Temin, Peter. *Iron and Steel in Nineteenth Century America; An Economic Inquiry*. Cambridge: Cambridge University Press, 1961.

Urofsky, Melvin I. *Big Steel and the Wilson Administration; A Study in Business–Government Relations*. Columbus: Ohio State University Press, 1969.

U.S. War Department. *Proceedings of a Court of Inquiry Convened at Washington D.C., November 9, 1868, by Special Orders No. 217, War Department, to Examine into the Accusations against Brigadier and Bvt. Major General A.B. Dyer, Chief or Ordnance*. 2 vols. Washington: Government Printing Office, 1869.

Wall, Joseph Frazer. *Andrew Carnegie*. New York: Oxford University Press, 1970.

Warren, Kenneth. *The American Steel Industry 1850–1970; A Geographical Interpretation*. Oxford: Clarendon Press, 1973.

Wiebe, Robert. *The Search for Order, 1877–1920*. New York: Hill and Wang, 1967.

ARTICLES

Adams, John W. "The Influences Affecting Naval Shipbuilding Legislation; 1910–1916." *Naval War College Review* 22, no. 4 (December 1969): 41–70.

Ainsworth, W.L. "U.S. Naval Ordnance Plant, Charleston, W. Va." *Proceedings of the United States Naval Institute* 46, no. 2 (February 1920): 238–43.

Allin, Lawrence C. "The Naval Profession Challenge and Response 1870–1890 and 1950–1970." *Naval War College Review* 28, no. 4 (Spring 1976): 75–90.

"American Steel For the New Cruisers." *Proceedings of the United States Naval Institute* 13, no. 3 (1887): 490–97.

"Armor Question Puzzles." *[The Engineer, June 16, 1893]*, *Proceedings of the United States Naval Institute* 19, no. 3 (1893): 318–19.

Barber, F.M. "A Practical Method of Arriving at the Number, Size, Type, Rig, and Cost of the Vessels of Which the U.S. Navy Should Consist in Time of Peace." *Proceedings of the United States Naval Institute* 12, no. 3 (1886): 418–22.

Becker, William H. "Foreign Markets For Iron and Steel, 1893–1913; A New Perspective on the Williams School of Diplomatic History." *Pacific Historical Review* 44, no. 2 (May 1975): 233–61.

Buhl, Lance C. "Mariners and Machines; Resistance to Technological Change in the American Navy, 1865–1869." *Journal of American History* 61, no. 4 (December 1974):703–27.

Cooling, B. Franklin. "The Formative Years of the Naval-Industrial Complex: Their Meaning for Studies of Institutions Today." *Naval War College Review* 27, no. 5 (March/April 1975): 53–62.

————— "Making of a Navalist: Secretary of the Navy Benjamin Franklin Tracy and Seapower." *Naval War College Review* 25, no. 1 (September/October 1972): 83–90.

Cowles, Alfred. "Aluminum Bronze for Heavy Guns." *Proceedings of the United States Naval Institute* 13, no. 4 (1887): 601–79 and 14, no. 1 (1888): 235–47.

Dashiell, R.B. "Report on the Test of a 14-inch Nickel Steel Harveyized Armor Plate." *Proceedings of the United States Naval Institute* 19, no. 1 (1893): 117–20.

Davenport, Russell W. "Gun Forgings and Armor Plate in the United States." *Proceedings of the United States Naval Institute* 19, no. 4 (1893): 485–86.

————— "Trial of Schneider's Nickel Steel Armor for Russia." *Proceedings of the United States Naval Institute* 19, no. 4 (1893): 491–92.

Dorsey, Edward B. "Steel For Heavy Guns." *Proceedings of the United States Naval Institute* 13, no. 1 (1887): 2–125.

Eaton, J.G. "Notes on Steel Inspection of Structural and Boiler

Material." *Proceedings of the United States Naval Institute* 14, no. 4 (1888): 641–53.

Garrett, Wendall. "John Davis Long, Secretary of the Navy, 1897–1902: A Study in Changing Political Alignments." *The New England Quarterly* 31, no. 3 (September 1953): 291–311.

Gleaves, Albert. "Review of Rogers Bernie, Gun-Making in the United States." *Proceedings of the United States Naval Institute* 14, no. 2 (1888): 465–69.

Hagen, Kenneth. "Admiral David Dixon Porter, Strategist for a Navy in Transition." *Proceedings of the United States Naval Institute* 94, no. 7 (July 1968): 140–43.

Hattendorf, John B. "Technology and Strategy: A Study in the Professional Thought of the U.S. Navy, 1900–1916." *Naval War College Review* 24, no. 3 (November 1971): 25–48.

Herbert, Hilary. "The Lesson of the Naval Review." *North American Review* 156 (June 1893): 641–47.

Hoff, William Bainbridge. "A View of Our Naval Policy and a Discussion of its Factors." *Proceedings of the United States Naval Institute* 12, no. 2 (1886): 121–38.

Hovgaard, C.W. "Submarine Boats." *Proceedings of the United States Naval Institute* 14, no. 1 (1888): 249–57.

Jaques, W.H. "Description of the Works of the Bethlehem Iron Company." *Proceedings of the United States Naval Institute* 10, no. 4 (1889): 531–40.

————. "The Establishment of Steel Gun Factories in the United States." *Proceedings of the United States Naval Institute* 10, no. 4 (1884): 531–868.

Karsten, Peter. "The Nature of 'Influence': Roosevelt, Mahan, and the Concept of Sea Power." *American Quarterly* 23, no. 4 (October 1971): 585–600.

Kimberly, L.A. "Report of the Board on the Competition Trial of Armor Plate." *Proceedings of the United States Naval Institute* 16, no. 4 (1890): 620–45.

Livermore, Seward W. "The American Navy as a Factor in World Politics, 1903–1913." *American Historical Review* 63, no. 4 (July 1958): 863–79.

Long, John D. "The Birth of the New Navy." *Outlook*, September 1902, 490–91.

Luce, Stephen B. "Annual Address." *Proceedings of the United States Naval Institute* 14, no. 1 (1888): 1–8.

————. "Our Future Navy." *Proceedings of the United States Naval Institute* 15, no. 3 (1889): 541–57.

Mahon, John K. "Benjamin Franklin Tracy, Secretary of the Navy 1889–1893." *New York Historical Quarterly* 44, no. 2 (April 1960): 179–201.

McAlpine, William J. "The Most Suitable Metal For Naval Guns." *Proceedings of the United States Naval Institute* 13, no. 2 (1887): 141–46.

Metcalf, William. "Steel: Its Properties; Its Uses in Structures and Heavy Guns." *Proceedings of the United States Naval Institute* 14, no. 2 (1888): 445–53.

Reisinger, W.W. "Torpedoes." *Proceedings of the United States Naval Institute* 14, no. 3 (1889): 483–538.

Richards, W., and J.A. Potter. "The Homestead Steel Works." *Proceedings of the United States Naval Institute* 15, no. 3 (1889): 431–44.

Sampson, William T. "Outline of a Scheme for the Naval Defense of the Coast." *Proceedings of the United States Naval Institute* 15, no. 2 (1889):169–232.

Schubert, H.R. "The Steel Industry." in Charles Singer et. al., editors. *A History of Technology. Vol. 5, The Late Nineteenth Century, 1850–1900.* Oxford: Clarendon Press, 1958.

Seager, Robert II. "Ten Years before Mahan: The Unofficial Case for the New Navy, 1880–1890." *The Mississippi Valley Historical Review* 40, no. 4 (December 1953):491–512.

Simpson, Edward. "A Proposed Armament for the New Navy." *Proceedings of the United States Naval Institute* 7, no. 2 (1881):165–82.

————. "The Navy and Its Prospects of Rehabilitation." *Proceedings of the United States Naval Institute* 12, no. 1 (1886):20–22.

Spector, Ronald. "Roosevelt, the Navy, and the Venezuela Controversy, 1902–1903." *The American Neptune* 32, no. 4 (1972):257–63.

Stillson, Albert C. "Military Policy without Political Guidance: Theodore Roosevelt's Navy." *Military Affairs* 25, no. 1 (Spring 1961):18–31.

Urofsky, Melvin I. "Josephus Daniels and the Armor Trust." *North Carolina Historical Review* 45, no. 2 (July 1968):237–63.
Very, Edward W. "The Development of Armor for Naval Use." *Proceedings of the United States Naval Institute* 9, no. 3 (1883):349–583.
Vroom, Guysbert, and William Oliver Stevens. "The Fate of the Dreadnought." *Proceedings of the United States Naval Institute* 47, no. 2 (February 1921):191–200.
"Wire Wound Guns." *Proceedings of the United States Naval Institute* 19, no. 4 (1893):486–89.
Yerxa, Donald A. "The State of Maine and the New Navy 1889–1893." *Maine Historical Quarterly* 14, no. 4 (Spring 1975):183–205.
Zalinski, E.I. "The Naval Uses of the Pneumatic Torpedo Gun." *Proceedings of the United States Naval Institute* 14, no. 1 (1888):10–55.

UNPUBLISHED STUDIES

Allard, Dean. "The Influence of the United States Navy upon the American Steel Industry, 1880–1900." M.A. thesis, Georgetown University, 1959.
Brandt, Walter I. "Steel and the New Navy, 1882–1893." Ph.D. dissertation, University of Wisconsin, 1920.
Brinker, William. "Robert W. Shufeldt and the Changing Navy." Ph.D. dissertation, Indiana University, 1973.
Brooks, Edward H. "The National Defense Policy of the Wilson Administration 1913–1917." Ph.D. dissertation, Stanford University, 1950.
Buhl, Lance C. "The Smooth Water Navy; American Naval Policy and Politics, 1865–1876." Ph.D. dissertation, Harvard University, 1968.
Cooling, Benjamin Franklin. "Benjamin Franklin Tracy; Lawyer, Soldier, Secretary of the Navy." Ph.D. dissertation, University of Pennsylvania, 1969.

Costello, Daniel. "Planning for War: A History of the General Board of the Navy 1900–1914." Ph.D. dissertation, Fletcher School of Diplomacy, 1968.

Finnegan, John P. "Military Preparedness in the Progressive Era, 1911–1917." Ph.D. dissertation, University of Wisconsin, 1969.

Hammett, Hugh Bernard. "Hilary Abner Herbert: A Southerner Returns to the Union." Ph.D. dissertation, University of Wisconsin, 1969.

Hangen, Rolf N. "The Setting of Internal Administrative Communication in the United States Naval Establishments, 1775–1920." Ph.D. dissertation, Harvard University, 1953.

Hessen, Robert Allen. "A Biography of Charles M. Schwab, Steel Industrialist." Ph.D. dissertation, Columbia University, 1969.

Jenkins, Innis LaRoche. "Josephus Daniels and the Navy Department, 1913–1916: A Study in Military Administration." Ph.D. dissertation, University of Maryland, 1960.

Kaufmann, John H. "Estimation of Requirements for War; A Case Study of Steel." Ph.D. dissertation, Harvard University, 1952.

Kurth, Ronald James. "The Politics of Technological Innovation in the United States Navy." Ph.D. dissertation, Harvard University, 1970.

Rilling, Alexander W. "The First Fifty Years of Graduate Education in the United States Navy, 1909–1959." Ph.D. dissertation, University of Southern California, 1972.

Ropp, Theodore. "The Development of a Modern Navy, French Naval Policy, 1871–1904." Ph.D. dissertation, Harvard University, 1937.

Stillson, Albert C. "The Development and Maintenance of the American Naval Establishment; 1901–1909." Ph.D. dissertation, Columbia University, 1959.

Index

DuPont Company, 108, 208

Earle, Ralph, 210
Electric Boat Company, 158, 168
Ellis-Brown Steel Plate, 24, 25
Emory, William, 102
Endicott Board, 59
Ericsson, John, 61
Evans, Robley D., 29

Firth-Sterling Steel Company, 168
Folger, F. M., 89, 91, 101, 103, 132
Fore River Engine Company, 168, 199
Fox, Gustavus, 18
France, Armor/Ordnance, 20, 24, 25, 42, 44, 45, 50, 60–61, 66–68, 77, 89, 92, 93, 96, 101–2, 119, 125, 128, 178, 192, 193, Appendix Table 7
France, Navy, 20, 24, 25, 42, 44, 45, 49, 86, 135–36, 157
France, Warships: *Admiral Duperre*, 86; *Gloire*, 24
Frick, Henry Clay, 103, 118, 148
Fritz, John, 53, 66, 75, 82–83, 142

Gaines, John W., 190
Garfield, James A., 27, 28
Gary, Elbert H., 183, 200, 217
Gas Engine and Power Company and Charles Seabury and Company Consolidated, 156, 168
Gatling Gun Company, 168
General Board of the Navy, 165, 172, 208
Germany, Armor/Ordnance, 20,

22, 42–44, 60, 89, 119, 120, 129, 146–47, 150, 157, 167, 189, 192–93, Appendix Table 7
Germany, Navy, 49, 135–36, 157, 171, 185, 198
Getty Board, 30
Grace, Eugene, 166, 188, 200, 203
Great Britain, Armor/Ordnance, 22, 23, 24, 25–26, 40–41, 44–46, 50, 52, 60, 66, 68, 74–75, 80–82, 91, 94, 120, 125, 129, 191, 192–93, 196, Appendix Table 7
Great Britain, Navy, 17, 19, 22, 79, 86, 90, 96, 99, 135–36, 157, 158, 165, 171, 199
Great Britain, Warships: *Anson*, 86; *Bellerophon*, 20; *Camperdown*, 86; *Dreadnought*, 171, 178; *Howe*, 86; *Invincible*, 18; *Iris*, 20; *Mercury*, 20; *Rodney*, 86; *Warrior*, 24
guerre de course, la, 17, 23, 81
gunpowder production, 108, 179, 190, 197, 208
Gun Foundry Board (Simpson Board), 41–48, 52–56, 62, 66, 83–84, 92, 133

Hadfield, Sir John, 196, 198, 206
Hale, Eugene, 50, 87, 90, 100, 108, 124, 141, 148, 150, 178
Harlan and Hollingsworth Company, 10, 12, 28, 37, 38, 156, 168
Harrah, C. J., 75, 149, 172, 212, 217
Harrison, Benjamin, 85, 102, 108, 139, 217
Harrison Loring Company, 38

86010

VF
373
.C66

Cooling, B.
Franklin.
Gray steel and
blue water Navy

DATE DUE

FEB 2 6 2007	

Fernald Library
Colby-Sawyer College
New London, New Hampshire

GAYLORD   PRINTED IN U.S.A.